"*Understanding Contemporary Brazil* provides an accessible, informative and engaging overview of Brazil. Chapters on topics such as 'Social Movements and Protest' and 'Environmental Contexts and Challenges' draw readers into the complex and contested issues of Brazilian politics and culture, revealing both the dynamism and conflict of the nation. This book is an excellent introduction for those beginning to study Brazil, and a useful overview and synthesis for those seeking greater insight into how transformations in recent economics, politics and culture fit together."

— *Dr. Bryan McCann, Professor of History and President of the Brazilian Studies Association (2016-2018), Georgetown University, USA*

"'Brazil is not for beginners,' as the musical luminary Tom Jobim once remarked, but one has to start somewhere. And there is no better primer than *Understanding Contemporary Brazil*. Both historically grounded and up-to-date, this study covers a dazzling array of issues—from Brazil's notorious inequality and violence to its insurgent social movements; from its pay-to-play multiparty coalition system to recent anti-corruption campaigns; from the authoritarian inclinations of its governing elite to the democratizing triumphs of civil society; from its chronic domestic unrest to its principled reliability on the world stage. In short chapters packed with eye-opening data and marvellous insights, Garmany and Pereira have produced a multidisciplinary study that will enlighten and inform 'beginner' as well as 'advanced' students of Latin America's largest nation."

— *Dr Christopher Dunn, Professor of Spanish and Portuguese and Africana Studies, Tulane University, USA*

"This is an excellent introduction, for researchers, teachers and students, to the economy, government and politics, society, culture, environment and international relations of contemporary Brazil by two engaged Brazilianists – an urban geographer and a political scientist – at the Brazil Institute, King's College London. The authors demonstrate a keen awareness of the influence of Brazil's unique history on contemporary Brazil and their analysis of contemporary issues is firmly based on the scholarly debates about Brazil among social scientists, not least in Brazil itself."

— *Professor Emeritus Leslie Bethell, former Director of the Centre for Brazilian Studies at the University of Oxford, UK (1997-2007), and editor of the* Cambridge History of Latin America

D1590366

Understanding Contemporary Brazil

Brazil has famously been called a country of contradictions. It is a place where narratives of "racial democracy" exist in the face of stark inequalities, and where the natural environment is celebrated as a point of national pride, but at the same time is exploited at alarming rates. To people on the outside looking in, these contradictions seem hard to explain. *Understanding Contemporary Brazil* tackles these problems head-on, providing the perfect critical introduction to Brazil's ongoing social, political, economic, and cultural complexities. Key topics include:

- National identity and political structure.
- Economic development, environmental contexts, and social policy.
- Urban issues and public security.
- Debates over culture, race, gender, and spirituality.
- Social inequality, protest, and social movements.
- Foreign diplomacy and international engagement.

By considering more broadly the historical, political economic, and socio-cultural roots of Brazil's internal dynamics, this interdisciplinary book equips readers with the contextual understanding and critical insight necessary to explore this fascinating country. Written by renowned authors at one of the world's most important centers for the study of Brazil, *Understanding Contemporary Brazil* is ideal for university students and researchers, yet also accessible to any reader looking to learn more about one of the world's largest and most significant countries.

Jeff Garmany is a Senior Lecturer in the Department of Geography and the King's Brazil Institute, King's College London, UK.

Anthony W. Pereira is Professor and Director of the King's Brazil Institute, King's College London, UK.

Understanding Contemporary Brazil

Jeff Garmany and Anthony W. Pereira

Routledge
Taylor & Francis Group
LONDON AND NEW YORK

First published 2019
by Routledge
2 Park Square, Milton Park, Abingdon, Oxon OX14 4RN

and by Routledge
52 Vanderbilt Avenue, New York, NY 10017

Routledge is an imprint of the Taylor & Francis Group, an informa business

British Library Cataloguing-in-Publication Data
Names: Garmany, Jeff, author. | Pereira, Anthony W., author.
Title: Understanding contemporary Brazil / Jeff Garmany and Anthony
W. Pereira.
Description: Abingdon, Oxon ; New York, NY : Routledge, 2019. |
Includes bibliographical references and index.
Identifiers: LCCN 2018033496 (print) | LCCN 2018045651 (ebook) |
ISBN 9781315175959 (eBook) | ISBN 9781138039322 (hbk) |
ISBN 9781138039339 (pbk) | ISBN 9781315175959 (ebk)
Subjects: LCSH: Brazil--Civilization--21st century. | Brazil--Economic
conditions--21st century. | Brazil--Politics and government--21st
century. | Brazil--Social conditions--21st century.
Classification: LCC F2538.3 (ebook) | LCC F2538.3 .G36 2019
(print) | DDC 981.06/5--dc23
LC record available at https://lccn.loc.gov/2018033496

Library of Congress Cataloging-in-Publication Data
A catalog record has been requested for this book

ISBN: 978-1-138-03932-2 (hbk)
ISBN: 978-1-138-03933-9 (pbk)
ISBN: 978-1-315-17595-9 (ebk)

Typeset in Goudy
by Integra Software Services Pvt. Ltd.

Contents

Figures

Tables

Acknowledgments

This book represents more than just two lifetimes of academic work and research. It represents the accumulated knowledge of all those we have worked with going back to our undergraduate years. This includes teachers, colleagues, students, research collaborators, and research participants, and the knowledge is an ever growing and always evolving collection of ideas, arguments, beliefs, insights, and so on. It is a co-productive process, it includes a multitude of people and resources, and just as often as it is wonderful, it is also humbling. We are indebted to so many that a full accounting could fill this whole book. Likewise, as we write in Chapter 1, bibliographic citations and notes often fall short when trying to acknowledge the co-productive processes behind academic scholarship. So again, this book represents much more than the hard work of just two authors. It represents the hard work and generosity of countless people, some living, some not, whose paths intersected with ours over the years.

At King's College London, where we first began collaborating in 2011, we wish to thank all those who were part of, and participated with, the King's Brazil Institute. In particular, we wish to thank (in alphabetical order) Jaqueline Armit, Leslie Bethell, Francisco Bethencourt, Vinicius Carvalho, Andre Cicalo, Alvaro Comin, Maite Conde, Felipe Botelho Correa, Thomas Deckker, Octavio Ferraz, Any Freitas, Paolo Gerbaudo, Sónia Gonçalves, Toby Green, Iain Hannah, Keith Hoggart, Oliver Marshall, Fred Moehn, Nancy Naro, Joanna Newman, Funmi Olonosakin, and David Treece. Crucial to the Brazil Institute have always been the students, and we want to recognize their efforts in making the Brazil Institute a dynamic, exciting, and fun place to work. Many of them read and provided feedback on early drafts of these chapters, and their efforts helped to improve the work.

Anthony wishes to thank a number of people, starting with his graduate school professors, Jorge Domínguez, Robert Fishman, Merilee Grindle, Frances Hagopian, and John Womack, as well as his former colleagues at Tulane University, Rebecca Atencio, Idelber Avelar, Christopher Dunn, Ludovico Feoli, Mauro Porto, Tom and Carole Reese, Aaron Schneider, and Edie and Justin Wolfe. He would also like to thank Brazilian, Brazilianist, and Latin Americanist colleagues in the UK, including Cath Collins, Mahrukh Doctor, David Doyle, Par Engstrom, Paul Heritage, Cathy Hochstetler, Peter Kingstone,

Fiona Macaulay, Ana Margheritis, Cathy McIlwaine, Kevin Middlebrook, Linda Newson, Francisco Panizza, Leigh Payne, Tim Power, Alfredo Saad-Filho, Diego Sánchez-Ancochea, Marco Vieira, and Andrew Whitehead. He would also like to thank colleagues in the Brazilian Studies Association (BRASA): Marshall Eakin, Jan Hoffman French, John French, Jeff Lesser, Bryan McCann, Gladys Mitchell, Kenneth Serbin, and Matthew Taylor, as well as colleagues in the Association of Brazilianists in Europe, Edmund Amann and Monica Schpun. Anthony also thanks the Brazilian Embassy in London, including Ambassador Eduardo dos Santos, former Ambassador Roberto Jaguaribe, DCM Ana Maria Bierrenbach, cultural attaché Hayle Gadelha, and education attaché Juliana Bertazzo. He wishes also to thank his fellow councillors at the Brazilian Chamber of Commerce of Great Britain.

Numerous colleagues and friends have helped Anthony and shaped his understanding of Brazil. These include Paulo Abrão, Sergio Adorno, Eneá de Stutz de Almeida, Maria Hermínia Tavares de Almeida, Hulda Alves, Leonardo Avritzer, Ricardo Borges, Maria do Socorro Sousa Braga, Cristiane Carneiro, Marcos Faro de Castro, Ernani Rodrigues de Carvalho Neto, Tiago and Raíra Alves Cavalcanti, Sidney Chalhoub, Marilena Chaui, Pedro Dallari, Liana de Paula, Paulo Esteves, Caio Farias, Pedro Feliú, Louissia Penha Musse Felix, Paulo Fontes, Jaime Ginzburg, Terrie Groth, Marcos Guedes, Michael Hall, Olaya Hanashiro, Francisco Foot Hardman, Kai Kenkel, John Lear, Kai Lehmann, Renato Lessa, Renato Sérgio de Lima, Maria Regina Soares de Lima, Felipe Loureiro, James Manor, Cecilia Mariz, Carlos Milani, João Roberto Martins Filho, Marcelo Medeiros, Alexandre Morelli, Jairo Nicolau, William Nylen, Amancio Oliveira, Janina Onuki, Jahnavi Phalkey, Letícia Pinheiro, Paulo Sergio Pinheiro, Leandro Piquet, Flávio da Cunha Rezende, Matias Spektor, Oliver Stuenkel, Louise Tillin, Marcelo Torelly, Arthur Trindade, Emilia and Maristela Vasconcelos, Kyrialie Vasconcelos Morant, Rafael Villa, Cliff Welch, Jorge Zaverucha, and Emilio Zebadua.

Anthony and Jeff would also like to thank their students. It is impossible to thank them all, but mention should go to Amna Bajwa, Christopher Barton, Kim Beechno, Daniel Buarque, Roxana Cavalcanti, Mathilde Chatin, Rob Coates, Thomas Froehlich, Anna Grimaldi, Marketa Jerabek, Christoph Harig, Matthew Richmond, Fernanda Odilla, Alexandre Pereira, Andreia Reis do Carmo, Roberta Sakai, Matheus Soldi Hardt, Grace Iara Souza, and Kayla Svoboda. Thanks also to Orion Sufi Noda and Ana Balbachevsky Guilhon Albuquerque for comments on drafts of chapters 10 and 11 (Orion) and 5 (Ana), respectively. We also appreciate the comments of two anonymous reviewers for Routledge, who commented on the entire book manuscript.

Finally, Anthony would like to thank his wife, Rita, children, Bela and Bevan, and cat, Sagwa, for their forbearance in putting up with his frequent trips to Brazil and long periods of isolation in his study working on this book.

Jeff wishes to thank, beginning with the University of Arizona, J.P. Jones, Sallie Marston, Sarah Moore, Tim Finan, Elizabeth Oglesby, along with friends and colleagues from the School of Geography and Development. Thank you for helping to sharpen my work. Deserving special mention is Bert Barickman, whose influence looms large over this book. Former students of Dr. Barickman are sure to note this across several chapters. (Even though there is no mention of singing competitions and reasons for why Hill is better than River.) Dr. Barickman was an outstanding scholar of Brazilian history, and, like others who had the privilege of working with him, I miss him and wish he was still here.

Others deserving special mention include (in alphabetical order) Vivien Kogut Lessa de Sa, Christina Baum, John Burdick, Michelle Domingues, Gabriel Feltran, Ana Paula Galdeano, Donna Goldstein, Melinda Gurr, Helena Hurd, Wilson Korol, Luciana Lago, Sarah Miller, Jeovah Meireles, Roberto Santos, Rolf Malunga de Souza, and Leila Walker. Bill Calhoun in Fortaleza has long had an important presence in my life, and I thank him for his mentorship and friendship. Close friends who have helped to make this work possible include Augusto, Patricia, and Flávia in São Paulo, and Fabio, Viviane, Clauberto, Seu Dutra, and Dona Pretinha in Rio de Janeiro.

In particular I wish to thank Oélito, Ceissa, Melissa, and Miguel in Fortaleza, who welcomed me into their home so many times. I cannot thank them enough for their generosity and love. Included here is the support of Tia Zenilda and her family, and Dona Francisca and her family, along with so many others in Pirambu. I am also very grateful for the love and support of my family in the United States, my sogros in Jundiaí, and most of all my partner, Elisabeth, who, in addition to making my life better every day, *also* read and provided feedback on chapters in this book!

1   Introduction

Aims of the book and frames of analysis

The title of this book is an ambitious one. Trying to *understand* contemporary Brazil, or, for that matter, any country, is a process that remains at best only partial. Even Brazil's most famous social scientists, from Gilberto Freyre to Darcy Ribeiro, to Caio Prado Júnior to Celso Furtado, would find plenty to disagree over. Today, Brazil is one of the largest countries in the world, with a territory bigger than the continental United States, a population greater than Russia's, and an economy ranked within the global top ten (see Figure 1.1). It has experienced enormous demographic, environmental, economic, political, social, and cultural change in recent decades. Important also to consider are historical processes and their connections to present day contexts. For example, Brazil's legacies of colonization, slavery, political governance, inequality, economic development, and globalization are crucial for making sense of the present. So again, how can one possibly hope to *understand* contemporary Brazil?

Our goal in this book is to provide context and analysis for making sense of contemporary Brazil from a multidisciplinary and international social science perspective. More directly, we want this book to serve as a critical toolkit for understanding social, cultural, political, and economic issues in present day Brazil. Rather than *describing* what Brazil is like, or providing a general overview of current events, we seek to offer critical insight on key subjects and debates. To do this, we draw on a host of academic contributions, merging insights from Brazilian scholars with those of *brasilianistas* (i.e., foreign scholars of Brazil[1]) to shed light on contemporary issues. Again, our goal is to provide the reader critical tools useful for drawing her or his own conclusions. The book is meant to provoke and engage, and, as such, it tends towards *analysis* rather than description.

There is no single analytical framework we make use of, yet, as we note in the next section, there are several key themes addressed across the chapters. Our approach is also multidisciplinary, and we draw on a host of socio-theoretical perspectives. This reflects our own scholarly diversity and different disciplinary backgrounds. This is not to say, however, that this book lacks arguments or shies away from academic debates. To the contrary, each chapter

Figure 1.1 Map of Brazil showing federal and state capital cities.

Source: UN Office of the Coordination of Humanitarian Affairs (OCHA) and optimized by Alice Hunter, Wikimedia commons: https://commons.wikimedia.org/wiki/File:BrazilLocation_Map UNOCHA_(optimized).svg

seeks to provide critical insight by challenging surface-level observations and oft-held presumptions. In particular, we draw attention to five central points of analysis when trying to understand contemporary Brazil:

1. **Brazil's colonial history** – and subsequent postcolonial present – is important for seeing the roots of ongoing inequalities, including broader processes of economic development, environmental management, and political governance.
2. **Processes of national identity formation and nation building** are key to understanding Brazilian culture and remain important for understanding social and political struggle as well as racial, ethnic, and gender discrimination.

3. **Globalization** and the ways Brazil shapes and is shaped by international processes and actors is critical for seeing how and *why* Brazil looks and operates as it does today.
4. **The organization of Brazil's federalist political structure** must be accounted for when trying to explain contemporary democratic processes, including bureaucratic inefficiencies, the (un)rule of law, and problems of corruption.
5. **The central role of informality** cannot be overlooked when considering processes of social and economic development, urbanization, and even state governance.

We are reluctant to call these criteria our theoretical framework or a formal analytical structure, yet we highlight them here to note their importance to our overall approach. They are the central pillars of our analysis – like meta-themes that extend across each chapter – and are useful, we argue, as guiding principles for social scientists investigating Brazil.

Like many bits of scholarship, this work emerged from our own teaching and research experience. In 2011, we began offering courses at the King's Brazil Institute at King's College London, teaching undergraduate and graduate-level classes on Brazil in contemporary global perspective. We wanted to write a book that could anchor our reading lists, as well as contextualize existing debates, provide background and critical insight, and spark discussion between students and researchers alike. Crucially, our goal was to put multiple scholars in conversation, both Brazilian and *brasilianista*, to help link existing debates and foreground the contributions of Portuguese-language texts. We also wanted to introduce and situate the work of scholars such as Caio Prado Júnior, Raymundo Faoro, Boris Fausto, Florestan Fernandes, Milton Santos, Marilena Chaui, Ermínia Maricato, Candido Mendes, Celso Furtado, Sérgio Buarque de Holanda, along with several others whose work exists mostly in Portuguese. While we hesitate to call this a "textbook," there is no denying it was provoked in the first instance by our own teaching needs.

In addition to teachers and students, this book should also prove useful for social science researchers looking to expand their knowledge of Brazil. Again, the objective is not to provide an overview of Brazilian current events, but instead to help *explain* contemporary social contexts. By providing crucial background information, as well as situating key issues within academic debates, our goal was to produce a unique resource for a wide range of social science researchers. Whether one has little background knowledge of Brazil, or indeed if one is already an expert – that is, Brazilian, *brasilianista*, or Brazil-curious – this book should prove useful for educating and sparking new ideas.

These are the aims of the book; what we mean by *understanding* contemporary Brazil. In the remaining sections of this introductory chapter, we detail important themes and questions addressed throughout the book, including issues of source material, as well as the co-production of knowledge that constitutes a work like this. We then provide an overview of the chapters, noting key topics and debates covered across each one. By the end of this book, our hope is that readers feel stimulated *and* challenged by the work, and that, ultimately, it serves to provoke new arguments, ideas, and research agendas that push forward existing debates involving Brazil and the social sciences.

Key themes

With respect to the content of each chapter, our choices were influenced by two main factors: we wanted to focus attention on issues that, on the one hand, were highly relevant to contemporary Brazil, and, on the other, were regularly addressed in academic debate. This way, each chapter considers several topical issues and also connects to broader theoretical questions. This helps to explain the focus and substance of each chapter, as well as reasons for why this book should prove especially useful for students and social science researchers.

To understand contemporary Brazil, as promised in the title of this book, it is important to keep in mind key historical details and background context. For this reason, each chapter engages critically with a host of historical factors useful for making sense of the present. Like other postcolonial contexts, Brazil's history of colonization, exploitation, independence, oligarchic governance, slavery, and violence – as well as integration into global processes of capitalist development – is hugely important for understanding *why* Brazil exists as it does today. Our purpose here is not to recount Brazilian history purely for the sake of background knowledge, but instead to be mindful of historical details in our examination of the present. Readers may be surprised how much history is included in a book about contemporary Brazil, but again, our goal here is to provide critical analysis useful for understanding present-day contexts.

Stemming from this engagement with key historical factors comes analysis of nation building efforts and Brazilian national identity. Brazil is well known for its geographic and population diversity, even celebrating these features as points of national pride. It is also famous for claims of "racial democracy," where, supposedly, racial prejudice is reduced thanks to historical and sociological factors. How these narratives have been constructed, the ways they hold the nation together, and also how they exclude and suppress oppositional groups, is crucial for shedding light on contemporary debates and social conflict. These are questions addressed in several chapters throughout the book.

Connected here are issues of inequality, as well as a host of contradictions that have come to define Brazil's legacy. Economist Edmar Bacha (1974, cited in Richmond, 2015, p. 24) famously described Brazil in the 1970s as "Belíndia": A country that combines in small pockets the 'first world,' industrial society of Belgium within a sprawl of widespread poverty akin to 'third world' India. Making sense of this context, and in particular the roles of globalization, informality, and uneven development, is another important theme throughout the book. We consider from several angles how these processes have been produced and maintained over time – including, for example, ongoing legacies of racial inequality, urban segregation, and social resistance – as well as recent social policies introduced to assuage these inequalities. Troubling histories of violence are also significant here, and in several chapters we explore how violence and fear are present in the daily lives of many Brazilians.

Though poverty in Brazil is often associated with urban environments, rural areas are where poverty is, in fact, most severe. Exploring the roots of this, as well as its consequences, is another point of focus throughout the book. This helps to explain, for example, problems of environmental degradation, as well as the rise of one of Latin America's largest social movements, the MST (*O Movimento dos Trabalhadores Rurais Sem Terra* – The Landless Rural Workers Movement). Related here are conflicts over natural resources and the rise of Brazil's increasingly powerful agro-industrial lobby. Seeing the connection points between these processes and capitalist development, inequality, and the natural environment is crucial for understanding Brazil's political ecologic future.

Part and parcel of this are questions of political governance, public policy, and federalism in Brazil. The role of the state, as well as the rule of law and democratic processes, is key to broader debates that span every chapter in this book. In recent years, Brazil has proven especially keen to engage in international diplomacy, participating with the United Nations and trying to establish a leadership role among developing countries by promoting Brazilian public and social policies. Through the early years of the twenty-first century, as the Brazilian economy grew and the middle 'C' class expanded, Brazil appeared well positioned to achieve these goals. But more recent economic and political turmoil has complicated these efforts, revealing Brazil's still precarious position in a globalized economy. What Brazil is doing to address these concerns, including ongoing academic debates over development, political economy, and globalization, are also important points of focus throughout the book.

Brazil is also well known for its cultural attributes, combing a unique mixture of indigenous, African, European, and Asian influences, as well as showing distinct regional and state identities across the country. How this socio-cultural context was created and why it remains significant today are debated in several chapters, along with major cultural influences such as television and social media. For example, the *Rede Globo* entertainment network has for several decades been Brazil's most significant cultural forum, and remains still today a central force in shaping attitudes, perspectives, and understandings of contemporary society. Considering the effects of such influences, including how new technologies, social media platforms, and patterns of mass consumption might alter Brazil's cultural landscape in years to come, are key questions addressed in the book.

Related to this is religious and spiritual change in Brazil, and the growing presence of evangelical Christian groups. In some respects, Brazil is becoming more secular, yet many people remain intensely spiritual and fluid in their religious identities. In recent years, this has sparked increasing debate over issues such as abortion, same-sex marriage, and gender equality. Such conflict is by no means confined to religious discussions, and today spills over into political and social debate more generally. As in other countries, Brazilian civil discourse appears increasingly vitriolic, helping to shed light on recent and dramatic political change. Considering these issues, along with processes of social resistance, public protest, and the diverse ways social movements are responding, are also important points of consideration in several chapters.

Finally, yet another key objective of this book is to cultivate multidisciplinary and international debate. As mentioned already, many of the best scholarly works on Brazil exist only in Portuguese, alienating readers not fluent in the language and inducing parochial effects on academic debates within Brazil. Similar to researchers who become straightjacketed by their own disciplinary boundaries, so, too, do non-Portuguese-speaking academics become cut off from key debates among Brazilian scholars. One of our goals in this work is to help break down some of these boundaries, between both language and discipline. By engaging critically with Brazilian and *brasilianista* scholars from a variety of disciplinary perspectives, this book seeks to lower the walls, as it were, between different academic camps, as well as Portuguese and English-speaking audiences.

It should also be noted that a book like this represents decades of academic co-production and collaborative work. This is to say that far beyond us, the two authors, this book reflects countless ideas, arguments, insights, and observations from others we have worked with and learned from over the years. Key influences include some of our former teachers and supervisors, as well as current and former colleagues and students at universities where we have worked. Bibliographic citations never fully acknowledge the co-productive processes behind academic scholarship, and as we move on in the next section to outline the content of each chapter, we want to recognize the valuable and ongoing contributions of our critical interlocutors.

Outline of chapters

Before detailing the subject matter of each chapter, we feel it important to note some key issues *not* addressed as singular, individual chapters within the book. The first is inequality, which, beyond simply being the focus of a given chapter, could be the topic of an entire book series. This issue is addressed across every single chapter in the book, and therefore not something we chose to focus upon in just one chapter. Related to this is gender inequality and critical perspectives of gender in Brazil, which, more so than any other topic, is perhaps most deserving of its own, individual chapter. On the one hand, like socio-economic inequality, this is a topic we address in several chapters, with specific emphasis in Chapters 7 and 11. More generally, critical perspectives of gender are ones we feel should intersect, critique, and engage with *all* social science debates, and, thus, we are hesitant to corral such insights within one individual chapter. Much like research about Brazil should not be cordoned off within "Area" or "Latin American Studies," feminist and queer critiques should not remain bound within "Gender" and/or "Women's Studies." Compartmentalizing such debates within individual paradigms and topics of study not only constrains them – placing them in academic ghettos, as it were – it also limits the scope and dynamism of other areas of research.

On the other hand, our decision not to dedicate a specific chapter to critical perspectives of gender and gender inequality in Brazil reflects our own limits of academic expertise, as well as decisions regarding the overall length of the book. This is not to make excuses, but instead to explain that key topics such as gender, geopolitics, biodiversity and ecology, business and international trade, literature and language, etc., receive lesser attention *not* because we believe they lack importance, but because the book is, of course, limited by our own scholarly knowledge and specific areas of study. These are also topics about which we continue to learn and research with our students, and ones we hope will continue to grow in future years.

We begin in the next chapter by considering questions of national identity and processes of nation building in Brazil. These factors are crucial for binding any nation together, particularly ones as large and diverse as Brazil. What calls attention in this case, however, is how Brazil as a *nation* is, in fact, a relatively recent creation. Many of the traits today considered quintessentially Brazilian were actually strategically identified and made significant within the last century. This is relevant not only for seeing how Brazil makes sense of its own history, but also for understanding ongoing processes of inequality and social exclusion. By drawing on key historical factors, this chapter sheds light on contemporary social and cultural debates in Brazil. It also sets the stage for subsequent chapters by providing relevant historical context and introducing several themes addressed throughout the book.

Chapter 3 provides an overview of Brazil's political structure and processes of government. It explores the roots of contemporary political processes and the strengths of, and challenges facing, Brazilian democracy. Beginning with historical patterns of centralization and decentralization (e.g., regionalism), the chapter details the gradual formation of Brazil's central state. It then moves on to consider how and why Brazilian democracy has been so fragile, accounting for the rise of an authoritarian military dictatorship in the twentieth century, and the subsequent return to democracy and struggle for rights with the 1988 constitution. The chapter concludes with a discussion of contemporary political challenges – most notably corruption – and the ways Brazilians today are articulating their citizenship rights. The chapter also focuses on the 2016 impeachment of President Dilma Rousseff, and the political polarization that contributed to, and was exacerbated by, this political process.

Chapter 4 examines economic development and social policies in Brazil, questioning why a country so rich in natural resources should remain starkly unequal and underdeveloped. Several key theories of economic and social development are considered alongside Brazil's history of economic development, with particular attention paid to Brazil's historical dependency on external markets and late industrial development and construction of national infrastructure. The chapter then moves on to consider questions of human capital (e.g., Brazilian public education and healthcare), and recent social policies launched to address poverty and socio-economic inequality (e.g., the *Bolsa Família* conditional cash transfer program). Rather than providing a descriptive account of Brazil's recent economic rise and fall, this chapter attempts to analyze different theoretical perspectives on contemporary Brazilian economic development.

In Chapter 5, we turn our attention to race, ethnicity, identity, and issues of prejudice and stigma in Brazil. This chapter explores the meanings and effects of racial identities in Brazil, starting with historical understandings of race and moving on to see how racial identity has been constructed over time. These historical roots are crucial for making sense of Brazil's supposed "racial democracy," and more recent developments that acknowledge racism and attempt to address it (e.g., university quotas for students of African and indigenous descent). Not to be overlooked here are a host of other racial/ethnic identities in Brazil (e.g., Brazilians of Japanese, Turkish, Lebanese, German, and Dutch descent), and the ways these populations fit – or not – within traditional constructions of race and identity in Brazil.

Chapter 6 considers urban development in Brazil. Like other countries in Latin America, Brazilian cities are (in)famous for poverty and informality, in both housing and modes of economic production. This chapter traces the underlying causes for these characteristics, accounting for Brazil's history of slavery and socio-economic inequality. High levels of urbanization are not new to Brazil, yet Brazilian cities still show a significant lack of urban infrastructure and public services. These problems have begun to boil over in recent years, erupting in massive street protests that also reveal Brazil's changing class structure. Related to this are issues of public security, violence, and crime, and the growing presence of private security and organized crime in Brazilian cities. Again, by considering the historical and structural roots of these problems, this chapter helps to explain *why* Brazil continues to confront these issues well into the twenty-first century.

In Chapter 7, we address social movements and protest in Brazil. Although Brazil might have a reputation as an easy-going, fun-loving country, it also has a long history of intense social conflict and collective mobilization. Social movements have long faced difficult struggles, battling an authoritarian and often violent state apparatus (particularly during the twentieth century), as well as hegemonic and nationalist discourses that undermine their efforts. Since Brazil's return to democracy in the 1980s, social movements have grown enormously and today play significant roles in social and political debate. Alongside struggles for land, housing, and resources are numerous groups challenging Brazil's legacy of racial discrimination, gender inequality, and homophobia. Not to be overlooked are new technologies such as social media that are having profound impacts on the ways social movements organize, evidenced by Brazil's 2013 street protests. We consider these questions in this chapter, suggesting that collective mobilization may be entering a new phase thanks to new organizational strategies and increasing attention paid to intersectional identities.

The purpose of Chapter 8 is to investigate deeply rooted environmental challenges in Brazil. It begins by considering how the environment and landscape have been historically constructed, and showing why these constructions are important for understanding contemporary contexts. It then moves on to examine issues of environmental degradation in Brazil, showing important links with processes of globalization and capitalist development. Brazil's rich history of environmental activism is also explored, showing why international activists have struggled in many cases to connect with Brazilian activists. Contemporary questions of energy production and deforestation are also considered, making connections between Brazilian history, current networks of globalization, and future concerns such as political responses to global climate change.

Chapter 9 tackles two large and admittedly complex issues: Brazilian culture *and* spirituality. It begins by exploring the roots of Brazil's diverse cultural mix, focusing specifically on characteristics that distinguish different geographic regions. Keeping these factors in mind, it then shows why these traits are important for understanding contemporary literature, music, cinema, and cultural celebrations such as Carnival. These traditions are crucial for defining Brazilian culture, yet they also reveal brutal histories of slavery, inequality, and exclusion. Crucial here is also Brazil's diverse religious landscape, and, in the second half of this chapter, we focus our attention on contemporary Brazilian spirituality. We pay particular attention to the growth of evangelical Christianity, as well as religion's role in society and politics. Today, for example, evangelical groups are establishing a stronger presence in political decision-making processes, and recognizing these changes and their cultural roots is important for understanding current political and social debates in Brazil.

In Chapter 10, we address Brazil's dynamic role in contemporary international relations. Historically speaking, Brazil has a reputation for savvy diplomatic relations. It bears noting that Brazil has maintained historically peaceful relations with nearly all of its neighbors, a feat even more impressive when one remembers Brazil shares a border with ten different countries. This history is important for understanding ongoing developments, whereby Brazil has sought in recent decades to expand its global engagement, even hoping for a permanent seat on the United Nations Security Council. Still, Brazil is by no means a military power, raising questions about whether a country that lacks nuclear weapons can, in fact, become a world leader in the twenty-first century. By exploring these questions, and working to explain *why* Brazilian foreign policy operates with complex and shifting patterns of cooperation with other states and non-state actors, this chapter provides key insight into several debates regarding Brazil's role in the world.

Finally, in Chapter 11, we turn our attention to soccer. Brazil is, of course, internationally renowned when it comes to soccer, yet rarely is the history of Brazilian soccer and its connections to social class and urban development ever considered. Important also is soccer's role in constructing regional and national identity, and the sometimes tense debates involving soccer, democracy, and social justice. This final chapter considers these questions, showing the broader importance of soccer in Brazilian society.

In the brief Afterword that concludes the book, we reflect on Brazil's 2018 presidential election. This election was, for several reasons, one of Brazil's most significant political events in recent years. It followed the very contentious impeachment of President Dilma Rousseff in 2016 (what many Brazilians called a coup), the equally contentious presidency of Michel Temer from 2016–2018, and the rise of populist right-wing candidates like Jair Bolsonaro. Many Brazilians were pessimistic about their presidential options in 2018, and perhaps about the state of Brazilian democracy more generally, revealing a concerning shift in electoral politics. We contemplate these issues in the Afterword, as well as the immediate outcome of the 2018 election.

A final note on sources and readings

As mentioned already, one of this book's major objectives is to draw attention to key pieces of scholarship on Brazil. This is one reason why each chapter has extensive bibliographic references that include top Brazilian and *brasilianista* scholars in their respective fields. Readers wanting to further explore a given topic are encouraged to note relevant authors, and then pursue additional source material using the list of references as a guide. We understand, however, that many readers are not fluent in Portuguese, and/or might appreciate a short list of central references for each chapter. As such, at the end of each chapter, we provide a short list of "suggested English readings" for readers wanting further insight. These lists should prove especially useful for researchers, teachers, and students looking for additional source material in English.

Yet another source referenced on several occasions in this book is the Brazilian Institute of Geography and Statistics (*Instituto Brasileiro de Geografia e Estatística* – IBGE). The IBGE is Brazil's national agency responsible for collecting demographic, geographic, cartographic, and environmental information, as well as conducting the national census every ten years. It is an excellent data source for social scientists, providing greater detail and analysis (for Brazil) than sources like the World Bank, the United Nations, or the Central Intelligence Agency. Their website even has a link for English-speaking users. Readers will note that we cite IBGE data in several instances, and those wanting additional information are encouraged to visit their website at www.ibge.gov.br.

Finally, as we draw this introductory chapter to a close, we want to mention the Scientific Electronic Library Online (SciELO). SciELO is a digital library for scientific journals published in many Portuguese and Spanish speaking countries (and also South Africa). It serves as a bibliographic database and a platform for open access publishing, with links to journal collections from participating countries. Again, for researchers, teachers, and students seeking resources in virtually *any* subject area, SciELO is an excellent resource. The main website can be found at www.scielo.org, with Brazil's specific homepage at www.scielo.br.

Note

1 It should be noted that the term *"brasilianista"* is a complicated one with a fraught history. Readers seeking further insight are encouraged to read Almeida, 2001 and Weinstein, 2001.

References

Almeida, P.R. de (2001). Os estudos sobre o Brasil nos Estados Unidos: A produção brasilianista no pós-Segunda Guerra. *Estudos Históricos*, 27, 31–61.

Bacha, E. (1974). O rei da Belíndia: Uma fábula para tecnocratas. Available at: www.scribd. com/document/55498998/O-Rei-da-Belindia-Edmar-Lisboa-Bacha, accessed 20 February 2018.

Richmond, M.A. (2015). Favela, network, and identity in a complex city: A comparative neighbourhood study in Rio de Janeiro. PhD dissertation. King's College London.

Weinstein, B. (2001). Sou ainda uma Brazilianist? *Revista Brasileira de História*, 36(72), 195–217.

2 National identity and nation building

Tall and tan and young and lovely ...[1]

One of the best descriptions of Brazil comes from the great jazz composer Tom Jobim. As legend has it, Jobim, one of the founders of the Bossa Nova movement, once said of his own country, "Brazil is not for beginners" (Monteiro, 2012, p. x). Rarely is such insight summed up in five simple words. Something nearly everyone with much experience in Brazil tends to agree with, whether foreign or native, is that Brazil can be difficult to navigate and to understand. It is big, diverse, and historically unique from other countries, including its own neighbors in South America. That Brazil as we know it today even exists is surprising, particularly when one considers how rarely Brazil has gone to war, either with itself or with its neighbors. This is not to say Brazil exists without conflict or violence – very much to the contrary – but instead to point out how remarkable it is that today we can talk about a singular place called Brazil, complete with some sense of national identity crucial for holding countries together. To begin to understand this process is to dig down to the roots, as anthropologist Roberto DaMatta might say, of "what makes brazil, Brazil?" (1986). It is crucial for understanding why and how Brazil exists as it does today, including the ways different groups are beginning to challenge some of these narratives in the twenty-first century.

National identity is often a dangerous topic. So, too, are debates over nation states, and the ways historical narratives are used to construct ethnic and cultural heritages within any given country. Brazil provides a stark example of this. Is it, today, a country with a remarkably harmonious blend of European, African, and indigenous heritages, or is it instead a country imprisoned by its legacy of slavery and genocide? Could it be some of both? These are questions that continue to weigh heavily on debates over what it means to be Brazilian, and, to be fair, Brazil is not the only country facing these questions.

Nation states and what we think of today as national identity are, in fact, very recent constructions historically speaking, and Brazil's seemingly schizophrenic sense of self – as a country rich with cultural and ethnic diversity *and* a horrific historical past – is by no means unique. Nearly every country is built on similarly uneven terrain. In particular are countries in the Americas and other former colonies, where discourses of national unity were pieced together over every sort of social injustice imaginable. What is interesting about contexts like Brazil is how recently the tropes of national identity were identified and constructed, and yet today these characteristics appear somehow timeless. To critically interrogate this history, what Marilena Chaui calls Brazil's "founding myth" (2000), is to peel back the layers of what today holds Brazil together.

Our goal in this chapter is to initiate this investigation. Here, we explore processes of nation building and national identity in Brazil, shedding light on key factors that explain why Brazil looks the way it does today. This chapter is primarily historical, so as to provide important background for subsequent chapters, but it is not intended as a generic historical overview or even an outline of Brazil's political history. Our purpose here is to drill down to the very core of *brasilidade* – that is, "Brazilianness," and, more specifically, those societal characteristics imagined to be truly authentic and unadulterated (Philippou, 2005) – to better understand what social and cultural factors bind Brazil together.

We begin by considering the process of colonization, Brazil's independence from Portugal and subsequent civil conflicts, and the transition from empire to republic. Important national myths come from this period – again, just as in any country – but national heroes, perhaps surprisingly, are much harder to come by. Brazilians, generally speaking, are notoriously iconoclastic, especially with respect to their own history and narratives of grandeur. The writer Nelson Rodrigues famously drew attention to this when he described Brazil's "mongrel complex" (*complexo de vira-lata*), or what could generally be described as an international inferiority complex, following Brazil's World Cup finals loss (at home) to Uruguay in 1950. As Candido Mendes points out, this also connects with, on the one hand, current-day tendencies to hyper-valorize all things European and North American, and dismiss anything indigenous and/or Brazilian (Mendes, 2010). On the other hand, it also reflects contemporary Brazil's peculiar fascination with international perceptions of Brazil, and, in particular, how Brazil is portrayed in international media outlets (again, mostly in North America and Europe; see also Buarque, 2013; Jiménez-Martínez, 2017).

Moving on, we explore Brazil's unique regional identities, as well as diverse immigration histories that flourished after the abolition of slavery. Even though Brazil, by the early part of the twentieth century, looked on the map very similar to how it does today, internally the country was not a recognizably cohesive whole. Much of this was achieved over just a few decades in the middle twentieth century, and, almost like magic, Brazil became a *nation* – not just a place – complete with a sense of national culture, heritage, geography, and so on. This history is crucial for understanding contemporary social debates, and the ways Brazilians continue to struggle over what it *means* to be Brazilian, including who has the power to make such claims. Far from being fixed or timeless, national identity is always in flux, and by working in this chapter to untangle these processes, we aim to demystify some of what makes Brazil so baffling for beginners.

The colonial legacy

Consider a seemingly straightforward question: is Brazil part of Latin America? On the map, it lies in South America, but are South America and Latin America synonymous? More directly, are Brazilians *Latinos*? And what makes someone *Latino* anyway? Is it an ethnic distinction? Surely it cannot indicate race, as people from 'Latin America' are as racially diverse as anywhere on the planet. Does it simply refer to people from a given geographic space? If so, does it include the English, Dutch, and French speaking countries of Guyana, Suriname, and French Guyana? And what about the Caribbean? If Cuba and the Dominican Republic are Latin American countries, then Jamaica and Trinidad and Tobago should be too, right? Nowadays, the term "Latin America" is used with little second thought, but what it actually means is very ambiguous. For example, if what it means to be *Latino* includes sharing the same language, or having Iberian ancestry, or even a common colonial heritage, then most Brazilians are definitely not *Latinos* (see, for example, Bethell, 2010). Neither is it a term that most people *in* Brazil are likely to use or even recognize. Then again, there are plenty of Brazilians who self-identify as *Latinos*, whether for personal reasons or external pressures. In particular are those who live abroad and may experience prejudice similar to others from Central and South America. The reasons for this are myriad – remember, "not for beginners" – and in order to understand them, we start here with the one feature perhaps more significant than any other for distinguishing Brazil from its neighbors: It is the only country in the Americas that was colonized by the Portuguese.

From a contemporary perspective, Portugal might seem an odd colonial match for Brazil. Differences between the two countries are easy to spot, and ethnic jokes about the Portuguese are a common trope in Brazilian society. Yet, beyond the Portuguese language itself – which, in fact, is crucial for understanding what binds Brazil together and differentiates it from neighboring countries – Portugal's colonial legacy carries on in a host of ways. Brazilian scholars are famously critical of this, linking Brazil's colonial history to ongoing problems with political democracy (Buarque de Holanda, 2012), social inequality, and economic underdevelopment (Prado Jr., 2011), a culture of patronage, inefficient bureaucracy, and inconsistent application of law (Faoro, 1975), and so on. More recently, researchers have cast this critical light in new directions, showing how Brazil's legacy of inequality and social injustice – what Chaui calls an "authoritarian society" (Chaui, 2000) – stem also from internal power structures as well as processes of globalization and capitalist development (Cardoso and Faletto, 1979; Fausto, 1999; Furtado, 2007). Such debates are useful for illustrating the ways national identity has been constructed over time, the emergence of national myths, and some of the features that distinguish patriotism in Brazil from countries elsewhere.

While Brazilians today may reflect critically on the effects of Portuguese colonization, when Brazil actually became independent from Portugal in 1822, many people in Brazil were ambivalent about the prospects of independence.

On the one hand were questions of regional diversity and differentiated economic and political interests, religious sentiment and loyalty to the crown, and fears over what independence might change with respect to social structure (e.g., slavery). On the other hand was Brazil's colonial history, and methods undertaken by the Portuguese – some virtually by accident – that helped to ward off colonial rebellion. We consider first the latter reasons (i.e., important colonial aspects), and then return to engage the former ones in order to show why Brazilian national identity, as we might think of it today, was so slow to emerge.

Portugal may have officially claimed Brazil as a colony in 1500, but actual settlement efforts were slow to follow. Brazil was an immense space to colonize and to govern, and along the coastline both the Spanish and French worked to establish their own settlements, ignoring Portuguese claims. Mindful that they were at risk of losing bits of the colony, Portugal finally sought to populate and administer Brazil in the 1530s. Called "the captaincies," the Portuguese crown divided Brazil into a series of massive land grants and bestowed them on recipients who were meant to settle, develop, and administer their own territory (see Figure 2.1). This semi-feudal system of hereditary rule was mostly an economic failure, but the captaincies nonetheless established a long-standing tradition of decentralized governance, where power and local authority became concentrated in the hands of landed elites.

The legacy of the captaincies can still be noted today in at least two key ways. The first is how landed elites continue to wield political power in their own localities, particularly in certain regions like the Northeast. Often referred to as *coronéis* (literally, "colonels" in the National Guard), landed elites held virtual political sway over their own territories well into the twentieth century (some would say they still do today). The second relates to individual Brazilian states, many of which still bear the names of the original captaincies. Bureaucratically, states in Brazil do not have as much legal autonomy as in some federative republics such as the USA, but, culturally speaking, they maintain a strong sense of individual state identity. This legacy has complicated constructions of national identity over time, as state identities are often more significant for most Brazilians than sentiments of national identity. The origins of this extend back to the sixteenth century, and so significant are Brazilian state identities that they appear similar in some ways to individual ethnic identities (cf. Ribeiro, 2000).

Along with Brazil's legacy for regional diversity and oligarchic rule come two other significant developments from this period: the arrival of Catholic missionaries and the growth of slave labor. In many respects, these two went hand in hand, and they were to have important consequences for the future of Brazil as a nation. From the sixteenth century to the early years of the seventeenth century, Portuguese colonists attempted to enslave Brazil's indigenous population. Sugar was the primary export, and slave labor was used to run the plantations, along with most other aspects of domestic life. This period also saw the arrival of Jesuit missionaries, who, in addition to helping establish Brazil as a

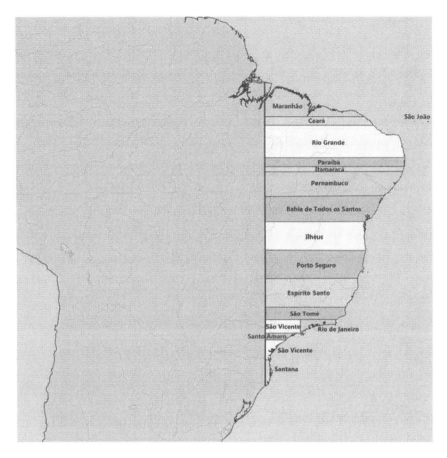

Figure 2.1 The colony of Brazil in 1534 showing the original 15 captaincies. It should be
noted that while the map appears to denote 16 captaincies, the captaincy of
Paraíba was, at the time, subordinate to the captaincy of Itamaracá.

Source: Showdowxfox, Wikimedia commons: https://commons.wikimedia.org/wiki/File:Brazil_
(1534).svg

Catholic country, also played a key role in the fate of indigenous people. Once
remembered as allies of the Indians, historians have since argued that the Jesuits
also relied heavily on indigenous slave labor to carry out their missionary work
(Monteiro, 1994). This helps to explain why indigenous people virtually disappear
from Brazil's historical record for centuries. They were ill suited for slave labor,
dying quickly from European diseases and the harsh conditions of living in
captivity. Many fled from both the colonists and the missionaries, moving into
Brazil's hinterland, and, in some cases, avoiding contact with Europeanized people
until the twenty-first century.

To meet this labor shortage, colonists began importing slaves from Africa, beginning a process that would, across the following centuries, forcibly transport nearly *five million* people from Africa to Brazil. Until recently, historians estimated this number at roughly four million people (e.g., Fausto, 1999, p. 18). But more recent research published by the Trans-Atlantic Slave Database (slavevoyages.org) suggests 4,864,374 African slaves actually disembarked in Brazil. A further 667,746 people died during the voyage.[2] By way of some context, this represents almost half of all people who came to the Americas aboard slave ships (nearly 10.7 million), and dwarfs the number of 388,745 who arrived in the USA.

Such was the growth of colonial Brazil. Until nearly the end of the nineteenth century (well after Brazil's independence from Portugal), slave labor fueled exports of sugar, gold, coffee, and other primary commodities. Raw materials formed the backbone of Brazil's economy, and little effort was made to industrialize or develop. For example, the Portuguese actually discouraged literacy and higher education for fear they might lead to revolution (Fausto, 1999). But by the late 1700s, Brazil's economy had grown more significant than Portugal's, and their colonial relationship was showing signs of strain. Plans were even made for a revolt against the Portuguese in 1789. Called the *Inconfidência Mineira* (the Minas Gerais conspiracy), the revolt was discovered by colonial authorities while still in the planning phase, and the leaders were arrested and imprisoned. One of the leaders, Tiradentes, was executed – not coincidentally, among the rebel leadership he was the only one who was not an aristocrat – and while today he is remembered as a national martyr, his legacy was not established until *many* years later (Skidmore, 2010).

As the nineteenth century dawned there were further rumblings of independence, but what really draws attention is how divided Brazil was at the time (Maxwell, 2004). Many Brazilian elites were unsure about the prospects of independence, and, in most cases, they were even less enthusiastic about forming a united, independent empire with the rest of the colony. Regional differences were hugely significant, and just like the legacy of Portuguese territorial administration, slavery, and the influence of Catholic missionaries, these differences remain important for understanding Brazil today (Bethell, 1985).

From empire to the Republic of the United States of Brazil

Reflecting on nineteenth-century Brazil, one might logically ask why Brazil never fractured into several smaller countries, or how, unlike in the USA, a major civil war was somehow avoided. After all, as Rodrick Barman notes (1988), the country comprised six different regional economies more closely connected to the Atlantic market than to one another. Furthermore, many people still had strong roots in Portugal, and there existed almost no common frame of mind among Brazil's incredibly diverse population. Even Brazil's independence in 1822 created little in the way of nationalist sentiment. There were no major battles with the Portuguese, and the first leader of independent

Brazil was Pedro I, a Portuguese prince and heir to the crown in Lisbon. As Thomas Skidmore notes, Brazil is the only former colony to choose its first monarch from the royal family of the same country against which it rebelled (Skidmore, 2010, p. 45)!

Different from colonial independence movements elsewhere, Brazil's was not one of radical social change. To the contrary, Brazilian elites were wary of what they saw in other countries. The French revolution had brought major changes to the country's social structure, something Brazilian elites had no desire to see repeated. And while the USA offered a slightly better alternative, where elites maintained power through the revolution, the abolition of slavery in several American states was not something Brazil wanted to replicate. Even more terrifying to Brazilian elites was Haiti's successful slave revolt in 1791, as they realized how vulnerable Brazil was to a similar revolution. And so Brazil waited, for decades, at first growing more significant economically than Portugal, and then even becoming the center of the Portuguese empire in 1808, when the royal family fled Lisbon to escape Napoleon's invasion of Spain and Portugal. When Brazil finally became independent in 1822, it did so very conservatively, taking care not to stir the flames of social reform. A strong sense of nationalist spirit could have been threatening to elites, since, in nineteenth-century Brazil, a majority of the population was non-white and poor. Thus, Brazil continued to wait, resisting change and holding onto both the monarchy and slavery until nearly the end of the nineteenth century.

With few obvious external foes,[3] Brazil had little traction upon which to build national identity. Without some sort of national enemy, externalized other, or at least a common national goal, it is difficult to conceptualize and construct much in the way of national unity. During the nineteenth century, Brazil was at first a colony, and then an empire, and then a republic, but never really did it become a "nation" like so many other countries at that time. Even as the twentieth century began, what might be called the "imagined community" of Brazil (cf. Anderson, 1983) was built mostly upon a sense of dynasty (e.g., the Braganza family and Portuguese roots) – and what made someone Brazilian was loyalty to that dynasty – rather than a unique sense of national identity. Individual state and regional identities remained far more significant than any sense of Brazilian national identity.

With few printing presses and very low literacy levels, there were few methods for constructing national identity, especially across such an enormous and diverse geographic space. Moreover, Brazilian elites who attended university often went to Coimbra in Portugal, creating a sense of homogeneity and social cohesion at the top of Brazil's social hierarchy (Carvalho, 1982). International enemies were also not sufficient for building nationalist sentiment: Portugal was by no means vilified, as many Brazilians still had strong Portuguese roots and no intention of forsaking their mother country. Conflicts with neighboring countries were few and far between, and very often took on a regional character (e.g., gauchos in the south of Brazil) rather than a national one. Even Brazil's bloodiest international conflict is often remembered ingloriously: Brazil partnered with archrival Argentina (*and*

Uruguay) to wipe out Paraguay in the Triple Alliance War of 1864–1870. With the benefit of hindsight, it is not surprising that by the start of the twentieth century, Brazil had little in the way of national heroes or widespread patriotic sentiment.

Rather than fight against non-Brazilians, Brazil instead became bound in a series of civil conflicts that, arguably, continue into the present day. Nowadays, Brazilian independence is typically remembered as a peaceful transition, but such mainstream perspectives overlook several internal rebellions that reflected the social and political tensions of the times. Between 1822 and 1850, tens of thousands of people lost their lives in major uprisings all over Brazil (see Figure 2.2). In some cases, these conflicts represented resistance to imperial rule; in others they erupted over regional disputes and, in at least one case, there was a major slave rebellion (Reis, 1993). The countryside was also dotted with hundreds of *quilombos*, communities of escaped slaves that existed all over nineteenth-century Brazil. When Brazil finally abolished slavery in 1888, and then, one year later, overthrew the monarchy and sent Emperor Dom Pedro II into exile, it had little to build on in terms of a nationalist legacy. The past was fraught with splintering divisions. Instead, the new republican government looked to the future, inspired by positivism and the influence of logic and rationality (e.g., Carvalho, 1990). The Brazilian population, it was presumed, would warm to the new Republic of the United States of Brazil (nowadays referred to as the Old Republic) for reasons of natural social evolution. To resist would be irrational and backwards.

Resistance, of course, was soon to follow, most famously in the Canudos War of 1897. For decades, historians have debated the roots of this conflict (see, for example, Levine, 1988), yet there is at least general consensus as to the government's reasons for wanting to annihilate the messianic rebel leader Antônio Conselheiro and his followers. The northeastern settlement, occupied by roughly 20,000 rural poor, refused to acknowledge the legitimacy of the new republican government. One of their objections was to the republic's formal

---

Confederação do Equador (1824): States of Pernambuco, Ceará, and Paraíba

Cabanada (1832–1835): States of Pernambuco and Alagoas.

Revolta dos Malês (1835): Slave rebellion in Salvador, Bahia

Cabanagem (1835–1840): State of Pará

Sabinada (1837–1838): State of Bahia

Balaiada (1838–1841): State of Maranhão

Farroupilha (1838–1845): State of Rio Grande do Sul

Praieira (1848–1849): State of Pernambuco

Figure 2.2 Rebellions within Brazil, 1822–1850.
Source: Skidmore, 2010

separation of church and state. Moreover, the very existence of this community in the *sertão* (rural backlands) undermined the positivist discourses of the Brazilian state. Here were the peasant farmers, ex-slaves, nomads, and religious fanatics who would not conform to the state's positivist vision for Brazil's future, and, thus, existed as a living reminder of Brazil's "backward" past. Their fate was a brutal one: they were exterminated by federal troops – not a single male resident was left alive – and the few dozen women and children who survived were sent mostly to brothels in nearby Salvador (Robb, 2004). It remains the single greatest slaughter of Brazilians at any one moment in history. Even those like writer Euclides da Cunha who were meant to glorify the republic – in essence, to extol the government's victory over the outcast rebels – were traumatized by what they saw. Brazil entered the twentieth century politically intact, but socially and culturally it remained deeply divided.

There was resistance to national cohesion and state positivist initiatives elsewhere, too. Many local and regional holidays, for example, stood in opposition to nationalist narratives (see, for example, Kraay, 1999), and widespread medical interventions were viewed with skepticism, in some cases leading to all-out riots (Chalhoub, 1993; Meade, 1986). The state was equally unsatisfied with the population, and, influenced by scientifically racist ideologies common at the time, sought to "whiten" Brazil's population by encouraging increased European immigration. The new immigrants, it was believed, would make Brazil more progressive and developed. Heavy immigration from Europe had already begun in the latter decades of the nineteenth century, and, as the twentieth century began, there came another significant wave. Most numerous were migrants from Italy, Portugal, and Spain, many of whom provided São Paulo coffee growers a substitute for slave labor. Included here were also many Jewish migrants from the former Russian and Austrian–Hungarian Empires, as well as plenty of non-European migrants from Japan, Lebanon, and Syria. They settled overwhelmingly in the Southeast and South of Brazil, and still today one can see this legacy in Brazilian racial demographics (e.g., the populations of these states typically have lighter skin tones, for example, than people in the North and Northeast of Brazil – cf. Lesser, 1999). These migrants also spurred urban growth in the regions they settled, and cities like São Paulo transformed rapidly, while new cities like Belo Horizonte (founded in 1897) sprouted and took off.

The economy in the early 1900s continued to rely on non-durable commodity exports – most notably coffee and rubber – and, despite discourses of "order and progress," Brazil remained agrarian and overwhelmingly illiterate. In many respects, little had changed from past centuries. Many people still lived without running water, electricity, or sewerage. However, like elsewhere in Latin America, politics were changing. The oligarchies and regional alliances that had maintained power since colonial times were no longer proving capable. Growing urban populations and the rise of labor unions were challenging existing power structures (e.g., the influence of landed elites), and, in Brazil especially, national political institutions were being challenged by state ones (including their respective military forces). There was a host of factors that brought about Brazil's revolution of 1930 (for the best account, see Fausto, 1975), yet, for the purposes of this chapter, the outcomes are perhaps most significant. In particular was the rise of dictator Getúlio Vargas (see Figure 2.3). While political changes undertaken in the early 1930s may have gone largely unnoticed by most Brazilians (Skidmore, 2010), the Vargas era proved enormously significant for Brazil as a *nation*.

A dictator, a democratic regime, and a military coup

Like Juan Perón in Argentina, or Lázaro Cárdenas in Mexico, Getúlio Vargas in Brazil had a keen understanding of the new socio-political context of the 1930s. It would be unfair to call him a visionary, but he realized that what had kept countries like Brazil glued together in the past was proving insufficient for the future. There was a growing urban working class, and marginalized groups such as landless peasants, Afro-Brazilians, and people of indigenous descent –which altogether numbered in the tens of millions! – had seen very few improvements or social change since the nineteenth century. These were people that had previously been shut out of politics, and now they were growing restless and beginning to demand a voice in political decision-making processes.

The combined presence of these groups represented a majority of the population, and, due to economic, political, and social change occurring both nationally and globally, governments in South and Central America were finding it increasingly untenable to govern as they had in the past (e.g., by largely excluding these populations). Brazil's Revolution of 1930 came about, in part, in response to these social changes, but it was by no means a revolution of the masses. On the contrary, it was led by elites who understood it was necessary to appease an incipient middle class while also co-opting the working classes through both populist and authoritarian measures.

This is what Vargas seemed to grasp better than most of his contemporaries, or perhaps he realized that these formally excluded groups needed at least to feel included as part of the nation (Levine, 1998). Most Brazilian elites were skeptical about outright democracy (Vargas included), yet there was space to create among the lower classes a sense of belonging without guaranteeing equal rights. Wide open as the possibilities for nationalist discourses may have been, the challenge of creating a united Brazil – which is to say a truly *national* sense of identity – must have seemed daunting. Beyond massive regional differences and strong state identities that continued to persist, the positivist/racist legacy of the Old Republic complicated the realm of nationalist discourses. For example, Brazil's idealized national image as a fully modern, Europeanized country in the tropics (viz., an advanced "white" country) not only clashed with everyday realities; it blatantly excluded a great majority of the population. How does one steer such a problematic construction of national identity in a new direction, such that formerly excluded people feel welcome, yet traditional elites will not reject it? On Vargas's side here was that both the future *and* the past in Brazil were essentially unwritten. There was very little in the way of a

Brazilian nationalist narrative, and what was, from one perspective, a seemingly impossible challenge was, from another, a wide-open landscape of possibilities.

Consider, for example, any number of attributes one might call "essentially Brazilian." The list very likely includes things such as samba, Carnival, soccer, feijoada (the national dish), caipirinhas (the national drink), and so on. These are features that today help to define Brazil, providing recognizable cultural cues helpful for establishing national cohesion, while also distinguishing Brazil from countries elsewhere. Virtually every country has these features, and, as in other

Figure 2.3 Getúlio Vargas in 1930.

Source: Governo do Brasil, Wikimedia commons: https://commons.wikimedia.org/wiki/File:Getulio_ Vargas_(1930).jpg

countries, what makes them effective is how they appear somehow "natural" and omnipresent, as if they were organic elements within Brazil's sociological DNA. As in other countries, however, and especially those in the Americas, these attributes were socially constructed very recently, and in Brazil's case we can look specifically to the legacy of Getúlio Vargas.

Under Vargas, the *Estado Novo* government ("New State" – 1937–1945) identified specific cultural practices as nationally significant, and then invested in and cultivated them to national prominence. One example is the Portuguese language: despite Brazil's vast cultural and ethnic diversity, the *Estado Novo* worked to ensure that *everyone* in Brazil spoke Portuguese. Two other well-known examples are Brazil's national soccer team and Rio de Janeiro's Carnival celebration, including with it Rio's samba schools, still famous today. The *Estado Novo*'s patronage of samba and other *carioca* (i.e., from Rio de Janeiro) art forms provides a clear illustration of how certain cultural attributes are accentuated over others in processes of national identity formation. That samba and *choro* might today be called "national" musical genres (McCann, 2004; Vianna, 1999), whereas others like *maracatu* and *frevo* remain "regional" ones, reveals the not-so-organic roots of Brazilian national identity.

Not to be overlooked here is the issue of race. Where in the past Brazil had projected itself to the world as a "white" country, in the 1930s the *Estado Novo* began to embrace Brazil's legacy of miscegenation. The (supposed) harmonious mixture of European, African, and indigenous people was regarded as something uniquely Brazilian, and a virtue – both genetic and cultural – upon which Brazil could build as a nation. Important here was the scholarly work of Gilberto Freyre, who, in 1933, published *Casa-Grande & Senzala* (in English, *The Masters and the Slaves*, 1964), arguably the most significant work of history ever published in Brazil. Freyre's account has since been widely criticized (Moura, 1988; Silva, 1995), and most famously for the way he connected contemporary race relations in Brazil to its slave history. According to Freyre, Brazil's legacy of positive race relations – what was later called Brazil's "racial democracy," though Freyre was not the one to coin this term – could be explained by the more fluid and compassionate social relationships that (supposedly) existed between slaves and slave owners in Brazil. Freyre's understanding of the past, *and the present*, were, of course, deeply flawed, but his book was quickly recognized as a national master-piece and played a key role in nation building. For Vargas and the *Estado Novo*, such narratives were crucial for reaching out to marginalized populations without actually addressing head on issues of inequality.

Hand in hand with Vargas's populism, nationalism, and cultivation of national identity was also a strong authoritarian streak. From the Revolution of 1930 until 1945 he ruled Brazil as both president and dictator (mostly the latter), and then returned as an elected president between the years of 1951 and 1954. Vargas's approach was similar in many ways to European fascists such as Mussolini and Salazar, using the police to intimidate and keep order in the streets, while also suppressing his opposition and anything that looked like communism or socialism. His political strategy was corporatist, whereby industrialists *and* labor unions were effectively co-opted and corralled, and there was little room for political resistance or collective bargaining and mobilization (e.g., strikes were outlawed in Brazil between 1937 and 1946). He also worked to repress ethnic diversity among immigrants, and his "campaign of nationalization" (*campanha de nacionalização*), launched in 1938, went so far as to try to prohibit speaking foreign languages in public spaces (Seyferth, 1999). By 1954, however, growing economic problems meant Vargas began to lose control over his vertically assembled political support, and he confronted having to either resign the presidency or face a military coup d'état. He chose instead to commit suicide, shooting himself through the heart in August 1954. The effect was dramatic, likely as Vargas had planned. His suicide garnered widespread sympathy among the working classes, and he was celebrated as a national hero and champion of the poor, while his enemies (most notably the journalist and politician Carlos Lacerda) confronted severe public backlash.

Though Vargas's suicide and the political fallout left Brazil on somewhat shaky ground, what could be called the *nation* of Brazil emerged stronger than ever. There now existed a broadly recognizable sense of nationhood – albeit a very hegemonic one – and with it specific cultural attributes identifiable on a national scale. From the mid-twentieth century onward there were real moments of national pride and celebration (Brazil's World Cup victories in 1958 and 1962), as well as ones of national tragedy (Brazil's World Cup loss in the finals, at home, to Uruguay in 1950). Brazil *as a nation* had come together over just a few decades, and all this despite deep-seated socio-economic inequality and low levels of industrial development.

Brazil's next significant leader, Juscelino Kubitschek, sought to address the latter of these two issues (industrialization, not inequality), and in 1956 assumed the presidency with promises of large-scale national development. He prioritized heavy industry, the establishment of multinational manufacturing firms (especially the automobile sector), and construction, building roadways to better connect Brazil's vast hinterland. Most famously he oversaw the construction of Brasília in order to open up and populate Brazil's interior (along with other political motives), and in 1960 it was inaugurated as the new national capital. While Vargas is the one credited most with Brazilian nation building, Kubitschek played no small role himself. When his five-year term ended in 1961, Brazil had undergone a significant transformation, though not without mounting problems of debt, inflation, and a host of socio-economic tensions. So significant were these issues they proved too much for Kubitschek's successors, and, indeed, for Brazilian democracy itself.

Authoritarianism and resistance

From a historical perspective, one can identify some interesting parallels between the causes of the Revolution of 1930 and factors that led to the military coup in 1964. Both saw elites rally around anti-leftist rhetoric, and in both cases elites were wary of a popular rebellion from the underclasses. This is not to suggest the coup of 1964 can be explained by the same factors as the Revolution of 1930, or that Brazil was the same country more than three decades later. On the contrary, Brazil had changed immensely over the middle part of the twentieth century, and the events of 1930 and 1964 were distinguished by important political and economic factors. Still, what brought elites together in both cases, in both urban and rural contexts and from across different regions in Brazil (particularly in 1964), was a growing fear of the underclasses. Just as elites had looked to Haiti in 1791 and been wary of a similar slave uprising in Brazil, so, too, did they look to Cuba in 1959 and fear a similar revolution in Brazil. Part and parcel of this was also the influence of the USA and, in 1964, the context of the Cold War. But significant most of all was the preservation of Brazil's social hierarchy. Brazil as a *nation* had grown more inclusive between 1930 and 1964, at least discursively, but the actual *country* of Brazil was still highly unequal and resistant to social change.

Unlike the period following the Revolution of 1930, however, when the *Estado Novo* cultivated Brazilian national identity through populism and nationalism, the military dictatorship of 1964–1985 was marked more by cultural subversion than national cohesion. Artists such as Carmen Miranda and Pixinguinha, for example, saw their careers flourish alongside Brazil's growing sense of national identity under the *Estado Novo*, whereas artists like Gilberto Gil and Caetano Veloso were arrested by the military dictatorship and went into exile because of their counter-cultural musical stylings (i.e., *Tropicália* – see Dunn, 2001).

Much more so than the *Estado Novo*, the military dictatorship is remembered for violently oppressive tactics, and for a period of nearly ten years, beginning in the late 1960s, *tens of thousands* of Brazilians were imprisoned, tortured, murdered, and/or sent into exile by the dictatorship (Coelho Filho, 2012). As the years of military rule dragged on, opposition began to mount, and as the 1980s dawned – and Brazil's external debt ballooned, as it did in many countries in the region – the dictatorship lost legitimacy. 1984 saw yet another decisive moment in Brazil's national history, as millions took to the streets demanding direct presidential elections (i.e., the *Diretas Já!* movement). This established a new precedent in Brazilian solidarity and national unity, where people came together on a truly nationwide scale to denounce Brazil's political leadership (see Figure 2.4).

In terms of nation building and national identity, arguably the most important feature to emerge from the military dictatorship was the Globo television network (in Brazil, *Rede Globo*). Launched in 1965, TV Globo was supportive of, *and* supported by, the dictatorship, quickly growing to become the world's fourth largest TV network in just 20 years (Skidmore, 2010). By the 1980s, nearly every household in Brazil was watching Globo programming, a trend that continues well into the twenty-first century. Whether for news, entertainment, sport and leisure, etc., Globo remains unrivaled in its media dominance of Brazil. As a trend-shaping force and cultivator of national identity, Globo is, without doubt, one of the most significant actors in Brazil's history.

Figure 2.4 Protesters of the Diretas Já! movement in Brasília in 1984.
Source: Agência Brasil, Wikimedia commons: https://commons.wikimedia.org/wiki/File:Diretas_Já.jpg

In 1985, as the military dictatorship gave way to democracy, Brazil saw a new surge in social activism. Millions of historically marginalized people, including Afro-Brazilians, indigenous groups, rural peasants, women, LGBT groups, the urban poor, etc. (lumped together, a significant portion of the population), began to mobilize. This has been a slow process, but one that has been growing and making modest gains over the years. Simply put, the discourses of inclusion and unity established during the first half of the 1900s were wearing thin by the end of the century, as Brazil's historically marginalized populations continued to suffer disproportionate levels of discrimination, poverty, violence, and so on. More than just pushing for equal rights, these groups have worked to challenge what might be called the Brazilian national psyche, exposing the ways hegemonic narratives produce social inequality (e.g., how the myth of "racial democracy" or being "different but united" impedes social change – see, for example, DaMatta, 1991; Hanchard, 1999).

The Brazilian constitution of 1988 was in every way a progressive and ambitious document, and while Brazil has endured significant political and economic shifts since it was established, Brazilian democracy has remained intact.[4] 2002 saw the election of Luiz Inácio 'Lula' da Silva of the Workers' Party (the PT, *Partido dos Trabalhadores*), a truly momentous occasion where for the first time someone from Brazil's labor movement became president. Since then, Brazil has gone through extreme economic highs and lows, along with several major political corruption scandals that included the contentious impeachment of President Dilma Rousseff in 2016. Not to be overlooked here is that Rousseff is not the first president to be impeached since the 1988 constitution – there was also Fernando Collor de Melo in 1992 – yet both cases came to pass without serious threat of another military dictatorship. This, however, is not to say that Brazilian democracy exists without deep-rooted concerns. For more on this, with special attention paid to Brazil's 2018 presidential election, please see Chapter 4 and the Afterword at the end of the book.

These events have not come without consequence for Brazil as a nation, where signs of tension and disillusionment are becoming evident. For example, where Brazil's streets filled with protestors from diverse socio-economic backgrounds in what might be called a spontaneous (and national) popular uprising in 2013, less than two years later protests had grown clearly divisive, pitting those for and against Rousseff's impeachment against one another, as well as those for and against the PT more generally. Such divisions have grown increasingly obvious on a national scale, where from one perspective there exists a clear split between north and south. Very crudely, wealthier Brazilians who live in the southern half of the country and vote against the PT, and poorer Brazilians who live in the northern half and vote *for* the PT (see Figure 2.5). While Brazil appears in no danger of political fragmentation (unlike several

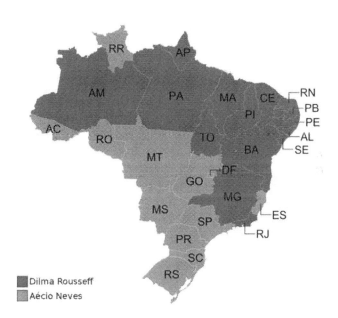

Figure 2.5 Second round presidential election results by state from 2014 showing strong support for Dilma Rousseff (Workers' Party) in the North and Northeast and equally strong support for Aécio Neves (PSDB) in the South, Southeast, and Central West.

Source: Felipe Menegaz, Wikimedia commons: https://commons.wikimedia.org/wiki/File:2014_Brazilian_ presidential_election_map_(Round_2).svg

countries in Europe, for example), such differences are, nonetheless, representative of significant social and demographic changes in the twenty-first century.

Related to this are growing rifts in what might be called Brazil's national body. For example, whereas Brazil is historically known as a Catholic country, surging conversion rates to evangelical and Pentecostal faiths are changing the face of Brazil's spiritual and cultural identity. Likewise are differences of opinion over issues such as civil rights, gender equality, discrimination, public education, environmental protection, human rights, and so on. Hot topics include abortion, same-sex marriage, affirmative action in higher education, and police violence and public security. It could be argued that Brazil – again, like many countries – appears to be at a crossroads regarding its national future. On the one hand are those who prefer increased privatization and reduced public expenditures, and on the other are those who want the state to take a more active role in addressing social inequality by improving public services and national infrastructure. Brazil's sense of nationhood and what it means to be Brazilian is very much at stake here, both in the ways people harness these discourses in different ways during public debate, as well as how these discourses change over time and the diverse effects they tend to produce.

Conclusion

Bringing this chapter back to where it began and what makes Brazil challenging for beginners, consider yet another (seemingly) straightforward question regarding national identity: Who are Brazil's national heroes? Nearly every country has them, and often they can be traced back to independence movements, social conflict, and struggles for civil and political rights. There are hundreds of national heroes in countries throughout the Americas, with obvious examples being Simón Bolívar, George Washington, José de San Martín, Susan B. Anthony, Martin Luther King, Frida Kahlo, Che Guevara, and so on. While not without controversy, national heroes play important roles in the ways countries remember their histories. So again, who are Brazil's? Is Chico Mendes one? Or Tiradentes? What about Zumbi or Machado de Assis? More to the point, of all Brazil's "national heroes" – for example, Joaquim Nabuco, Maria Bonita, Santos Dumont, Princess Isabel – who really stands out? Is there *anyone* known throughout all Brazil, perceived to embody Brazil's national spirit, who can actually be identified by most Brazilians?

The obvious answer is Pelé, the soccer star, which, in fact, is revealing in all sorts of ways. Pelé is about the least controversial national hero one can imagine. That Pelé is probably Brazil's most recognizable national hero exemplifies in many ways something DaMatta calls attention to:

> Everything suggests that we Brazilians see conflicts as omens of the end of the world, as signs of unbearable failure that make it difficult for us to accept them as part of our history, especially as part of the official versions of that history with its idealized and understandable emphasis on our

solidarity. This is why we always prefer to put more stress on our universalist and cosmopolitan tendencies, in the process sidestepping a more penetrating and accurate look at our problems.

(DaMatta, 1991, p.139)

There are good reasons to question DaMatta's argument here, and not least for his somewhat reductionist reading of Brazilian history and culture. To be sure, many Brazilians are critical of their own country, and this helps to explain increasing levels of social protest and polarization considered in several chapters throughout this book. Still, there remains compelling insight in DaMatta's argument that Brazilians prefer to see common ground between heterogeneous groups rather than identifying points of difference and inequalities. Particularly when trying to identify Brazil's national heroes. For example, given Brazil's diversity and history of struggle, trying to identify non-divisive national heroes is nearly impossible. This is not to say Brazilians lack patriotism, but simply that patriotism in Brazil exists differently than in countries elsewhere. For example, that "Brazil is not for beginners" is often endearing to many Brazilians, as it plays on a shared sense of national pride. It appeals to broader sentiments that *because* of Brazil's problems, Brazilians themselves tend to be clever, creative, and improvisational. They can find a way (i.e., *jeitinho*) under impossible circumstances. Such sentiments bring people together – again, emphasizing commonalities rather than conflicts – as well as turning nationwide problems (e.g., ongoing daily struggle) into positive and character-shaping attributes.

So why is Brazil like this? Throughout this chapter, we have considered a host of historical factors helpful for understanding Brazilian national identity, and in particular the slow and conflict-ridden process by which Brazil came together as a nation. Portuguese colonization established important pillars of language and religion, yet colonial traditions of governance, slavery, illiteracy, and loyalty to Portugal also meant that Brazil's sense of national identity was slow to emerge. When independence came in 1822, Brazil was still deeply divided – and still a long way from what could realistically be called a nation – evidenced by numerous civil conflicts waged throughout the nineteenth century. As both slavery and the monarchy came to an end, the new republican government sought to build Brazil on positivist foundations, hoping that European immigration would help "modernize" and whiten the population.

By 1930, however, it became clear that Brazil's tradition of oligarchic governance was incapable of keeping the country together, thus setting the stage for Getúlio Vargas and a host of "invented traditions" that helped forge the *nation* of Brazil (McCann, 1999). Still, it was not until the emergence of TV Globo several decades later that Brazilians would have so many tangible examples of what *being* and *feeling* Brazilian was supposed to look like. Since Brazil's return to democracy in the 1980s, these sentiments have, on some occasions, combined with deep-seated frustration, exploding in unprecedented moments of nationwide protest. Though highly critical of state actors, these popular manifestations have, nonetheless, played important roles in national cohesion.

All this helps to shed light on why the nation of Brazil looks as it does today, yet predicting how Brazil might look in the future is a different question altogether. Cultural and historical precedents are only partially useful, especially when one considers the profound influences of globalization, technology, and social media. Add to this the impacts of migration and demographic shifts, along with regional and global political change, and it is possible Brazil could look very different by the middle part of the twenty-first century. For example, ongoing processes of outward and inward migration remain significant, and, just as in many countries, they play important roles in political debate and discourses of national identity. Right now, as we enter the 2020s, both the country *and* nation of Brazil are very much in flux. Social, political, and economic tensions are arguably running higher than at any point in recent history, and, much like 100 years ago, the solutions of the past seem insufficient for the future. Like many countries, it could be said Brazil is facing an identity crisis, and the way in which Brazilians understand and make sense of their own country – including visions for what type of country they want to live in – will factor significantly into Brazil's future as a nation.

Notes

1 It bears noting that the first few lines in the English translation of Jobim's *Garota de Ipanema* bear little resemblance to the original Portuguese lyrics. Here is another example of how Brazil is often misunderstood internationally and the ways it can be difficult for beginners.
2 This number accounts for all Brazilian regions, including Amazonia, considered by the Trans-Atlantic Slave Trade Database (slavevoyages.org).
3 To be fair, conflict with the Spanish – and then later Argentina – was not insignificant along Brazil's southern border. But such rivalries were most intense for those in southern Brazil, and not necessarily significant for those elsewhere in the country.
4 Several readers might take issue with this claim, particularly with respect to president Dilma Rousseff's impeachment in 2016 and charges brought against former president Lula da Silva leading up to the 2018 presidential elections. These are fair objections, and ones we address more specifically in Chapter 4 and in the Afterword at the end of the book.

Suggested English readings

Barman, R.J. (1988). *Brazil: The Forging of a Nation*. Stanford: Stanford University Press.
Buarque de Holanda, S. (2012). *Roots of Brazil*. Translated by G.H. Summ. Notre Dame, IN: University of Notre Dame Press.
DaMatta, R. (1991). *Carnivals, rogues, and heroes: An interpretation of the Brazilian dilemma*. Notre Dame, IN: University of Notre Dame Press.
Eakin, M. (2017). *Becoming Brazilians: Race and national identity in twentieth-century Brazil*. Cambridge: Cambridge University Press.
Fausto, B. (1999). *A concise history of Brazil*. Cambridge: Cambridge University Press.
Freyre, G. (1964). *The masters and the slaves: A study of the development of Brazilian civilization* [*Casa-Grande & senzala: Formação da Família Brasileira sob o regime da economia patriarcal* (1933)]. Translated by Samuel Putnam. 4th ed. New York: Knopf.

Levine, R.M. (1998). *Father of the poor? Vargas and his era.* Cambridge: Cambridge University Press.

McCann, B. (2004). *Popular music in the making of modern Brazil.* Durham, NC: Duke University Press.

Ribeiro, D. (2000). *The Brazilian people: The formation and meaning of Brazil.* Gainesville: University Press of Florida.

Skidmore, T.E. (2010). *Brazil: Five centuries of change.* 2nd ed. Oxford: Oxford University Press.

Vianna, H. (1999). *The mystery of samba: Popular music and national identity in Brazil.* Chapel Hill: University of North Carolina Press.

References

Anderson, B. (1983). *Imagined communities: Reflections on the origin and spread of nationalism.* London: Verso.

Barman, R.J. (1988). *Brazil: The forging of a nation.* Stanford: Stanford University Press.

Bethell, L. (1985). The independence of Brazil. In: L. Bethell, (ed.), *The Cambridge History of Latin America* (Vol. 3). Cambridge: Cambridge University Press, pp. 157–196.

Bethell, L. (2010). Brazil and "Latin America". *Journal of Latin American Studies*, 42(03), 457–485.

Buarque, D. (2013). *Brazil: Um País do Presente.* São Paulo: Alameda.

Buarque de Holanda, S. (2012). *Roots of Brazil.* Translated by G.H. Summ. Notre Dame, IN: University of Notre Dame Press.

Cardoso, F.H. and Faletto, E. (1979). *Dependency and development in Latin America.* Berkeley: University of California Press.

Carvalho, J.M. de (1982). Political elites and state building: The case of nineteenth-century Brazil. *Comparative Studies in Society and History*, 24(03), 378–399.

Carvalho, J.M. de (1990). *A formação das almas: O imaginário da República no Brasil.* São Paulo: Companhia das Letras.

Chalhoub, S. (1993). The politics of disease control: Yellow fever and race in nineteenth-century Rio de Janeiro. *Journal of Latin American Studies*, 25(3), 441–463.

Chaui, M. (2000). *Brasil: Mito Fundador e Sociedade Autoritária.* São Paulo: Fundação Perseu Abramo.

Coelho Filho, P. (2012). Truth commission in Brazil: Individualizing amnesty, revealing the truth. *Yale Review of International Studies* (Feb. 2012). Available at: http://yris.yira.org/essays/440 [accessed 27 March 2018].

DaMatta, R. (1986). *O que faz o brasil, Brasil?* 2nd ed. Rio de Janeiro: Rocco.

DaMatta, R. (1991). *Carnivals, rogues, and heroes: An interpretation of the Brazilian dilemma.* Notre Dame, IN: University of Notre Dame Press.

Dunn, C. (2001). *Brutality garden: Tropicália and the emergence of Brazilian counterculture.* Chapel Hill: University of North Carolina Press.

Faoro, R. (1975). *Os donos do poder: Formação do patronato político Brasileiro.* 2nd ed. São Paulo: Editora da Universidade de São Paulo.

Fausto, B. (1975). *A Revolução de 1930: Historiografia e História.* São Paulo: Brasiliense.

Fausto, B. (1999). *A concise history of Brazil.* Cambridge: Cambridge University Press.

Freyre, G. (1964). *The masters and the slaves: A study of the development of Brazilian civilization* [*Casa-Grande & Senzala: Formação da família brasileira sob o regime da economia patriarcal* (1933)]. Translated by Samuel Putnam. 4th ed. New York: Knopf.

Furtado, C. (2007). *Formação econômica do Brasil.* São Paulo: Companhia das Letras.

Hanchard, M. (1999). Black Cinderella? Race and the public sphere in Brazil. In: M. Hanchard, (ed.), *Racial politics in contemporary Brazil*. Durham, NC: Duke University Press, pp. 59–81.

Jiménez-Martínez, C.A. (2017). Nationhood, visibility and the media: The struggles for and over the image of Brazil during the June 2013 demonstrations. PhD. London School of Economics and Political Science.

Kraay, H. (1999). Between Brazil and Bahia: Celebrating dois de Julho in nineteenth-century Salvador. *Journal of Latin American Studies*, 21(2), 255–286.

Lesser, J. (1999). *Negotiating national identity: Immigrants, minorities, and the struggle for ethnicity in Brazil*. Durham, NC: Duke University Press.

Levine, R.M. (1988). "Mud-hut Jerusalem": Canudos revisited. *Hispanic American Historical Review*, 68(3): 525–572.

Levine, R.M. (1998). *Father of the pPoor? Vargas and his era*. Cambridge: Cambridge University Press.

Maxwell, K. (2004). *Conflicts and conspiracies: Brazil and Portugal, 1750–1808*. London: Routledge.

McCann, B. (1999). The invention of tradition on Brazilian radio. In: R.M. Levine and J. J. Crocitti (eds), *The Brazil reader: History, culture, politics*. Durham, NC: Duke University Press, pp. 474–482.

McCann, B. (2004). *Hello, hello Brazil: Popular music in the making of modern Brazil*. Durham, NC: Duke University Press.

Meade, T. (1986). "Civilizing Rio de Janeiro": The public health campaign and the riot of 1904. *Journal of Social History*, 20(2), 301–322.

Mendes, C. (2010). *Subcultura e mudança: Por que me envergonho do meu país*. Rio de Janeiro: Topbooks Editora.

Monteiro, J.M. (1994). *Negros da terra: Índios e bandeirantes nas origens de São Paulo*. São Paulo: Companhia das Letras.

Monteiro, P.M. (2012). Foreword. In: Buarque de Holanda, S. *Roots of Brazil*. Translated by G.H. Summ. Notre Dame, IN: University of Notre Dame Press, pp. ix–xx.

Moura, C. (1988). *Sociologia do negro Brasileiro*. São Paulo: Editora Ática.

Philippou, S. (2005). Modernism and national identity in Brazil, or how to brew a Brazilian stew. *National Identities*, 7(3), 245–264.

Prado Jr., C. (2011). *Formação do Brasil contemporâneo*. São Paulo: Editora Companhia das Letras.

Reis, J.J. (1993). *Slave rebellion in Brazil: The Muslim uprising of 1835 in Bahia*. Baltimore: Johns Hopkins University Press.

Ribeiro, D. (2000). *The Brazilian People: The Formation and Meaning of Brazil*. Gainesville: University Press of Florida.

Robb, P. (2004). *A death in Brazil: A book of omissions*. New York: Picador.

Seyferth, G. (1999). Os imigrantes e a campanha de nacionalização do Estado Novo. In: D. Pandolfi, (ed.), *Repensando o Estado Novo*. Rio de Janeiro: Fundação Getúlio Vargas, pp. 199–228.

Silva, M. (1995). *Racismo à Brasileira: Raízes históricas*. 3rd ed. São Paulo: Anita Garibaldi.

Skidmore, T.E. (2010). *Brazil: Five centuries of change*. 2nd ed. Oxford: Oxford University Press.

Vianna, H. (1999). *The mystery of samba: Popular music and national identity in Brazil*. Chapel Hill: University of North Carolina Press.

3 Political structure and government

Introduction

Brazil is the fourth largest democracy in the world after India, the USA, and Indonesia. It has also experienced enormous political change in its modern history, including wrenching industrialization and urbanization; oscillation between military and civilian rule; mass movements demanding a variety of civil, political, and economic rights; and contested constitutional, legal, and political reforms. Although formally federal in its institutional design, the Brazilian state is more centralized than that of many other federal structures, and it combines an unusual electoral system with a form of presidentialism that involves the creation of large and complicated coalitions in Congress.

Colonized by Portugal in the sixteenth century, Brazil became politically independent in 1822. It has had six political regimes since then: the Empire (1822–1889); the Old Republic (1889–1930); the Vargas era (1930–1945); the Second Republic (1945–1964); the military dictatorship (1964–1985) and the New Republic (1985–present). Some features of Brazil's political history are distinctive when compared to those of its neighbors in Spanish America. For example, many of its decisive political transitions were accomplished with a relatively high degree of inter-elite consensus and bargaining, and relatively little bloodshed. That is not to say that Brazil's political history has been non-violent; however, most of the violence has been employed from the top down against the subaltern, the marginalized, and the poor.

This chapter briefly analyzes the central institutions and rules of the contemporary political system, as well as some important moments in Brazil's political history. Its themes include the existence of a large gulf between rulers and ruled; the belated emergence of a capable national state in the mid-twentieth century; the fragmentation of political representation under democracy, with an extreme version of multipartyism; and the strengthening of official accountability institutions embodying the ideal of equality of citizenship after the creation of the 1988 constitution. In contemporary Brazil, glaring economic inequalities and long-standing patterns of personalism, clientelism, corruption, and social hierarchy coexist with innovative participatory institutions, vibrant social movements demanding a variety of reforms, and robust political competition at election time.

Since Brazil's return to democracy in the second half of the 1980s, three waves of analysis of Brazil's political system can be observed. The first wave of the 1980s and early 1990s was quite pessimistic about Brazil's prospects. Scholars observed the conservative nature of the Brazilian transition to democracy and many of them feared that Brazil was vulnerable to an authoritarian regression. Some critics pointed to the alleged dysfunctionality of Brazilian electoral rules, the amorphous nature of Brazil's political parties, and the high costs of coalition-building in a multiparty system, which stymied much needed reforms (Ames, 2001; Mainwaring, 1999; O'Donnell and Schmitter, 1990; Stepan, 1999; Weyland, 1996).

A second wave of scholarship reflected the unexpected stability and policy consensus of the 1995–2010 period. This literature was largely positive about Brazil's "coalitional presidentialist" system (Abranches, 1988), in which the president's party never won more than 20% of the seats in either house of the national Congress, but in which governments were capable of creating working multiparty majorities (see, for example, Alston, Melo, Mueller, and Pereira, 2016; Limongi and Figueiredo, 1999; Melo and Pereira, 2013). Finally, the "third wave" of scholarship has reverted to pessimism again, in reaction to the discontent expressed in the mass protests of 2013, the recent political deadlock that saw the impeachment of President Dilma Rousseff in 2016, and renewed questioning of the costs of coalitional presidentialism (Avritzer, 2017; Mello and Spektor, 2017).

The political system

Anyone who understands the structure of the political system of the USA will find the Brazilian system familiar. There is a directly elected President who serves a four-year term, with the possibility of one re-election.[1] There is a national Congress with a lower house in which representation is based on population and a Senate with a fixed number of Senators for each state (although, unlike the USA, the federal district is represented in Congress). As in the USA, there is a separation of powers between the Congress, the presidency, and the judiciary, the latter represented at its apex by the Federal Supreme Court (with eleven, rather than nine, judges). Similarly, state governments have directly elected governors and state legislatures, and cities have directly elected mayors and city councils. As in the USA, state governments have their own constitutions.

However, there are features of Brazil's politics that will look very unfamiliar to an observer of the USA. For example, Brazil's 1988 Constitution is far more detailed than its USA counterpart, with nine major sections and 250 articles specifying, sometimes in minute detail, the rights and obligations of citizens and the powers and responsibilities of the respective branches of government and the agencies within them. Furthermore, as of the end of 2017, the constitution had been amended 99 times in 29 years, for an average of more than three amendments per year. While amendments require a three-fifths majority in both houses in two separate votes, in practice this has been relatively easy to achieve for most governments.

The party system is another example of difference with the USA. Rather than two parties, Brazil has 32 political parties represented in Congress and 35 registered with the Superior Electoral Tribunal or TSE, Brazil's highest electoral court. (In addition to these 35, a further 56 parties are trying to register with the TSE; two of these might obtain registration before the 2018 elections, bringing the total in the electoral system to 37.)[2] This makes Brazil an extreme case of multipartyism, facilitated by an electoral system that is permissive when it comes to the creation of new parties and the representation granted to small parties.

To form a new party, a relatively small number of signatures – 0.5% of the valid vote in the last election for the lower house of Congress – must be presented to the TSE. In 2014, this was 484,169 signatures, hardly an insurmountable barrier in a country of 208 million people.[3] New parties, once registered by the TSE, immediately get access to the electoral fund (Special Fund for Campaign Finance), public money allocated to parties for their campaigns. (This was R$1.7 billion in 2018, or roughly US$514 million at the exchange rate of R$3.31 to the dollar in March 2018.)[4] In October 2017, a barrier clause was created for political parties. Starting with the 2018 elections, parties will have to obtain a minimum of 1.5% of the national vote (or elect lower house deputies from nine different states) to qualify for public financing and free television and radio time in the campaign. This threshold will rise to three percent by 2030, and, starting in the 2020 elections, parties will no longer be able to form alliances with other parties with whom they do not share a program (Pereira, 2018, p. 148). As such, the growth of Brazil's political parties may have peaked, but it has peaked at a level that still amounts to extreme multipartyism when compared to the party systems of other democracies.

Like most other Latin American countries, Brazil also has a gender quota in its elections. Political parties are required to make sure that at each election, 30% of their candidates for office are women (Gatto, 2017, p. 249). Although Brazil was an early adopter of electoral gender quotas, passing the law before 2000 (Gatto, 2017, p. 247) and later revising it, the quotas have not had the impact on representation that some people had hoped for. After the 2014 elections, women had only 14% of the seats in the Senate and ten percent of the seats in the Congress, the lower house.[5] This compares unfavorably to the 32% of seats held by women in the UK House of Commons in 2018, for example, or the 19% and 22% of seats held by women in the USA's House of Representatives and Senate, respectively, both in 2018. (In some countries, over 40% of the seats in the national legislature were held by women in 2018; these include Bolivia, Costa Rica, Sweden, Mexico, South Africa, Finland, and Norway.)[6] There are several reasons why the candidate quota has not resulted in greater representation of women in Brazil's national Congress. Some parties put women up in races that they are unlikely to win; women's access to campaign financing is often limited; and party leaderships are still dominated by men (Gatto, 2017).

Loyalty to, and identification with, parties is almost non-existent in the Brazilian electorate, with the exception of members and sympathizers of the

Workers' Party (*Partido dos Trabalhadores*, or PT). Most parties are also amorphous in ideological and programmatic terms. Politicians often regard parties as
temporary vehicles of convenience, switching their allegiance from one to
another several times during their careers. As mentioned earlier, candidates to
the lower house of the national Congress (as well as state deputies and city
councillors) win election on the basis of open list proportional representation
(Nicolau, 2016). The vote for national congressional deputies takes place at the
state level for all candidates, rather than in smaller districts, as in the US and
UK electoral systems. That means that, if elected, deputies represent the voters
of their entire state, rather than any particular locality within it. Critics argue
that this increases the distance between voters and their representatives, and
allows the latter to dodge responsibility for particular local problems. Supporters
of the system argue that it guarantees that multiple parties represent the same
state in Congress, thus ensuring pluralism and the inclusion of a variety of
different voices in the legislature. Notwithstanding this debate, deputies serve
four-year terms with no limit on their re-election. Representation in the lower
house is capped at 70 seats (the largest state, São Paulo, has this number,
although, on the basis of its population, it is under-represented) and the
minimum is eight seats (over-representing the small states such as Roraima and
Amapá). The total number of lower house deputies is 513.

Unlike the USA, representation in the lower house is not reapportioned on
the basis of the census every ten years in Brazil. Representation is highly unequal
(Nicolau, 2015, p. 242). While São Paulo has one lower house deputy for every
644,000 citizens, Roraima, the smallest state, has one for every 64,000 people
(Pereira, 2018, p. 148). Senators are elected using a simple majority system
(Nicolau, 2015, p. 237). Every state and the federal district have three senators,
who serve eight-year terms (as with deputies, there is no limit on re-election).
There are a total of 81 senators. At four-year intervals, one-third and then two-
thirds of the Senators are elected, while all lower house seats are contested at
each election every four years (see Table 3.1).

Brazilian political campaigns are notoriously expensive. Exact figures on
campaign expenditure are hard to come by, because illegal off-the-books
campaign financing is common. The average district size – the state electorate
– is five million but ranges enormously, from 325,000 in Roraima to 32 million
in São Paulo. In big states, the costs of campaigning are particularly high.
Candidates in the 2014 election officially reported spending one billion *reais*,
or more than US$302 million. Ten large companies financed the campaigns of
70% of candidates elected to the lower house of Congress. These firms were in
construction, banking, mining, and food, and all were recipients of government
financing and/or government contracts. In 2015, the Federal Supreme Court
ruled that donations to political campaigns by companies were unconstitutional,
and since then only donations by individuals (up to a limit of ten percent of the
individual's income in the prior year) has been allowed.[7]

The parties that compete for power, and the coalitions that form at the state
level, are different across states. This is confusing for voters and gives Brazil a

Table 3.1 The three branches of Brazil's federal government.

	EXECUTIVE	LEGISLATIVE	JUDICIAL
Power vested in	President of the Republic	National Congress comprises two bodies: the Federal Senate and the Chamber of Deputies	Federal Supreme Court (along with lower-level Superior, National, and Regional courts)
Composition	Directly elected president/head of state; governs in multi-party coalition (e.g., Vice-President is often a member of coalition party)	Federal Senate comprises three senators from each of Brazil's 26 states and the federal district – for a total of 81 senators. Chamber of Deputies are elected by proportional representation from each state (and the federal district) for a total of 513 deputies	11 Federal Supreme Court judges (called ministers). The President of the court is elected by his fellow judges and this traditionally goes to the longest-serving judge on the court.
Appointment	National election	State-level elections	Appointed by president and confirmed in the Senate
Time in office	4 years; can serve multiple terms but not more than two consecutively	Senators serve 8-year terms with no term limits; Deputies serve 4-year terms with no term limits	Permanent, but with mandatory retirement at age 75

Source: The authors.

higher level of political fragmentation, and a lower degree of party system nationalization than many other Latin American countries. However, Brazilian presidents are relatively powerful and certain features of the Brazilian system strengthen the importance of presidential elections. For example, the winner of the presidential election has to win 50% of the vote or more. If no one reaches that threshold in the first round, a second-round run-off is held four weeks later (Nicolau, 2015, pp. 242–243). Presidents, therefore, start off their terms with popular majorities and a mandate that gives them leverage over Congress.

Furthermore, since 1994, presidential, gubernatorial, and legislative elections at the state and federal level have concurred in Brazil, strengthening the alignment between national and subnational election outcomes (Borges and Lloyd, 2016, p. 107). With the exception of small groups of indigenous people, Brazil does not have territorialized ethnic identities, and this increases the homogeneity and cohesion of the electoral process (Borges and Lloyd, 2016; Schakel, 2013). (Unlike in India, for example, in Brazil regional parties representing specific linguistic or ethnic communities are not significant.) Furthermore, the Workers'

Party is a truly national party with representation in almost all of Brazil's *municípios* (counties). Presidential politics shape state politics because, as Borges and Lloyd (2016, p. 104) argue, "No candidate for subnational executive office receives as much media attention or as many campaign contributions as the top presidential contenders do."

At the national level, a system of "coalitional presidentialism" helps to achieve coordination within Congress despite the high number of parties (Melo and Pereira, 2013). As mentioned earlier, this arrangement has elements of a parliamentary system, in that presidents are elected from parties that never have majorities in either house, and, therefore, have to stitch together complicated multiparty coalitions in order to govern. As the party system has fragmented in recent years, those coalitions have grown in size. In the government of Dilma Rousseff (2011–2016), the coalition was made up of ten different parties. Presidents try to placate the parties in their coalition and maintain their support by awarding them ministerial posts (sometimes with the right to appoint large numbers of people at lower levels of the ministry) and federal resources for their home states.

President Rousseff's impeachment in 2016 was a major event in Brazil's young democracy. On April 17–18, the lower house of Congress voted on whether to refer the case to the Senate. 367 deputies voted in favor, with only 172 against. President Rousseff then stepped aside, provisionally replaced by her Vice-President, Michel Temer, and an all-male, all-white cabinet. On 31 August, after several days of deliberation, the Senate voted 61 to 20 to remove the President from office. The Temer administration formally began, with a formal mandate until the end of 2018, controversial origins, and a very low rate of popularity (Pereira, 2017, p. 153).

The impeachment probably had more to do with President Rousseff's mismanaging the economy and losing her majority in the lower house than it did with the alleged budgetary improprieties she was accused of. In this sense, her impeachment had some of the characteristics of a parliamentary vote of no confidence, even though Brazil's is a presidential system. Defenders of the impeachment argued that it followed constitutional procedures, was conducted by members of Congress who had been elected, and was presided over by a Federal Supreme Court with a majority of judges appointed by President Dilma Rousseff and her predecessor, President Lula. Critics argued that the demands to remove the President started right after her re-election in 2014, and, thus, preceded the constitutional justification for the impeachment. Some of these critics called Rousseff's removal a "coup," pointing out that many in Congress who opposed her faced serious charges of personal corruption, and appeared to have been motivated by a desire to stop the investigations and legal proceedings against them.

It is hard to escape the conclusion that the impeachment, while legal and popular, was not legitimate. In ruling that the budgetary maneuvers for which Dilma was removed was a crime of responsibility worthy of removal from office, Congress ignored a history of permissiveness with regard to the budget by executive branch leaders in Brazil that includes former presidents, state governors, and mayors. The impeachment weakened the presidency, involved a highly selective invocation of the rule of law, and did not address the problem of systematic corruption among the major parties and in Congress. Furthermore, in a deal that seemed to defy article 52 the 1988 constitution, which specifies that a presidential impeachment should result in the deprivation of the president's political rights for eight years, the then-President of the Federal Supreme Court, Ricardo Lewandowski, and the Senate allowed Dilma Rousseff to keep her political rights. This deal reinforced the perception among the Brazilian electorate that rules – even constitutional ones – can be played with by elected officials, that there is one rule for the powerful and another for the powerless, and that the self-interest of politicians usually comes before any conception of the public good.

While President Rousseff proved to be incompetent in maintaining a governing coalition, her successor, Michel Temer, a veteran member of Congress, showed himself to be much more able, successfully defeating a motion in the lower house to allow him to be tried for corruption in the Supreme Court in August of 2017. This occurred despite the then-Prosecutor General of the Republic, Rodrigo Janot, bringing charges in the Supreme Court against President Temer of corruption, obstruction of justice, and racketeering (Pereira, 2018, pp. 146–147).

In recent years, the coordination of parties at the national level has been supported by a trend of fiscal recentralization. Under the new constitution that was promulgated at the end of the military dictatorship in 1988, Brazil entered an era of decentralization. Because the dictatorship had centralized power in many areas, there was popular pressure and regional political interest in decentralizing. Decentralization became associated with democratization. However, this process began to be partially reversed in the 1990s, in part because state spending got out of control, jeopardizing the fiscal equilibrium of the federal government. Under President Fernando Henrique Cardoso, a fiscal responsibility law, passed in 2000, reined in state spending.

In the same period, Cardoso's government decentralized expenditure responsibilities to the municipal level in order to make it more difficult for state governors to divert revenues towards patronage (Dickovick, 2007). New center-local linkages helped the federal government restrain governors who had been empowered in the process of democratization. Significantly, social policy was the most substantial area of expenditure responsibility to be transferred to the municipalities (Dickovick, 2007; Fenwick, 2016). Thus, the federal government reduced the spending capacity of the states while also enhancing fiscal space at the federal level by expanding taxation.[8] New revenues collected by the federal government were increasingly directed towards the social sector from Cardoso onwards (Campello and Neri, 2013, 2014; Melo, 2008, p. 176; Schneider, 2015), and were directed via municipalities rather than the states (Fenwick, 2016).

Alfred Stepan (1999) described Brazil as sitting at one end of what he called a *demos constraining* to *demos enabling* continuum. By this he meant that institutional features of Brazilian federalism such as the over-representation of small states in the Senate, the strong powers of the Senate *vis-à-vis* the lower house, and the embedding of the allocation of inter-governmental powers in the constitution, undermine the ability of the central government to pass reforms on the basis of popular majorities and increase the powers of minority interests.

Trust in politicians and political parties is low in Brazil, and the gap between representatives and those who are supposed to be represented is wide. This gap is exacerbated by unusual privileges enjoyed by Brazilian elected officials. For example, at the top of the federal government, members of Congress, the cabinet, the President and Vice President – about 700 people in all – have what is called a "privileged forum" (*foro privilegiado*). This means that they can only be tried by the Federal Supreme Court; this privilege extends to anything they might be charged with, not just crimes committed in connection to their office. In practice, conviction of these individuals in the Supreme Court is very rare.

A recent study of privileged forum cases dealt with by the Supreme Court concluded that fewer than one percent of these cases resulted in a conviction. Because there were so many cases and the court was slow in dealing with them, many defendants were protected by statutes of limitation; in other instances, the cases were transferred to other courts when the defendant left public office (Falcão, Hartmann, Almeida, and Chaves, 2017, p. 9). The privileged forum is seen by some members of the public as an institution that delays judgment and provides impunity to politicians. In total, about 22,000 public officials have some version of the privileged forum in the Federal Supreme Court and other courts at the federal and state levels. To take one example of the impact of the privileged forum, as of March 2018 there were hundreds of cases involving politicians in the Federal Supreme Court. But in only 35 of those had charges been brought, and in only nine of them had charges been turned into criminal proceedings. In the words of a criminal defense lawyer, "The Federal Supreme Court does not have a vocation for making criminal judgments".[9] In 2018, the Supreme Court, in a series of judgments, began to reduce the scope of the privileged forum, excluding certain categories of office holders from its jurisdiction and limiting the crimes of legislators that can be heard in it to those linked to the exercise of their mandates.[10]

In addition to the traditional three branches of government (the executive, legislative, and judicial), Brazil has a Public Ministry that, since the promulgation of the 1988 constitution, has functioned as a virtual fourth branch of government. This Public Prosecutors' Office has the authority to protect the public interest by investigating and, if necessary, prosecuting individuals who may have harmed that interest. The scope for action of prosecutors in the Public Ministry, who have security of employment and cannot under ordinary circumstances be replaced or relocated, is very wide. The Public Ministry works closely with the Federal Police, an entity that has also gained autonomy and capacity in recent decades. The Federal Police is a national police force that supervises the entrance and exit of foreigners from the national territory, issues passports to Brazilian citizens, monitors national borders, and investigates federal crimes (see Power and Taylor, 2011).

This brief overview of Brazil's political system helps to explain how Brazilian democracy operates. However, to better understand *why* contemporary Brazil's political structure looks the way it does, important historical factors must also be accounted for. We consider these in the next section, and then move on to explore recent political corruption scandals that have rocked Brazil.

The late development of a national state

Brazil's political development has been marked by several characteristics, including the relatively late development of a national state, a large gulf between rulers and ruled, and a complex history of regionalism. Brazil was settled by the Portuguese in a South American continent dominated by the Spanish empire. South America has experienced less international war (measured by battle deaths) than any other major world region, and this has shaped the internal characteristics and foreign policies of its states. In South America, "state survival has been virtually guaranteed, wars have been rare, and legalization of disputes has been the norm" (meaning that border disputes have usually been settled by treaties) (Malamud, 2017, p. 153). Furthermore, "security has acquired a more domestic than international connotation" (Malamud, 2017, p. 153), and the armed forces have had important domestic roles in areas such as policing and the development of infrastructure.

Brazil's last major involvement in war was against Paraguay in 1865–1870, and its last remaining border disputes were settled peacefully under Foreign Minister José Maria da Silva Paranhos Júnior – better known as the Baron of Rio Branco – Brazil's most famous diplomat, from 1902 to 1912. Although Brazil has borders with ten other South American countries, the vast bulk of its population lives near the Atlantic coast at a great distance from those borders. Brazil has not faced serious security threats within its region, apart from a historical rivalry with Argentina, and its armed forces have focused inwards as much as they have engaged in the defense of the territory against external enemies (see Chapter 10).

The Portuguese seaborne empire that colonized Brazil was smaller and less bureaucratically capable than its Spanish rival. The Portuguese crown granted huge tracts of land (captaincies) to members of the nobility willing to settle in, and administer, the territory, and these rulers acquired near-absolute local powers, given their distance from Lisbon and the weaknesses of Portugal's colonial administration (for more on this, see Chapter 2). A refueling station on the way to the riches of the East and a source of some primary products such as brazilwood (used to dye clothes red) and sugar, Brazil, in the early part of its colonial history in the sixteenth and seventeenth centuries, was a backwater in its own region, which was dominated by the wealth of Peru, the center of the Spanish Empire in South America (Boxer, 1973). It was also a territory that supplied Europe with primary products; its name comes from the first of those exports.

Independent Latin American states arose in the early nineteenth century in much of the Spanish Empire through rebellions of American-born Spaniards and their irregular armies. In Brazil, however, independence was triggered by the royal family itself, and little fighting ensued. The Portuguese royal family and its court had moved to Brazil in 1808, with the help of the British Navy, to escape the occupation of Portugal by the French Army. Brazil became home to the only European monarchy in the Americas (aside from the brief and ill-fated interlude of Maximilian's rule in Mexico from 1864 to 1867). In 1820, most of the royal family returned to Portugal, but not before the King, João, named his son, Pedro, Prince Regent, leaving him in Brazil. Independence came about in 1822, with Pedro leading Brazil out of what had been the United Kingdom of Portugal, Brazil, and the Algarves and into what was called the Brazilian Empire.

Brazil's independence was, therefore, less an anti-colonial revolt than it was the separation of two strands of the same European royal dynasty. This conservative and imperial establishment of sovereignty contrasts with the republican and popular origins of the USA and most of the Spanish American republics (Simon, 2017, p. 9). It also stands in stark contrast to the revolutionary origins of Haiti, which achieved independence from France in 1804 after an uprising of slaves against their colonial masters.

The rulers of Brazil feared the Haitian example. At the beginning of the nineteenth century, Brazil had the largest slave population in the world – roughly 50% of its total population of 3 million (Eakin, 1998; Fausto and Fausto, 2014). The economy was based on slave labor in mining and plantation agriculture. Brazil exported coffee, sugar, tobacco, and other agricultural commodities. For most of the century, Brazil was ruled by Emperor Pedro II, the son of Pedro I (see Figure 3.1). The managers of the central state spent much of their time putting out the fires of secessionist and slave revolts and keeping the national territory together, largely through the selective deployment of the navy and army. Brazil was an archipelago of loosely connected provinces, but, unlike the remnants of the Spanish Empire after independence, it did not fragment into several small states. Brazil remained whole, and, in fact, expanded westward beyond its colonial territorial limits.

As noted in Chapter 2, one factor in the greater degree of cohesiveness of the former Portuguese empire was the education and socialization of the country's elites. Unlike the Spanish in the Americas, the Portuguese had prohibited the establishment of universities in their colony. Brazil's elites tended to study abroad, most notably law and engineering at the University of Coimbra in Portugal, and this common experience facilitated inter-elite communication and understanding, which in turn helped to maintain the empire (Carvalho, 1993). From 1865 to 1870, Brazil fought the bloodiest war of its history against Paraguay, in partnership with Uruguay and Argentina. In the early part of the war, military setbacks revealed Brazil's lack of preparation for a large-scale conflict. Over the course of the war, which compared in scale and ferocity to the Civil War in the USA (1861–1865), industrialization in São Paulo was spurred by the demands of the armed forces for weaponry and supplies.

The war also saw the strengthening of the armed forces within the state, and the armed forces subsequently played an important role in the abolition of

Figure 3.1 Emperor Dom Pedro II, monarch of the Empire of Brazil from 1831–1889, pictured here in 1876.

Source: Brady–Handy collection (United States Library of Congress), Wikimedia commons: https://commons.wikimedia.org/wiki/File:Pedro_II_of_Brazil_-_Brady-Handy.jpg

slavery in 1888. (Brazil became the last country in the Americas to abolish slavery, twenty-five years after the Emancipation Proclamation in the USA.) Abolition coincided with large-scale immigration to Brazil from Europe, especially Italy, Spain, and Portugal, and immigrant laborers replaced slaves in the vital coffee-growing heartland of São Paulo state. The armed forces also deposed the emperor and declared the establishment of the Brazilian republic in 1889. The officers who established the republic, many of whom were believers in the positivist philosophy of Auguste Comte, chose the Comtean motto "order and progress" for the nation – still seen today on Brazil's flag – and promulgated a constitution inspired in part by that of the USA.

The first phase of republican rule in Brazil from 1889 to 1930 was an oligarchical system based on the "politics of the governors." Powerful state machines competed and cooperated with one another to shape national politics; the central state was weak. The key alliance was between the two largest states of São Paulo and Minas Gerais, which alternated control of the presidency in an arrangement dubbed coffee with milk, in recognition of the main products of these states' economies. In this period coffee was Brazil's principal export and the USA its most important market.

Brazil's state was dualistic in the sense that it accommodated cosmopolitan, liberal, and outward-looking financial and export sectors in Brazil's principal cities, located on or near the coast. But it also represented provincial and more traditional landed elites based on the plantations of the countryside, where despotic landlord control over dependent laborers continued despite formal equality of citizenship (Topik, 2002). Elections were regular under the old republic, but they were often fraudulent and the franchise was very small. The number of people who voted in the old republic has been estimated at between one and five percent of the population (Nicolau, 2012, pp. 58–59).

The Wall Street crash of 1929 and the subsequent depression shook the political stability of most governments in Latin America as demand for exports plummeted. Governments fell throughout the region, and in Brazil the collapse of the São Paulo–Minas Gerais compromise led to a revolt spearheaded by the states of Minas Gerais, Rio Grande do Sul, and Paraíba. This revolt was known as the 1930 revolution, although it was not a social revolution (as in Russia in 1917, or in Mexico in 1910), but an inter-elite conflict. The former Governor of Rio Grande do Sul, Getúlio Vargas, came to power and subsequently ruled for fifteen years, mostly as an unelected president. The most authoritarian phase of his rule was the "New State", which was inaugurated by an auto-coup in 1937, in which the president and the armed forces canceled elections, closed Congress, and ruled on an emergency basis. The New State lasted until the end of the Second World War in 1945.

The Vargas years were pivotal for Brazil and saw the formation of many key state institutions that are still present today, as well as the growth of a powerful federal bureaucracy that centralized the loose coalition of ruling forces that had held sway during the Old Republic. Previously powerful state militias were subordinated to the army and, in a symbolic act of destruction, the Vargas regime burned the flags of the states in an attempt to replace the regionalism of the Old Republic with a new, more powerful central state. Again, as detailed in Chapter 2, the Vargas regime promoted the Portuguese language and symbols of Brazilian national identity such as football (soccer), samba, and the image of the President himself as the "father of the poor" (Levine, 1988).

The Vargas regime also recognized trade unions, creating a Ministry of Labor and a network of labor courts, and codified labor rights in the 1943 Con-solidated Labor Laws. Under Vargas, urban workers in the formal sector gained new rights to a minimum wage, pensions, and the opportunity to have their disputes with employers adjudicated in a labor court. These policies, dubbed "workerism" (*trabalhismo*), won Vargas the support of much of the expanding working class during this period. Vargas promoted Brazilian industrialization and gained American financing of a steel mill in Volta Redonda (Rio de Janeiro state). He also moved Brazil closer to the USA in the international arena (see Chapter 10).

Proportional representation, a feature of Brazil's rules for electing members of the lower house of the national Congress, was devised in the 1930s by the Vargas regime to prevent the establishment of dominant party machines at the state level.[11] Proportional representation, or PR, is an electoral system in which seats are distributed to parties based on their share of the vote. Used widely in continental Europe, it gives small parties opportunities they do not have in the first-past-the-post system of the USA and the UK. Open-list PR, introduced in Brazil in 1945 (Nicolau, 2015, p. 240), allows voters to choose their preferred candidates by name, as opposed to closed-list PR, in which party leaders rank the candidates in their party, so that votes go automatically to those who are ranked highest. With open-list PR, the control of party leaders over who gets elected is limited, candidates essentially run against everyone else, including candidates from their own party, and elections favor politicians with broad name recognition. As mentioned earlier, in the Brazilian system, districts are the entire state in elections for the lower house of Congress, making them far larger than those typically found in first-past-the-post systems.

The Vargas government enacted proportional representation in the early 1930s in reaction to the fraud and party politics of the Old Republic. The leaders of the 1930 Revolution wanted a system of representation that gave opportunities to minority parties that had been excluded by dominant state party machines under the old system (Pires, 2009, pp. 129–133). President Vargas knew the power of these machines very well. He started his political career as a loyal follower of republican party leader Borges de Medeiros, who was Governor (in those days called President) of Rio Grande do Sul for twenty-five years (1898–1908 and 1913–1928), winning elections that were sometimes fraudulent and violent.

There was another, more pragmatic reason why the leaders of the Vargas regime wanted to weaken the state party machines. They were keen to make sure that states could not combine to overthrow the government in the same way that they themselves had come to power. Open-list proportional representation leads to many parties gaining seats in the lower house from each state. It fragments regional representation, strengthens the power of the central state, and prevents the emergence of monopolistic state parties of the type that existed in the Old Republic.

Vargas was forced out of office by the high command of the armed forces in 1945, and the so-called Second Republic was born. This period was marked by the growth of urbanization and industrialization, the expansion of the electorate through the inclusion of the working class, and conflicts over Brazil's relationship with the USA and international investors. The armed forces intervened on several occasions to resolve political stalemates. Getúlio Vargas returned to the presidency after winning the election of 1950 and ruled from January 1951 to August 1954, when he committed suicide during a crisis. During this period, the state oil company, Petrobras, and the national development bank, the BNDE (then the National Bank for Economic Development, now the National Bank for Economic and Social Development or BNDES), were created.

Perhaps the most emblematic presidency of the Second Republic was that of Juscelino Kubitschek, "JK", who promised "fifty years of development in five" and was President from 1956 to 1961. During Kubitschek's presidency, foreign companies began producing cars in Brazil and the national capital was moved from Rio de Janeiro to a new, modernist city built from scratch in the interior of the country: Brasília (see Figure 3.2). Kubitschek's presidency is often seen as a time of optimism and innovation in Brazil, with the country gaining international recognition for its modernism in architecture and urban planning, music (especially Bossa Nova), and soccer (Brazil won the first of its five World Cups in Stockholm in 1958; see Chapter 11).

Kubitschek's successor, Jânio Quadros, was elected in 1960, but resigned unexpectedly in his first year in office and was replaced by his Vice President, João Goulart, a protégé of Vargas. Goulart's presidency was turbulent. Cold War divisions were exacerbated by the 1959 Cuban Revolution and the 1962 Cuban missile crisis. Goulart promoted the establishment of rural trade unions and promised land reform and other structural changes. At the end of March 1964, military officers moved against him in a coup d'état that had the support of the

Figure 3.2 The Palácio Nereu Ramos, Brazil's National Congress building in Brasília. It was designed by Oscar Niemeyer and completed in 1960.

Source: Mario Roberto Duran Ortiz, Wikimedia commons: https://commons.wikimedia.org/wiki/File:
Brasilia_Congresso_Nacional_05_2007_221.jpg

USA. The authoritarian regime that was subsequently established lasted for 21 years, with all presidents during that period being army generals. Congress was purged, the party system was reshaped, and repression was unleashed against dissidents and opponents of the regime, reaching its height in the late 1960s and early 1970s.

The dictatorship gradually began to liberalize, starting in the mid-1970s. In 1984, a mass movement for direct elections for president failed in its immediate aim but demonstrated the power of civil society. A revitalized trade union movement became more active. By 1985, a civilian president was indirectly elected in Congress, and in 1988 a new constitution (called by some a "citizens' constitution" – see Holston, 2009) was promulgated after an intensive process of constitution-making in 1987 and most of 1988 in which demands coming from civil society were presented in, and debated by, Congress. In 1989, a direct presidential election was held for the first time since 1960. Democracy had finally returned to Brazil. This time democracy was more inclusive than ever: for example, for the first time, illiterates could vote. The communist parties were legalized, and people aged 16 and 17 were also allowed to vote (although their vote was voluntary). For everyone else, voting was (and still is) compulsory. Voters who abstain by not appearing at the polls are subject to a small fine. Voters who have no preference can cast a blank vote, pressing the button for this option on the electronic voting machine that was first introduced in Brazil in 1996, or they can cast a null vote by putting in a number that does not exist, such as "00", and confirming their selection. In both of these instances the vote is not allocated to any candidate and is not considered valid.

The first few years of the new democracy were troubled as hyperinflation, fueled by deficit spending at the federal level, spiraled out of control. However, 1994 ushered in a period of relative economic and political stability with the imposition of the anti-inflationary Real Plan. Inaugurated during the presidency of Itamar Franco, who had succeeded Fernando Collor de Mello after the latter was impeached for corruption in 1992, the Real Plan contributed to the election of one of its progenitors, the academic-turned-politician Fernando Henrique Cardoso. Cardoso persuaded Congress to change the constitution and served two terms as President from 1995 to 2002, presiding over a period of liberal reforms of the economy, including the privatization of state owned firms, and of an increase in federal control of public spending. The stability brought about by the Real Plan is reflected in the terms of office of Finance Ministers. From 1985 to 1995, Brazil had twelve Finance Ministers; most left office in less than a year. From 1995 to 2015, Brazil had only three.

The years from 2003 to 2016 were ones in which the presidency was controlled by the Workers' Party, founded in 1980 by activists from trade unions and other social movements and middle-class intellectuals. The election of a Workers' Party candidate in 2002 was an important milestone for Brazilian democracy, showing that a formerly oppositional political party on the left could take power through peaceful means without military intervention or a capital strike. Ruling in coalition with other parties, first under President Luiz Inácio "Lula" da Silva and then under Lula's hand-picked successor, Dilma Rousseff, the Workers' Party changed Brazilian politics by substantially reducing poverty and (to a lesser extent) inequality. This was achieved through increases in the minimum wage, a conditional cash transfer program (*Bolsa Família*, or Family Allowance), and other social programs, and by increasing access to universities, technical education, and consumer credit (Pereira, 2015; Tillin and Pereira, 2017). In the 2000s, for the first time, the majority of Brazilians were in the middle of the income distribution. This was heralded as the emergence of the "new middle class", although many of the people in this category could more accurately be described as working class, albeit workers with enhanced prospects for access to credit and the ownership of homes, cars, and other consumer goods.

The Workers' Party years also saw the expansion of new forms of participation at the local, state, and federal level (Avritzer, 2002, 2009). Locally, participatory budgeting was initiated in many cities, allowing residents to influence the spending priorities of parts of the municipal budget. In the health and education sectors, councils were created in an attempt to institute social control over these public policies. Even at the federal level, councils were created to expand participation beyond the traditional and formal mechanisms of representative democracy (Avritzer, 2009).

At the end of his second term in 2010, Lula was one of Brazil's most popular presidents, with an approval rating hovering around 80%. For most of his period in office and for the first three years of Dilma Rousseff's term, Brazil combined growth with redistribution. But it was also a period of political business as usual, as the Workers' Party allied itself with many parties and ruled over a broad coalition. Additionally, while the Workers' Party long touted itself as free from deep-rooted legacies of political corruption, an important investigation later suggested that continued systematic corruption was part of this business as usual. The relative political calm and prosperity that had endured for nearly 20 years thus began to unravel.

A strong democracy?

In June and July of 2013, Dilma Rousseff's administration was shaken by nationwide protests that reflected a widening legitimacy gap between elected officials and the public, and revealed popular discontent about corruption, skewed governmental spending priorities, and the low quality of public services in education, health, transportation, and security. The protests were more anti-political than anti-government, but President Rousseff's popularity fell sharply and never fully recovered. She narrowly succeeded in winning re-election in 2014 as growth slowed and political polarization deepened, but, in the subsequent year, millions of people took to the streets to demand her impeachment and she lost control of her majority in the lower house of Congress. Reflecting this polarization, a recent edited volume about contemporary Brazilian democracy is titled *Democratic Brazil Divided* (Kingstone and Power, 2017).

In August 2016, Dilma Rousseff was impeached on the controversial charge of fiscal impropriety. Majorities in both houses of Congress voted for her removal on the grounds of creative bookkeeping, maneuvers in which the federal government's fiscal deficit was temporarily made to look smaller than it was. Dilma Rousseff's own Vice President, Michel Temer, was part of the coalition in favor of impeachment. Temer became President in a conservative restoration, ushering in policies of economic liberalization and fiscal austerity, supported by business interests and most of the mainstream media. His government passed a constitutional amendment freezing government spending in real terms for the next 20 years, reformed the labor laws by reducing workers' rights and making employment contracts flexible, and promised to reduce the fiscal deficit by reforming the pension system. It also embarked on a series of privatizations of state-owned enterprises, including airports, ports, roads, and the electricity company, Eletrobras.

The activities of a major anti-corruption investigation (called Carwash, or *Lava Jato*, because the initial investigation was into money laundering in a carwash in Brasília) involving the Federal Police, the Public Prosecutors' Office (*Ministério Público*), the tax authorities, and the federal judiciary, including the Supreme Court, led to charges being filed against many elected officials. The investigation, begun in March of 2014, also ensnared prominent executives of companies who had previously enjoyed impunity for crimes such as bribery, money laundering, and making undeclared and illegal campaign contributions. The Carwash investigation started by focusing on an alleged kickback scheme in the partially state-owned oil company, Petrobras, in which contracts were rigged. According to investigators, a percentage of the overcharged contracts was siphoned off in bribes to Petrobras executives and illegal (and sometimes legal) campaign contributions.

The Carwash investigations led to the conviction and imprisonment of – among others – former lower house President, Eduardo Cunha, former Governor of Rio de Janeiro, Sergio Cabral, and the former CEO of the major construction company that bears his family name, Marcelo Odebrecht. It has also led to the conviction of former President Lula in a federal court in Curitiba in 2017, a conviction that was upheld by an appeals court in Porto Alegre in January 2018. The then-Prosecutor General, Rodrigo Janot, also brought charges of accepting a bribe and attempting to obstruct justice against President Michel Temer in the Federal Supreme Court in 2017. Both of the latter developments are unprecedented in Brazil's political history: a former president convicted of, and a sitting president charged with, corruption.

Municipal elections took place in Brazil in October 2016. This was the first election in which the Federal Supreme Court's ban on corporate donations to candidates was in effect. The Workers' Party had its worst results in municipal elections in 20 years, winning in only one state capital, Rio Branco, in the state of Acre. The elections confirmed the advance of economic and social conservatism in Brazil (Gonçalves, 2016). The two main parties in coalition at the federal level, the Brazilian Democratic Movement Party (PMDB, now just the MDB), and the

Brazilian Social Democratic Party (PSDB), did well. João Doria, a conservative businessman of the PSDB, won the mayoralty of São Paulo, while a neo-Pentecostal bishop in the Brazilian Republican Party, Marcelo Crivella, won in Rio. Apathy also increased, as abstentions, blank and spoiled ballots totaled 32.5% of the electorate in the second round, up from 26.5% in 2012.

Brazil seems to have reached an impasse in its politics in the contemporary period. While, economically, many people have done well under democracy, with poverty declining markedly and social inclusion increasing, evidence of disenchantment with the political system is abundant. In the Latinobarometer survey, a major annual survey of public opinion in Latin America, Brazil had one of the lowest levels of support for democracy in the region in 2017 at just 43%. Only 13% of Brazilians polled in the same survey were satisfied with democracy, while 92% of Brazilians polled lacked confidence in their government.[12] While survey research regularly finds confidence in political parties and Congress to be low, in 2017 a survey found that 53.5% of Brazilians polled did not believe that the courts guarantee just decisions.[13]

One problem may be that Brazilians, despite the marked improvement in the performance of state institutions in recent decades, still tend to see their state as "patrimonial", as a vehicle for private interests, despite its apparently public façade and the formal commitment to equality of citizenship in the constitution (Pereira, 2016). Not all perspectives on the patrimonial state are equal. On the left, commentators talk about the state representing the "Casa Grande", the Big House, the interests of the traditional dominant class in Brazil, which they regard as irredeemably authoritarian.[14] On the right, commentators are more likely to accuse the PT of hijacking the state for its own purposes in the 2003–2016 period, conflating its own partisan interests with those of the nation and demonstrating an insufficient commitment to liberal democratic values (Lamounier, 2016; Vélez-Rodríguez, 2015). There are many versions of patrimonialism in between these two ideological poles, but what they share in their ubiquity is a denial of the public nature of many state actions, and skepticism about the ability of state institutions to represent popular interests.

It seems unlikely that the social inclusion accomplished in the 1995–2010 period, and especially in the 2000s, will be continued. The state has increased its capacity, and tax revenues as a percentage of the gross domestic product (GDP), at 37%, are above the average for rich countries in the Organization for Economic Cooperation and Development (OECD) (Melo, 2016a, p. 267). There is no appetite in Congress for tax increases even though the tax burden is spread unequally. Wealth is very lightly taxed, and because many taxes are on consumption rather than income, the rich often pay a smaller proportion of their income in tax than the poor. Social spending has been curbed and inequality and poverty are increasing rather than declining. Institutions of accountability and the rule of law seem to have been strengthened and are robust, but political polarization has increased and the legitimacy gap between elected officials and the public is large. Political reform is being discussed in Congress and on the streets, but there is no consensus as to what represents desirable or feasible reform. There is a political vacuum and plausible and viable leaders are thin on the ground. To understand Brazil's current political impasse, it is necessary to explore the anti-corruption investigations in more depth.

The Carwash corruption investigation

In recent years, there have been important changes in the legislation surrounding anti-corruption investigations in Brazil. A popular signature-gathering movement succeeded in pressuring Congress into passing an anti-vote buying law in 1999. In 2010, again bowing to popular pressures, Congress passed a clean file (*Ficha Limpa*) law, prohibiting candidates who have been convicted at the second level of the justice system from running for office. In subsequent years, new money laundering, anti-racketeering, and plea-bargaining laws were passed by Congress. Brazil also joined the OECD Anti-Bribery Convention in 2000 and passed the Clean Companies Act in 2013, imposing higher penalties on people in companies convicted of engaging in bribery, contract rigging, clandestine campaign finance, and other illicit acts.

The Carwash anti-corruption investigation, mentioned earlier, was facilitated by some of these legal changes and also shifts in the public mood towards a greater level of intolerance of and indignation about corruption. The heart of the Carwash investigation is the task force in Curitiba headed by federal judge Sergio Moro. As of March 2017, the Carwash probe had resulted in 746 searches and arrests, 183 requests for international cooperation, 155 agreements to cooperate with authorities on the part of those investigated, and ten agreements with companies. It had led to 56 charges against 260 people at the first level of the justice system, with 26 convictions for combined prison terms that exceed 1,300 years. These results suggest that Brazil is changing from a country in which impunity for high-level corruption was the norm to one in which the executives of big companies and top elected officials can be investigated, charged, and imprisoned for acts of corruption – in some cases.

The Carwash investigation divides opinion in Brazil. It is popular, because it has led to the conviction and jailing of people previously thought to be untouchable in Brazil's political system. In some accounts, Carwash – as well as the impeachment of President Dilma Rousseff – is depicted by observers as the unalloyed triumph of the rule of law, the strengthening of accountability institutions and a deepening of Brazilian democracy (Alston et al., 2016; Melo, 2016b; Melo and Pereira, 2016). However, such a narrative is simplistic. Carwash is unusual, in that it involves unprecedented cooperation between the federal judiciary, the Public Ministry, the Federal Police, and the tax authorities (*Receita Federal*). Congress has been trying to weaken the investigation, and it is not clear that this level of cooperation will continue indefinitely. Furthermore, it is not plausible that the judiciary, Public Ministry, auditing agencies, tax authorities, and Federal Police are completely free of political bias and corruption themselves. If systematic corruption exists in the legislative and executive branches, it is unlikely that such corruption has not also contaminated – to some extent – other branches and state agencies.

It is likely that versions of the kickback scheme in Petrobras that the Carwash investigation uncovered exist in other ministries and state-owned enterprises.[15] Since prosecution for crimes moves slowly, especially against those with a privileged forum, many politicians probably still calculate that they will be able to get away with corruption. It is notable that many of the alleged corruption cases uncovered in 2017 had been committed well after the beginning of the Carwash investigation in March 2014.

Those critical of Carwash – and the impeachment of President Dilma Rousseff – tend to accuse it of political bias (anti-PT) and depriving the accused of rights, through innovations such as plea bargaining and preventive detention (Avritzer, 2017). Some of the convictions in Carwash have been rushed, with questionable rulings. Figures in Carwash have also occasionally overstepped the legal limits on their actions, as when, in 2016, Judge Sergio Moro released tape-recorded conversations between then-President Dilma Rousseff and ex-President Lula to the press. Moro's conviction of ex-President Lula in July 2017 was seen by some as a political as well as a legal judgment. (This ruling was upheld by an appeals court in Porto Alegre in January 2018, and on the 7th of April 2018, Lula began serving a 12-year sentence in prison in Curitiba.) However, Carwash has clearly not only targeted the PT, but politicians from all the major political parties.

On its own, Carwash is probably incapable of uprooting corruption from the Brazilian political system. One of the federal prosecutors in Curitiba, Delton Dallagnol, said this:

> Many times people believe that Lava Jato is sufficient, that Lava Jato will transform Brazil. But … it is necessary to go beyond Lava Jato, because what Lava Jato does is a diagnosis of a serious situation, of a corruption that is extremely harmful to our society … we need, if we want a better country, to reform the justice system, reform the political system of our country …
> (Pavaneli and Kirsche, 2017)

Unless Congress passes political reforms, changing the rules and reducing the incentives to engage in illegal campaign finance and other forms of corruption, corruption is likely to persist in the Brazilian political system. Since so many members of Congress have themselves been accused of corruption, they are unlikely to want to reform the system.

Conclusion

There are some good reasons to be positive about Brazilian democracy. The country defied the pessimism of the first wave of analysis of its democracy, and its democratic institutions have endured. Whether the start of democracy is dated from the indirect election of a civilian president in 1985, the promulgation of the new constitution in 1988, or the direct election of the president in 1989, democracy has now outlasted the dictatorship that began in 1964. This is no small achievement.

However, it is difficult to give a resounding "three cheers" for Brazilian democracy because evidence suggests that satisfaction with democracy is low. Trust in elected officials and institutions vital for democracy, such as political parties and Congress, is also low. Even the judiciary, an important institution for the rule of law and a very powerful actor in Brazilian politics, is viewed with skepticism by many Brazilians. Almost a third of the electorate abstained or cast blank and null ballots in the second round of the municipal elections in 2016, suggesting widespread frustration on the part of voters at the choices elections are giving them.

The mass protests of 2013 were followed by a bitterly contested presidential election in 2014 and gridlock around the impeachment of President Dilma Rousseff in 2015 and 2016. For Rousseff's opponents, her impeachment was an act of fiscal probity and political common sense. For her supporters, it was a "coup" that weakened the constitutional foundations of democracy. The polarization around these contrasting narratives of the impeachment is still present in Brazilian politics. The Carwash corruption investigations have also sparked debates about the extent to which the judicial, prosecutorial, auditing, tax, and police bodies engaged in it are impartially enforcing the rule of law or, instead, selectively applying the law in their and others' interests.

Brazilian politics is at an important crossroads. The central state, which emerged as a capable actor in the mid-twentieth century, has become a significant force. As we have seen, it was, to a considerable extent, able to overcome the forces of regionalism and decentralization that enhanced the despotic power of traditional and landed interests in the countryside. With urbanization and industrialization, the state increased its capacity to deliver education and health services to the population, improving the quality of life of the Brazilian population. Democratization in the 1980s expanded participation, leading to new forms of social inclusion and the expansion of rights, not just civil and political rights, but also social and economic ones. But the state is also pockmarked with archaic privileges, vestiges of the old, unequal, social order, and riddled with systematic corruption.

As the tolerance of corruption has declined and accountability institutions strengthened, the state has been split, and gone to war with itself. The institutions entrusted with investigating corruption are removing members of the executive and legislative branches in a slow, deliberate, but devastating manner. What this means for the governability of the country and the legitimacy of its political institutions is uncertain. Carwash could come to be seen as a major change in Brazilian history, a process that moved the country to a new equilibrium in which impunity for corruption is no longer the norm. But it could also come to be seen, like the Clean Hands investigation in Italy in the 1990s, as a temporary aberration that changed little in the long term. It is too early to tell in which direction Brazilian democracy is moving. Much is at stake in the 2018 elections, but optimism about the outcome of those elections is not high, and no elections since those of 1989 have been as unpredictable.

Notes

1 In Brazil, unlike in the USA, there is no constitutional prohibition of a president who has served two terms running and winning office again, as long as there is a gap between his or her second and third terms.
2 In Venceslau and Hupsel Filho (2017).
3 "Resultado de Eleições – 2014", TSE.
4 In the 2018 elections, the lion's share of the party fund will go to the three largest political parties: R$305 million for the MDB, R$301 million for the PT, and R$259 million for the PSDB. From a presentation by political scientist Jairo Nicolau at the Fourth Best Legislative Practices workshop, Canning House, London, 16 March 2018.
5 From "Eleições 2016: mulheres representam mais do 30% dos candidatos" at Tribunal Superior Eleitoral, 2 September 2016, at www.tse.jus.br/imprensa/noticias-tse/2016/Setembro/eleicoes-2016-mulheres-representam-mais-de-30-dos-candidatos [accessed on 30 June 2018]; and Jamil Chade (2015) "Brasil tem menos mulheres no Legislativo que Oriente Médio" in O *Estado de São Paulo*, 6 March 2015, at https://politica.estadao.com.br/noticias/geral,brasil-tem-menos-mulheres-no-legislativo-que-oriente-medio,1645699 [accessed on 30 June 2018].
6 From the Inter-Parliamentary Union, Women in National Parliaments, 1 June 2018, at http://archive.ipu.org/wmn-e/classif.htm [accessed on 30 June 2018].
7 From a presentation by political scientist Jairo Nicolau at the Fourth Best Legislative Practices workshop, Canning House, London, 16 March 2018.
8 In 2016, the federal level of government collected 60% of all tax revenue, with the states getting 23%, and the municipal governments only 17% (Fucs, 2016).
9 In Shalders (2018). The criminal defence lawyer quoted was Pierpaolo Bottini, who has clients being investigated by the Carwash task force.
10 See "STF decide restringir foro privilegiado" in O *Globo*, 3 May 2018, at https://g1.globo.com/politica/ao-vivo/stf-discute-restricao-ao-foro-privilegiado.ghtml [accessed on 30 June 2018].
11 The system was established via the 1932 Electoral Code and Law 48 of 1935 (Pires, 2009, pp. 130–131).
12 In 2017 the Latinobarometer surveyed 20,000 people in 18 Latin American countries (Rivas, 2017).
13 The survey was conducted in April–May 2017 by the Barometer das Americas, conducted by Vanderbilt University (Barbosa, 2018).
14 See, for example, the editorial "É Golpe" in *Caros Amigos*, June 2016, p. 6.
15 Carwash itself uncovered kickback schemes in the electricity company Eletrobras, and the state banks the Caixa Econômica Federal and the Bank of Brazil, as well as Petrobras. See Quiz: Teste seus conhecimentos sobre a Lava Jato, que completa 4 anos, in *BBC Brasil*, 16 March 2018. Available at: http://www.bbc.com/portuguese/brasil-42477785 [accessed 18 March 2018].

Suggested English readings

Ames, B. (2018). *Routledge handbook of Brazilian politics*. Oxford: Routledge.
Fausto, B., and Fausto, S. (2014). *A concise history of Brazil*. 2nd ed. Cambridge: Cambridge University Press.
Holston, J. (2009). *Insurgent citizenship: Disjunctions of democracy and modernity in Brazil*. Princeton: Princeton University Press.
Kingstone, P., and Power, T. (eds). (2017). *Democratic Brazil divided*. Pittsburgh: University of Pittsburgh Press.

Needell, J. (ed.). (2015). *Emergent Brazil: Key perspectives on a new global power*. Gainesville: University Press of Florida.
Schneider, B.R. (ed.). (2016). *New order and progress: Development and democracy in Brazil*. New York: Oxford University Press.

References

Abranches, S. (1988). Presidencialismo de coalizão: o dilemma institucional brasileiro. *Dados*, 31(1), 5–38.
Alston, L.J., Melo, M.A., Mueller, B., and Pereira, C. (2016). *Brazil in transition: Beliefs, leadership, and institutional change*. Princeton: Princeton University Press.
Ames, B., 2001. *The deadlock of democracy in Brazil*. Ann Arbor: University of Michigan Press.
Avritzer, L. (2002). *Democracy and the public space in Latin America*. Princeton: Princeton University Press.
Avritzer, L. (2009). *Participatory institutions in democratic Brazil*. Baltimore: Johns Hopkins University Press.
Avritzer, L. (2017). The Rousseff impeachment and the crisis of democracy in Brazil. *Critical Policy Studies*, 4 August, 352–357. http://dx.doi.org/10.1080/19460171.2017.1363069
Barbosa, B. (2018). Por que condenações de Lula não afeteram seu bom desempenho nas pesquisas. *UOL Notícias*, 6 February. Available at: https://eleicoes.uol.com.br/2018/noticias/2018/02/06/por-que-condenacoes-de-lula-nao-afetaram-seu-bom-desempenho-nas-pesquisas.htm [accessed 21 March 2018].
Borges, A., and Lloyd, R. (2016). Presidential coattails and electoral coordination in multilevel elections: Comparative lessons from Brazil. *Electoral Studies*, 43(September), 104–114.
Boxer, C.R. (1973). *The Portuguese aeaborne empire 1415–1825*. London: Penguin Books.
Campello, T., and Neri, M. (2013). *Programa bolsa família: Uma década de inclusão e cidadania*. Brasília: IPEA.
Campello, T., and Neri, M. (2014). *Programa Bolsa Família: Uma década de inclusão e cidadania: Sumário executivo*. Brasília: IPEA.
Carvalho, J.M. de. (1993). Political elites and state building: The case of nineteenth-century Brazil. In: D. Levine (ed.), *Constructing Culture and Power in Latin America*. Ann Arbor: University of Michigan Press, pp. 403–428.
Dickovick, J.T. (2007). Municipalization as central government strategy: Central–regional–local politics in Peru, Brazil, and South Africa. *Publius: The Journal of Federalism*, 37(1), 1–25.
Eakin, M. (1998). *Brazil: The once and future country*. New York: Palgrave Macmillan.
Falcão, J., Hartmann, I., Almeida, G. F. de, and Chaves, L. (2017). *Supremo em números V: O foro privilegiado e o supremo*. Rio de Janeiro: FGV Direito Rio.
Fausto, B., and Fausto, S. (2014). *A concise history of Brazil*. 2nd ed. Cambridge: Cambridge University Press.
Fenwick, T.B. (2016). *Avoiding governors: Federalism, democracy, and poverty alleviation in Brazil and Argentina*. South Bend: University of Notre Dame Press.
Fucs, J. (2016). Hora de mudar. *O Estado de São Paulo*, 19 September. Available at: http://politica.estadao.com.br/noticias/geral,hora-de-mudar,10000076906 [accessed 28 March 2018].
Gatto, M.A.C. (2017). Gender quotas, legislative resistance and non-legislative reform. In D. Pedro Fortes, L. Boratti, A. Palacios, and T.G. Daly (eds), *Law and policy in Latin*

America: Transforming courts, institutions and rights. London: Palgrave Macmillan, pp. 239–255.

Gonçalves, M.A. (2016). Barry Ames fala sobre a direita e a guinada política no país. *Folha de São Paulo*, 22 May. Available at: www.folha.uol.com.br/illustrissima/2016/05/1773123 [accessed 13 August 2016].

Holston, J. (2008). *Insurgent citizenship: Disjunctions of democracy and modernity in Brazil*. Princeton: Princeton University Press.

Kingstone, P., and Power, T. (eds). (2017). *Democratic Brazil divided*. Pittsburgh: University of Pittsburgh Press.

Lamounier, B. (2016). *Liberais e antiliberais: A luta ideológica do nosso tempo*. São Paulo: Companhia das Letras.

Levine, R.M. (1998). *Father of the poor? Vargas and his era*. Cambridge: Cambridge University Press.

Limongi, F., and Figueiredo, A.C. (1999). *Executivo e legislativo na nova ordem constitucional*. São Paulo: Editora FGV.

Mainwaring, S., 1999. *Rethinking party systems in the third wave of democratization: The case of Brazil*. Stanford: Stanford University Press.

Malamud, A. (2017). Foreign policy retreat: Domestic and systemic causes of Brazil's international rollback. *Rising Powers Quarterly*, 2(2), 149–168.

Mello, E., and Spektor, M. (2017). Presidencialismo de coalizão condena país ao atraso, dizem pesquisadores. *Folha de São Paulo, Ilustríssima*, 3 Dec. Available at: www1.folha.uol.com.br/ilustrissima/2017/12/1939782-presidencialismo-de-coalizao-condena-pais-ao-atraso-como-mostra-lava-jato.shtml [accessed 28 March 2016].

Melo, M.A. (2008). Unexpected successes, unanticipated failures: Social policy from Cardoso to Lula. In: P. Kingstone and T.J. Power (eds), *Democratic Brazil revisited*. Pittsburgh: University of Pittsburgh Press, pp. 161–184.

Melo, M.A. (2016a). Political malaise and the new politics of accountability: Representation, taxation and the social contract. In: B.R. Schneider (ed.), *New order and progress: Development and democracy in Brazil*. New York: Oxford University Press, pp. 268–297.

Melo, M.A. (2016b). Crisis and integrity in Brazil. *Journal of Democracy*, 27(2), 50–65.

Melo, M.A., and Pereira, C. (2013). *Making Brazil work: Checking the president in a multiparty system*. New York: Palgrave Macmillan.

Melo, M.A., and Pereira, C. (2016). The good news from Brazil. *Foreign Policy*, 9 August. Available at: www.http://foreignpolicy.com/2016/08/09/the-good-news-from-brazil-dilma-rule-of-law/ [accessed 31 August 2017].

Nicolau, J. (2012). *Eleições no Brasil: Do império aos dias atuais*. Rio de Janeiro: Zahar.

Nicolau, J. (2015). Os sistemas eleitorias. In: L. Avelar and A.O. Cintra (eds), *Sistema político Brasileiro: Uma introdução*. São Paulo: Editora UNESP/Konrad Adenauer Stiftung, pp. 237–245.

Nicolau, J. (2016). *Representantes de Quem? Os (Des)caminhos do seu voto da urna à câmara dos deputados*. Rio de Janeiro: Zahar.

O'Donnell, G., and Schmitter, P. (1990). *Transitions from authoritarian rule: Tentative conclusions about uncertain democracies: Prospects for democracy: Volume 4*. Baltimore: Johns Hopkins University Press.

Pavaneli, A., and Kirsche, W. (2017). "É preciso ir além da Lava Jato", diz Deltan Dallagnol sobre combate à corrupção e à impunidade. *Globo.com*, 29 April. Available at: http://g1.globo.com/pr/parana/noticia/e-preciso-ir-alem-da-lava-jato-diz-deltan-dallagnol-sobre-combate-a-corrupcao-e-a-impunidade.ghtml [accessed 9 September 2017].

Pereira, A. (2015). Bolsa Família and democracy in Brazil. *Third World Quarterly*, 36(9), 1682–1699.

Pereira, A. (2016). Is the Brazilian state patrimonial? *Latin American Perspectives*, 43(2), 135–152.

Pereira, A. (2017). Brazil. In: D.S. Lewis and Wendy Slater (eds), *The 2017 Annual Register*. 258th ed. Ann Arbor, MI: ProQuest, pp. 152–155.

Pereira, A. (2018). Brazil. In: D.S. Lewis and Wendy Slater (eds), *The 2018 Annual Register*. 259th ed. Ann Arbor, MI: ProQuest, pp. 146–149.

Pires, J.M. (2009). *A invenção da lista aberta: O processo de implantação da representação proporcional no Brasil*. MA, IUPERJ. Available at: http://bd.camara.gov.br/bd/handle/bdcamara/4026 [accessed 28 August 2017].

Power, T., and Taylor, M. (eds). (2011). *Corruption and democracy in Brazil: The struggle for accountability*. South Bend: University of Notre Dame Press.

Resultado de Eleições – 2014. TSE. Available at: www.tse.jus.br/eleicoes/estatisticas/estatisticas-eleitorais-2014-resultados [accessed 31 August 2017].

Rivas, F. (2017). Apoio a democracia na America Latina cai pelo quinto ano consecutivo, de acordo com o Latinobarometro. *El Pais Internacional*, 28 October. Available at: https://brasil.elpais.com/brasil/2017/10/27/internacional/150913152_010672.html [accessed 21 March 2018].

Schakel, A.H. (2013). Congruence between regional and national elections. *Comparative Political Studies*, 46(5),631–662. http://dx.doi.org/10.1177/0010414011424112

Schneider, A. (2015). Political economy of citizenship regimes: Tax in India and Brazil. *UNRISD Working Paper*, no. 11 (July), 1–29.

Shalders, A. (2018). Por que a maioria dos politicos investigados não precisará se preocupar com a Lava Jato no STF em 2018. *BBC Brasil*, 4 January. Available at: www.bbc.com/portuguese/brasil-42561266 [accessed 18 March 2018].

Simon, J. (2017). *The ideology of Creole revolution: Imperialism and independence in American and Latin American political thought*. Cambridge: Cambridge University Press.

Stepan, A. (1999). Federalism and democracy: Beyond the US model. *Journal of Democracy*, 10(4), 19–34.

Tillin, L., and Pereira, A. (2017). Federalism, multi-level elections and social policy in Brazil and India. *Commonwealth and Comparative Politics*, 55(3),353–376.

Topik, S. (2002). The hollow state: The effect of the world market on state-building in Brazil in the nineteenth century. In: J. Dunkerley (ed.), *Studies in the formation of the nation state in Latin America*. London: Institute of Latin American Studies/University of London, pp. 112–132.

Vélez-Rodríguez, R. (2015). *A grande mentira: Lula e o patrimonialismo petista*. Campinas: Vide Editorial.

Venceslau, P., and Hupsel Filho, V. (2017). Eleição de 2018 pode ter dois novos partidos. *UOL Noticias*, 2 April. Available at: https://noticias.uol.com.br/ultimas-noticias/agencia-estado/2017/04/02/disputa-em-2018-pode-ter-dois-novos-partidos.htm [accessed 29 August 2017].

Weyland, K. (1996). *Democracy without equity: Failures of reform in Brazil*. Pittsburgh: University of Pittsburgh Press.

4 Economic development and social policy

Introduction

Brazil is the ninth largest economy in the world measured by nominal GDP, and the eighth largest measured by purchasing power parity. The economy has also changed dramatically in the past one hundred years. In the early twentieth century, Brazil's was an agrarian economy based on plantation agriculture. Coffee was the most important export. Most people lived in the countryside and engaged in physical labor for their livelihoods. Today, Brazil possesses an industrial sector that produces automobiles, airplanes, computer software, and pharmaceuticals, as well as agricultural and mineral commodities and a variety of basic and more sophisticated services. It is a high middle-income country that could join the ranks of the high-income countries in the coming years.

Brazil's economic development in the twentieth century was impressive. Its industrial production *quadrupled* between 1965 and 1980; by way of comparison, Japan's increased threefold during the same period (Vieira, 2017, p. 35). The Brazilian economy, however, suffers some chronic shortcomings, such as a low rate of savings and investment (less than 20% of GDP), low investment in infrastructure, and meager investment in research and development (around one percent of GDP, most of it public). The quality of its basic education is also low for a country of its wealth, and levels of economic inequality remain startlingly high. Brazil is one of the fifteen most unequal countries in the world, with significant pockets of poverty.

Brazilian economic development provokes passionate disagreement and debates. Some analysts lament the lost opportunities and disappointments of Brazil's economic trajectory, describing the latter as a "hen's flight", in which the country seems to be taking off, only to come crashing back down again (Valladão, 2013). Others emphasize Brazil's rapid industrialization of the mid-twentieth century and improvements in standards of living, as well as reductions in poverty and inequality, over the past few decades. These evaluations are based on different expectations and comparisons, and raise questions about what is the most reasonable baseline to use when assessing Brazil's economic development.

Like other late developers, Brazil strayed from economic orthodoxy in its path towards industrialization (Pereira, 1984). Beginning in the 1930s, the Brazilian state developed a variety of instruments with which to guide economic development, from planning agencies such as the Institute of Sugar and Alcohol (eventually abolished in 1990), to state-owned enterprises in strategic sectors that continue to play significant roles today. Examples include Brazil's partially state-owned oil company, Petrobras, and the national development bank, the BNDES (*Banco Nacional de Desenvolvimento Econômico e Social*), which allocates subsidized credit to selected companies. This approach to development, called national developmentalism, is one to which many prominent economists and politicians have adhered over time (particularly in the mid-twentieth century). It is based on a reading of Brazil's economic history that emphasizes Brazil's subservience to foreign markets and its dependence on capital, technology, and organizational know-how from abroad. Its basic tenets are that, in late development, the state needs to take on roles that were played by private entrepreneurs in countries that developed earlier. The state is, thus, required to solve coordination problems, channel investment to preferred sectors, stimulate the expansion of the domestic economy, and shield the economy from the negative effects of unfettered global capitalism (Ferreira, 2017, p. 185).

To provide context and insight for understanding Brazilian economic development and social policy, this chapter begins by focusing on three key perspectives regarding Brazil's economic development. The first is national developmentalism, the second is liberalism, and the third is post-developmentalism. The clash of these perspectives has shaped Brazil's development trajectory: its extraordinary growth and industrialization in the twentieth century, the increased economic stability and decline in poverty and inequality that occurred in the 1990s and 2000s, and the contemporary debates about the relationship between fiscal and social policy. Debates between proponents of these perspectives have generated divisions, especially between national developmentalists who want to use the state to promote industrialization and the growth of the domestic market and economic liberals in favor of macroeconomic orthodoxy. The third perspective, that of post-developmentalism, offers an important critique of both mainstream perspectives, although it is still a minority view in debates in Brazil. After reviewing these three perspectives, this chapter moves on to describe recent economic events in Brazil, including the extraordinary stability achieved by the inauguration of the Real Plan in 1994, innovations in social policy in the 1990s and 2000s, and the recession of 2015–2016.

Developmentalism

For developmentalists, the state has been essential in transforming the Brazilian economy. Developmentalist policies were crucial to developing countries that industrialized after the Second World War, when the opportunities for development were different than those faced by early developers. Furthermore, many countries that are now rich did not adhere to liberal policies in the early stages of their industrialization. In the USA, for example, the protection of infant industries was standard policy and "patriotic protectionism" the conventional

Table 4.1 Three perspectives on Brazilian economic development.[1]

	DEVELOPMENTALISM	LIBERALISM	POST-DEVELOPMENTALISM
Broad position	State guidance of the economy is necessary for successful "late" development	The "free market" is the best way to achieve development	"Free markets" *and* developmentalism should both be rejected
Ideological foundations	Social Democratic Internationalism; Realism; Nationalism; "Third Worldism"; Marxism; Dependency Theory	Liberalism	"Post-development" perspectives; post-colonialism; Marxism; various culturally particular movements
Representative thinkers	Friedrich List; Alexander Gerschenkron; Peter Evans; Ha-Joon Chang; Dani Rodrik; John Maynard Keynes	Jagdish Bagwati; Thomas Friedman	Arturo Escobar; Vandana Shiva; Mahatma Gandhi
Representative thinkers from Brazil	Teconio dos Santos; Celso Furtado; Caio Prado Jr.; Luiz Carlos Bresser-Pereira; Fernando Henrique Cardoso	Roberto Campos; Mario Henrique Simonsen; Gustavo Franco; Armínio Fraga; Maílson da Nobrega; Fernando Henrique Cardoso	João Pedro Stedile; José Lutzenberger
Use of developing/ developed countries as categories (and alternatives)	Sometimes (alternatives: Third World; BRICS; rising powers; Global South)	Yes (alternatives: market-friendly; economically "free"; "emerging markets")	No (alternative: Global South)
Are markets "natural"?	No	Yes	No

Primary concern	Alleviating absolute poverty and/or "catching up" to developed countries via various political initiatives (at the multilateral, national, and civil society level); industrializing via industrial policies	Realizing aggregate gains from "free" trade; further economic liberalization; securing property rights and contracts; strengthening institutions crucial to the functioning of markets	Resisting neoliberal globalization and multinational corporations in favor of local, communitarian forms of production, politics, and culture
Representative institutions or organizations	Group of 77; BRICS; agricultural G20; UNDP; UNESCO; UN ECLAC (CEPAL in Portuguese); UN General Assembly	World Bank; IMF; WTO; financial G20; World Economic Forum; UN Security Council	World Social Forum; Movimento dos Trabalhadores Rurais Sem Terra (Brazilian Landless Movement)
Colonial legacies	Surmountable, especially through South–South cooperation	Negligible or benign	Malign and ongoing

Source: the author.

wisdom in the nineteenth century. The country did not embrace "free trade" until it became economically dominant after the end of the Second World War. In the words of economist Ha-Joon Chang, the early developers "kicked away the ladder" for late developers by insisting on liberal rules on intellectual property and trade that they themselves had not followed in earlier stages of their own development, thus locking in their advantages and dominance of the global economy (Chang, 2003, pp. 1–9).

For developmentalists, most of Brazil's economic history prior to the 1930s was one of backwardness and dependency, in which the motor of development existed outside the domestic economy. A stunted domestic market coexisted with an overdeveloped export sector (and a financial system to service the export sector), and the direction and pace of the economy were conditioned by overseas markets, primarily Europe in the early period of Brazil's development, and the USA in the twentieth century. The labor market was based on crude forms of exploitation. Brazil was the largest slave-owning society in the world in the nineteenth century, and employers had little incentive to invest in the education and training of their workers, or to develop more efficient forms of production, preferring instead to derive easy profit from their ownership of land. In this vision, Brazil has historically been trapped in colonial and neo-colonial economic relationships in which it occupies a low rung in the division of labor of the world economy, supplying commodities produced with cheap labor to more advanced capitalist countries that dominate the production of high technology products and services and dictate the terms of trade to poorer countries.

For developmentalists, industrialization is the only way out of this trap, and industrialization cannot happen merely on the basis of free market prices and the supposed benefits of "static" comparative advantage. (Static comparative advantage is the idea that a country should specialize in the production of those goods that it already knows how to produce, and for which it has an abundance of the factors of production.) Instead, the state must play an active role and take up coordination functions unnecessary for states in already developed countries, inducing industrialization, shielding infant industries from potentially devastating competition from companies in advanced capitalist countries, and stimulating demand in the domestic market in order to encourage the substitution of industrial imports with domestically produced versions of the same products. For developmentalists, only in this way can Brazil gradually climb up the value-added ladder until it can compete in the export of sophisticated manufactured products. For developmentalists, dynamic comparative advantage must replace static comparative advantage. (Dynamic comparative advantage is the idea that a country can change what it is best able to produce through proactive policies that induce firms to enter sectors where they could be competitive.) A country is not condemned in perpetuity to rely principally on a commodity such as coffee. Instead, it can channel the surplus produced by coffee into science and technology and new exports by solving collective action problems that firms on their own, operating in an uncoordinated market, cannot solve themselves. For developmentalists, therefore, the panoply of development-oriented institutions at the federal level are not distortionary barriers to the full realization of the economy's potential, but instead vital enablers of this development (Pereira and Matei, 2015).

If, for liberals, the examples for Brazil to follow are principally the USA, the UK, and France, for developmentalists, a far more relevant and useful set of countries for Brazil to try to emulate are the East Asian newly industrializing countries (NICs) that developed in heterodox fashion after the Second World War (with the exception of Japan, which had industrialized significantly before the war). These East Asian NICs, including Taiwan, South Korea, and Singapore, as well as a later cohort including Malaysia, Thailand, and Vietnam, did not "get their prices right" or follow all the rules of the major Bretton Woods institutions such as the International Monetary Fund (IMF) and the World Bank. Instead, they priced credit differentially, rewarding good industrial performance with cheap credit and creating incentives for firms to become internationally competitive through a judicious combination of state planning, bureaucratic guidance, and market incentives (Amsden, 1992; Wade, 2004). Chalmers Johnson calls this a "plan rational" orientation (Johnson, 1982).

Developmentalism is a strong current in Brazilian thinking about development (Chilcote, 2014; Eakin, 1998; Fausto, 1999; Ioris, 2014). The historian, Caio Prado Júnior (1953), for example, found in Brazil's colonial period the roots of its underdevelopment, and recommended policies that would expand the domestic market and forge a truly national economic project that would lift the standards of living of the majority. Celso Furtado, an economist who came to direct the regional development organization of the Northeast (Sudene) under President João Goulart (1961–1964), had a similar conception (Furtado, 2007). In Rio de Janeiro in the 1950s, a group of intellectuals around the political scientist Helio Jaguaribe participated in the Superior Institute of Brazilian Studies (*Instituto Superior de Estudos Brasileiros*, ISEB) to promote the idea of developmental nationalism (Chilcote, 2014, pp. 10, 12). Developmentalists found an international voice when the United Nations Economic Commission for Latin America (ECLA in English, CEPAL in its Spanish and Portuguese variants), headed by the Argentine economist Raul Prebisch, published analyses in the 1950s that showed the terms of trade for agricultural and mineral commodities (the chief exports of Latin America at the time) falling behind those of manufactured goods produced by the capitalist core. The recipe for developmental success in the ECLA perspective was clear: exports of manufactured goods would enable Latin America to climb up the value-added chain, surmount the terms of trade problem, and become "developed." Creating larger domestic markets through regional economic integration was a key to developing competitive manufacturing sectors.

The largest Latin American economies, especially Mexico and Brazil, were able to develop strong manufacturing sectors that did engage in exports to some extent. However, these export sectors tended to be capital intensive, importing technology from abroad. Because they generated relatively low levels of unemployment, they contributed to dualistic economies, marked by small, privileged groups of formal sector workers with reasonably good wages, working conditions, and benefits, and larger segments of informal, vulnerable workers with lower wages, reduced job stability, and few benefits. In Brazil, this duality has been reduced in recent years but it is still a characteristic of the economy. (For more on the developmental state in Brazil, see Arbix and Martin, 2012; Hochstetler and Montero, 2012; Taylor, 2015.)

The developmentalist diagnosis of, and prescriptions for, Brazil's economic problems come in different varieties. However, most developmentalists would agree on the following: Brazil's principal economic challenges arise because the country has not been developmentalist enough, not because it has not been liberal enough. Developmentalist policies have been hampered by their half-heartedness and the schizophrenic co-existence of orthodox liberal policies with developmentalist ones. Brazil needs a more, not less, active state, one that can invest in basic education as well as science, technology, and innovation, promote leading sectors through industrial policy, steer credit to competitive companies through the national development bank, and boost domestic demand through fiscal incentives, social policy, and infrastructure programs. State owned enterprises should not be privatized across the board. With regard to trade, the Brazilian state should not unilaterally lower tariff barriers, but, instead, base tariffs on strategic considerations and a plan for national economic development. Liberal *laissez-faire* policies, rather than liberating the productive potential of the Brazilian economy, would instead accelerate deindustrialization, push Brazil more firmly into the ranks of second-tier commodity exporters, and make the country more vulnerable than it already is to the instabilities of the world's capital markets. For developmentalists, the fact that activist developmentalist policies in trade and technology can sometimes slide into a network of bureaucratic stagnation and corruption (as, arguably, they did under the presidency of Dilma Rousseff from 2011 to 2016), does not mean that those policies should be completely abandoned. In the words of the economist Ha-Joon Chang, "we do not stop flying aeroplanes because there is a chance that they might crash, or abandon all vaccination programmes because some children may die from allergic reactions" (Chang, 2003, p. 140). In Brazil, developmentalist thinking has been most clearly articulated by left-wing members of the Workers' Party (*Partido dos Trabalhadores*, or PT), although the Workers' Party-led coalition implemented a mix of liberal and developmentalist policies while in government (Morais and Saad-Filho, 2012).

Liberalism

National developmentalism has been a dominant approach to economic policy in Brazil since the 1930s, but, in recent decades, it has been challenged by advocates of economic liberalism. During the presidency of Fernando Collor de Mello (1990–1992) some liberal ideas began to be implemented, signaling a move away from state intervention (Doctor, 2017, p. 15). These reforms were accelerated under the presidency of Fernando Henrique Cardoso (1995–2002), when trade opening, privatization, and deregulation were at the heart of macroeconomic policy. The Cardoso years were followed by the presidency of Luiz Inácio "Lula" da Silva (2003–2010) when a new version of developmentalism co-existed with liberal approaches to economic policy.

For liberals, the propensity to "truck, barter and exchange" (in the words of Adam Smith) is as old as humanity itself. Markets are natural, while political institutions, including states, are not. The price mechanism is a unique tool with which to allocate scarce resources. Competitive markets establish an equilibrium between supply and demand and are self-correcting, in the sense that rising demand triggers rising prices which, in turn, induce increases in supply, while falling demand results in a similar movement in the opposite direction. Market failure, or the incapacity of a market to supply adequate amounts of a given item or service, are relatively rare in capitalist economies, according to liberals, and state intervention is often counterproductive, distorting the effect of the price mechanism, misallocating resources, and politicizing economic policymaking.

The liberal approach to Brazil's economic history is one that sees no inherent problem in the country's origin as a colonial supplier of raw materials to richer and more powerful countries. Liberals argue that other economies that began as colonial producers of raw materials, such as the USA and South Korea, became wealthy and innovators in leading sectors in the world economy, so there is no barrier to Brazil doing the same. In the case of Brazil, the raw materials sought by the Portuguese in the beginning of the colonial period were wood (*pau Brasil*, used as a red dye for clothing) and sugar. Other cycles of export production included gold, silver, and precious stones in the eighteenth century, cotton, tobacco, rubber, and, most of all, coffee, Brazil's major export in the second half of the nineteenth and first half of the twentieth centuries. For liberals, the best economic policies are efficient ones that allow for the undistorted allocation of capital to activities yielding the highest rate of return and that are open to the world economy, such that domestic prices align closely with world market prices. By implementing such policies, liberals believe, Brazil (and any other developing country) can climb the economic ladder, move into higher value-added forms of production, and catch up with the core of developed countries.

In this reading, Brazil's economic policies were prudent and reasonable in the late nineteenth and early twentieth centuries, after the overthrow of the monarchy and the establishment of the republic. Brazil pursued its comparative advantage in the production of coffee and respected the rules of the liberal international economic order of that period, which included the gold standard and a stringent approach to fiscal discipline. However, Brazil's reaction to the Great Depression, which involved the establishment of institutions that regulated the operation of the price mechanism and controlled markets, including the labor market, represent a deviation from liberal orthodoxy that the country has still not fully escaped, and which holds Brazil back from realizing its full economic potential (again, according to liberals).

It was under the rule of President Getúlio Vargas (1930–1945, 1950–1954) that the major institutions of what is now called national developmentalism were established. Like other Latin American countries, Brazil experienced a sharp drop in the demand for, and prices of, its principal commodity exports (including the number one export, coffee) after the stock market crash of 1929. Brazil's foreign exchange earnings declined, and its capacity to pay for imports dropped. State intervention was initially aimed at stabilizing the price of its major export commodities by regulating supply (including stockpiling and destroying crops), so institutes dedicated to the regulation of coffee and sugar were established. However, state regulation soon expanded to include the establishment of the Ministry of Labor, which registered trade unions and eventually regulated wages and working conditions (though the Consolidated Labor Laws, promulgated in 1943) and institutions to stimulate industrialization, technological innovation, and basic science.

For liberals, these institutions and policies created what Michael Barzelay (1992) has called a "politicized market economy," in which access to state favors and privileges became a key tool for businesses as they sought to survive the rigors of the market. The state intervened in markets with high tariffs and a complicated system of protection (including tax breaks, cheap credit, and other subsidies) and price regulation. Multinational corporations that chose to invest in Brazil were often induced to go into partnerships with local companies in an arrangement that Peter Evans calls the "tripé," or triple alliance, because it involved a partnership between multinational capital, the state, and domestic capital (Evans, 1979). For liberals, this state-led capitalism established market distortions and a vicious circle in which the state became increasingly involved in picking winners, usually on the basis of untransparent backroom deals based on political favors, nepotism, corruption, and patronage. In this reading of Brazil's economic history, developmentalism and Brazilian political practices such as clientelism, *coronelismo* (bossism), and patronage went hand in hand. From the liberal perspective, what is needed to unleash the productive potential of the economy is a sharp movement in the direction of *laissez-faire*, a lifting of the dead hand of a patrimonial, corrupt, and clientelistic state from the economy, thereby unleashing the entrepreneurial and innovative spirit of the business community (Reid, 2014, pp. 263–281).

The return to democracy in Brazil brought additional problems from a liberal point of view. The 1988 Constitution, called by some the "citizen's constitution" because of the popular participation involved in its creation, guaranteed a number of social and economic rights. These are "entitlements," from the perspective of many liberals, and they weigh down the state with obligations that lead inexorably to more and more state spending. In the disdainful words of the late diplomat, minister, and liberal thinker Roberto Campos, the Constitution of 1988 gave Brazil "Swedish social security with Mozambican resources" (Prado, 2017).

Liberals view the world economy in terms that are similar to their view of the domestic economy. For liberals, the world economy should be open and oriented towards free trade and the frictionless movement of goods and services across borders, facilitating comparative advantage and allowing for the maximization of aggregate gains. Liberals generally support global economic institutions that move the world in a *laissez-faire* direction, reducing tariff barriers and eliminating state subsidies, thereby promoting the diffusion of the best organizational and production practices in the world economy. From a liberal perspective, Brazil's membership in Mercosur, an economic bloc originally consisting of Argentina, Brazil, Paraguay, and Uruguay and formed in 1991, is a drain on its productive potential. This is because Mercosur is less liberal than other regional economic blocs such as the Pacific Alliance (Chile, Colombia, Mexico, and Peru, established in 2012), it forbids Brazil from signing its own trade agreements with other countries (instead, Mercosur must negotiate and agree as a group), and, in 2012, for political reasons, it accepted to the bloc Venezuela, a country with an illiberal approach to trade. (In 2016 Venezuela was suspended from Mercosur, but its having been admitted to the bloc still rankles with many economic liberals.) On the other hand, Brazil's recent application to join the Organization of Economic Cooperation and Development (OECD, a club of rich nations that Chile and Mexico have already joined) is a good move from a liberal point of view, because this will require Brazil to comply with financial, accounting, tax, and regulatory conventions approved of by the international business community and certify it as "market-friendly".

The liberal prescription for Brazil's economy is, therefore, clear. It includes opening up to world trade by lowering tariff barriers, eliminating subsidies and tax breaks to business, downsizing the national development bank (BNDES), and trying to create a "level playing field" in which capital of whatever national origin can compete on equal terms. Taxes should be simplified and reduced, labor markets deregulated to allow for easy hiring and firing of workers, state assets should be privatized, sold at auction to the highest bidder, and the bloated pension system should be reformed so as to reduce entitlements and become fiscally sustainable. Private property rights and the independence of the central bank should be strongly protected. No doubt these measures would cause discomfort to many privileged sectors, cossetted as they have been by almost 90 years of national developmentalism, but, argue liberals, the competitive shock provoked by a smaller state, a lighter touch regulatory regime with clearer and more fairly enforced rules, would boost productivity, clear out dead wood among companies, and deliver net gains to consumers and workers (Alston, Mueller, Melo, and Pereira, 2016). For liberals, what Brazil needs is a government that is courageous and independent enough to deliver this liberal shock. Parties of the right and center-right, including the PSDB (*Partido da Social Democracia Brasileira*), are most likely to articulate liberal ideas about the economy, although they do not always practice them in government. For liberals, the government of Michel Temer (2016–2018) is an improvement on the Workers' Party years (2003–2016), but it has not gone far enough.

Post-developmentalism

For post-developmentalists, both liberals and developmentalists are locked into mainstream thinking that ignores the devastation that the capitalist economy has inflicted on the planet. In this perspective, environmental degradation, climate change, the death of indigenous languages and cultures, and the growth of "McWorld", a soulless, standardized hodgepodge of consumer brands (Barber, 2011), are part of the price the world has paid for unfettered globalized capitalism. For post-developmentalists, the development "game" is dead. Post-developmentalists question the priority that both liberals and developmentalists give to huge infrastructural mega-projects such as dams, including Brazil's Itaipu and Belo Monte dams (the latter leading to the forced relocation of indigenous people in the Xingu River basin). What countries such as Brazil should do, in the post-developmental perspective, is avoid emulating the industrialized capitalist core and, instead, seek an alternative path to well-being, by protecting the environment, respecting cultural heterogeneity, and seeking to evolve towards a more peaceful and cooperative economy (Escobar, 1994; Sachs, 2009).

Post-developmental critiques of Brazil's economic history begin with nature. Nature is part of Brazilian national identity; pride in the beauty and abundance of the natural environment is one of the enduring elements of Brazilian patriotism (for more on this, see Chapter 8). In the Brazilian national anthem, the homeland is described as "lying eternally in a splendid cradle" (*deitado eternamente em berço esplêndido*), and its fields as having "more flowers," and its forests "more life." Despite these rhapsodies about nature, the Brazilian economy was, and still is, founded on the predatory exploitation and export of its natural resources, and the destruction of the natural environment.

The desire to "develop" and to "catch up" with the advanced capitalist countries stimulates the continued destruction of the environment and people who defend the environment. Over a period of 500 years, from 1500 to 2000, human activity resulted in the destruction of roughly 92% of Brazil's Atlantic rain forest, according to some estimates.[2] In the past 50 years, with far more destructive tools at their disposal, humans have destroyed almost 20% of the Amazon rain forest in Brazil.[3] If this trend continues, the results will be catastrophic for the entire planet. Post-developmentalism sees in these patterns the need for a fundamental rethinking of the ideas of development and progress.

Post-developmentalists critique economics as a discipline as well. While nineteenth- century political economists considered philosophical and moral questions to be central to economics, twenty-first-century economists tend to be highly specialized and unquestioning of the idea of maximizing the production of goods and services. Growth is good, while the destruction of the environment is an "externality" to be considered later or not at all. For post-developmentalists, economics, as a discipline, should return to its roots as a science of human behavior dedicated to human welfare and must consider the environmental and social consequences of the pursuit of economic growth at all costs.

Post-developmentalists also pay particular attention to agriculture in Brazil. For post-developmentalists, Brazil has missed an opportunity to pursue a small-scale, agrarian path to development. The 1964 military coup consolidated an approach to agriculture based on the conservative modernization of the sector. Cheap credit was funneled to large agribusiness enterprises that consolidated their holdings, invested in machinery and other forms of technology, and produced primarily for export. This resulted in the formation of one of the largest agribusiness complexes in the world. Brazil is today one of the biggest producers of soy, beef, chicken, oranges, sugar, and coffee on the planet. On the other hand, millions of smallholders, tenant farmers, and sharecroppers lost access to land and moved to cities. In a few decades after 1960, Brazil went from being primarily rural to a society in which 85% of the population live in cities.

For post-developmentalists, a better strategy than investing in agribusiness would have been to promote small-scale family farms, securing livelihoods in the countryside for people who now live in urban slums (*favelas*). More unused land held unproductively by large landowners should have been redistributed, giving opportunities to rural families who knew how to produce but lacked the access to land to try their hand at farming. Now that knowledge has largely been lost. Greater emphasis on small-scale family farming would have boosted domestic food production but also reduced violence in Brazilian cities by diminishing the flow of poor rural migrants to urban slums. Small-scale family farming, in this view, is better for the environment than large-scale agribusiness. This is because small farmers are generally committed to sustainable practices and have ties to local communities. Agribusiness, especially multi-national agribusiness, in contrast, views land as a factor of production and can move on after soil is degraded (Wright and Wolford, 2003).

The indigenous question is also of great interest to most post-developmentalists. Historically, indigenous groups have been treated as the human equivalent of the environment: useful if available for exploitation, and expendable if not. Many of the original inhabitants of Brazil have been driven into remote parts of western and northern Brazil by the steady encroachment of capitalist development throughout the territory. For post-developmentalists, the condition of indigenous people is indicative of the overall health of the economic system. For post-developmentalists, the plight of the indigenous in the 1950s, when the population declined and the destruction of indigenous communities was rife, revealed the poverty of assimilationist ideas and the blindness of both liberal and developmentalist approaches to growth (Hemming, 2004). Since Brazil's return to democracy in the 1980s, the situation has improved. The 1988 Constitution recognized some rights for indigenous Brazilians. Chapter VIII, article 231 of the Constitution recognizes the rights of the indigenous to their social organization, customs, languages, beliefs, and traditions. This was a step away from the assimilationist ideology that prevailed for much of the twentieth century, and which saw the indigenous in their native form as a threat to Brazilian civilization, and only useful to Brazilian national development if they could be made to speak Portuguese, wear Western clothing, and integrate with the rest of Brazilian society (Ramos, 1998).

The same article of the Constitution also required Brazil's federal government to demarcate and protect the lands that the indigenous have traditionally occupied. As a result of this, some large reserves, mostly in the Amazon region, have been demarcated, although the defense of the borders of these reserves is still a problem. The 2010 census saw an increase in the number of people who described themselves as indigenous (*índio*). For post-developmentalists, the increase in the respect for indigenous cultures and lands in Brazil's democracy needs to be taken several steps further. The Brazilian federal government needs to do more to defend indigenous reserves from encroachment by loggers and miners. It should also listen more to indigenous objections to large-scale infrastructure projects, such as the Belo Monte dam, which forced the relocation of indigenous groups in the Xingu river basin and deprived them of their traditional livelihoods (Hall and Branford, 2012).

Post-developmentalists are also concerned about Brazil's energy use and over-all approach to the environment. The Brazilian government claims to be a leader in sustainability, and its hosting of the Eco 92 conference in Rio de Janeiro in 1992 was the start of a greater global commitment to tackle climate change (a commitment that produced the COP 21 agreement at the Paris Climate Conference in 2015). Brazil's image as a sustainability leader is not entirely unjustified. It has an unusually green energy matrix. Around 47% of its electricity is produced by renewable forms of energy; mostly hydroelectric, but also biofuels. This is well above the OECD average of around 12%. But Brazil could do more to promote other forms of renewable energy, including solar and wind power. Furthermore, the discovery of large oil deposits below the salt bed offshore of the states of Rio de Janeiro and São Paulo threatens to burden Brazil with a "resource curse" and could lead the country to slide into an over-reliance on an energy source that is clearly unsustainable, and which the rest of the world has started to move away from. For post-developmentalists, the continued prevalence of liberal and developmentalist thinking will stymie Brazil's potential to be a leader of sustainable approaches to development, and will induce the country to opt for short-term solutions that maximize profit but neglect long-term and sustainable alternatives to the status quo.

Post-developmentalism, like liberalism and developmentalism, comes in many forms. Overall, however, its policy prescriptions are clear. Brazil should favor sustainability and the careful conservation of its vast array of natural resources, including the biodiversity of the Amazon rain forest. The assumption that growth and environmental sustainability are trade-offs should be rejected; instead, Brazil's future growth will be increasingly based on, rather than undermined by, its conservation of the environment. (Another stream in post-developmentalist thinking rejects the idea of economic growth altogether.) Brazil is well placed to avoid the mistakes of the already rich countries and transition to a low-carbon economy. It should avoid infrastructural mega-projects and over-reliance on offshore oil deposits and promote a decentralized, inclusive model of economic development that promotes and protects family farms, small and medium enterprises, and indigenous communities. While few actors in Brazilian politics fully articulate a post-developmental vision, the one that comes closest is the political party Rede and its spokesperson, Marina Silva, who ran for president in 2010, 2014, and 2018.

To better understand how liberalism, developmentalism, and post-developmentalism offer different perspectives on Brazil's economic development, a brief review of Brazil's recent economic history is helpful. We address this in the second half of the chapter, focusing on the creation of macroeconomic stability in the mid-1990s, the expansion of social programs in the 1990s and 2000s, and the recession of 2015–2016.

The consensus of 1995–2010

Brazil's model of economic development from 1930 to 1980 can be described as the developmentalist one of import-substitution industrialization, or ISI. In this model, the state promoted the domestic production of basic consumer and industrial goods that had previously been imported, such that Brazil gradually climbed up the value-added chain and began to produce goods such as raw steel, machine tools, automobiles, and airplanes. However, by the 1980s this model had been exhausted and Brazilian policymakers, concerned about the country's heavy burden of external debt and rapidly rising inflation rate, began to search for new approaches to economic policies.

The result, influenced by the "Washington Consensus," was to liberalize, lowering tariff barriers that had long protected the Brazilian economy and to privatize state-owned enterprises.[4] These moves, quite timid at first, were undertaken by President Fernando Collor de Mello (1990–1992), the first democratically elected president after military rule (1964–1985). Collor was impeached for corruption in 1992 and the rest of his term was served out by his Vice President, Itamar Franco, a politician with little interest in liberalizing the economy but tremendous concern about the hyperinflation then gripping the country. Inflation in 1993, President Franco's first year in office, was 2,477% (Alston et al., 2016, p. 101).

Franco's Finance Minister was Fernando Henrique Cardoso, a former sociologist and ambitious politician, who appointed a team of economists to study the problem of inflation. The team decided that Brazil's inflation had its roots in government deficits but it also had a large inertial component, meaning that widespread indexation of salaries and prices, predicated on the expectation of high future inflation, locked the country into an increasingly dysfunctional spiral of rising prices. This was a delicate collective action problem. The solution to it, devised by Cardoso's economic team, was the Real Plan. This plan pegged the Brazilian currency, the *cruzeiro*, to an abstract unit of value (the real unit of value), de-indexed the economy, and then, on the 1st of July 1994, introduced the new currency, the real (Alston et al., 2016, pp. 99–100).

The Real Plan worked, despite initial skepticism by many. Inflation came down and stayed low. Fernando Henrique Cardoso, buoyed by the success of the Real Plan, ran for, and won, the presidency in 1994 as the candidate of the PSDB, in alliance with a party of the right, the PFL (*Partido Frente Liberal*). By 1996, inflation was down to ten percent per year, and by 1997 it was five percent (Alston et al., 2016, p. 101). During the remaining years of the Cardoso presidency, until the end of 2002, the government was known for the maintenance of the Real Plan and also a trinity of economic policies. These were inflation targeting by the Central Bank that kept price rises within a band between 2.5 and 6.5% per year; a floating currency with an exchange rate largely determined by market forces; and a primary fiscal surplus, or a Federal government surplus before government debt payments are taken into account. These orthodox, liberal economic policies reassured investors and helped to make Brazil a major recipient of direct foreign investment in the globalizing world economy of the 1990s. The Cardoso administration also moved the Brazilian economy in a liberal direction by privatizing many state-owned enterprises.

The election of Luiz Inácio "Lula" da Silva of the Workers' Party in 2002 was an important step forward for Brazil's democracy, in that it showed that a center-left candidate could win without disruption to the political system. However, in economic terms, there was a considerable amount of continuity between the Cardoso and Lula presidencies. While the Lula administration did not carry out any major privatizations, it did maintain the trinity of inflation targeting, a floating exchange rate, and a primary fiscal surplus. This orthodoxy reassured investors and enabled the Workers' Party government to expand and create new social programs in order to appeal to its core supporters.

The expansion of social programs

The Lula administration started in January 2003 with a focus on ending hunger in Brazil. Its flagship program, Zero Hunger (*Fome Zero*), was based on the idea of distributing food to the malnourished and increasing the poor's access to food through school meals programs and other measures. It was also focused on reducing structural causes of hunger by engaging in land reform and support for family agriculture. And, like many other Workers' Party programs, it involved the creation of councils at the state and local level (food security and nutritional councils) in which representatives of civil society organizations and local authorities could learn about, monitor, and be consulted about the Zero Hunger program (Freire and Sydow, 2016, p. 325). Various problems with the design and implementation of Zero Hunger led to it being incorporated into the Family Allowance (*Bolsa Família*) program, launched in October 2003.

The *Bolsa Família* program was one of several social programs created or maintained during these years. The BPC (*benefício de prestação continuado*), for example, is a minimum wage payment for the elderly and disabled. Pro-Uni is a student loan scheme to provide low-income students with the opportunity to attend private universities. Pronatec is a program to provide students with technical skills that enhance their access to the job market. In Federal universities, affirmative action in admissions is now mandatory, giving places to qualified Afro-Brazilians, indigenous Brazilians, and students who went to state/public high schools.

Of all these programs, the *Bolsa Família* Program (BFP) is probably the best known, and it became something of a flagship for the Lula administration (Pereira, 2015). It was an amalgamation of various pre-existing measures. These were the *Bolsa Escola* program, which gave money to low-income families for keeping their children in school, the *Bolsa Alimentação* and *Cartão Alimentação* programs, income supplements to the poor for food, and the *Auxílio Gas*, a subsidy to the poor for the purchase of gas for cooking (Freire and Sydow, 2016, p. 327). The BFP was modeled on the *Progresa* program in Mexico and touted by the World Bank; it was liberal in its inspiration to the extent that it conformed to the market. It was a conditional cash transfer (CCT) to the poor that the beneficiaries could use to buy and consume more in the market, and it did not include participation by civil society, but was, instead, administered locally by mayors.[5] For these reasons, some activists within the Workers' Party considered the BFP to be too pragmatic and economistic to be fully consistent with the Workers' Party's historical commitment to the structural transformation of Brazilian capitalism (i.e., a post-development transformation).

The BFP is now one of the largest CCT programs in the world. It includes 13.8 million families comprising 49.6 million people, or 26% of Brazil's population. The program reaches beneficiaries in 99.7% of the 5,570 counties (*municípios*) of Brazil.[6] Like other CCT programs, the BFP involves a "cash transfer, a targeting mechanism, and conditionality" (Bastagli, 2009, p. 1). Payments are made on the basis of a vast database called the *Cadastro Único para Programas Sociais* (CadÚnico), or the single registry for social programs. CadÚnico contains data on 23 million low-income families, 13.8 million of which are beneficiaries of the BFP (Campello and Neri, 2014, p. 15).

Families are eligible for the BFP if their income falls below a certain threshold (R$150 per capita per month, or about US$39 at the rate of exchange of 3.90 Brazilian *reais* per US dollar) (Santos, 2013, p. 149).[7] A representative of the family must present documents to local authorities in order to qualify for the program. Once the family passes the means test, cash is transferred electronically onto ATM cards issued by the Federal savings bank, the *Caixa Econômica Federal* (Montero, 2014, p. 139). Payments range from R$32 to R$242 per month (US$8 to $62), depending on family profiles (Hunter and Sugiyama, 2017, p. 137). Ninety-three percent of BFP cardholders are women: the program prioritizes women on the reasonable assumption that they will spend the money more wisely, to the benefit of children, than will men. The program is relatively cheap, costing in 2013 about R$23 billion *reais* ($5.9 billion), or roughly 0.5% of the country's GDP (Campello and Neri, 2014, pp. 14–15, 31). This amounts to less than 3% of total social spending in Brazil, or one-tenth of the money spent every year servicing the government's debt.[8]

The conditionality of the BFP concerns schooling and health. Beneficiary families must keep their children aged 6–15 in school for 85% of the annual school days (this drops to 75% for those aged 16–17). They must also get their children younger than seven the inoculations required by the national immunization schedule, and allow the growth and development of their children to be monitored by professionals in the national health service (*Sistema Único de Saúde*). Pregnant women and nursing mothers aged 14–44 who are beneficiaries of the PBF also have to agree to periodic monitoring by a healthcare professional (Montero, 2014, p. 139; Santos, 2013, p. 149).

Under Lula's presidency, social assistance to the poor doubled (Montero, 2014, p. 138). *Bolsa Família* was part of an extraordinary period of pro-poor growth in Brazil. From 2003 to 2011, Brazilian per capita income increased 40%, from R$550 (US$141) per month to a little over R$770 ($197), while the Gini coefficient – which measures income inequality – fell by 9.2%, from 0.576 to 0.523 (Campello and Neri, 2014, p. 29). The incomes of the bottom decile rose much faster than the incomes of the top decile. The poverty rate fell from 37.13% in 2003 to 21.42% in 2009 (Montero, 2014, p. 133). In absolute terms, from 2001 to 2007, the population living in extreme poverty (with monthly per capita income below R$70, or roughly US$18) fell by 11 million people, while the number of people living in poverty (with a monthly per capita income below R$150, or about $39) declined by 13 million (Barros, Carvalho, Franco, and Mendonça, 2010, p. 137).

From 2003 to 2015, the number of people in the so-called "class C" – a marketing category consisting of those with a monthly family income between R$1,000 ($256) and R$4,000 ($1,026) – rose from about 38% (65.8 million people) to 60% (almost 120 million), becoming a majority of the Brazilian population (Power, 2016, p. 218). Commentators began to analyze the emergence of Brazil's "new middle class." Some hailed the new middle class as the harbinger of a major transformation in Brazil, while others argued that it was actually a new working class (Chaui, 2013; Neri, 2012; Pereira, 2010; Pochmann, 2012, 2014; Souza and Lamounier, 2010).

Important questions about this "new middle class" have yet to be resolved. For example, what are the divisions within Class C? What do people in Class C think about government redistribution? For instance, not just CCT programs such as *Bolsa Família*, but programs in health and education? These are crucial questions, because above a certain income threshold, families tend to opt out of public services, buying health insurance and education from private sector providers. While the growth of the middle class may generally be associated with a strengthening of democracy, in Brazil it may, instead, have exacerbated conflict over redistribution and contributed to an increase in political polarization.

The BFP was not the principal cause of these economic changes. Barros et al. (2010) argue that the drop in income inequality in Brazil between 2001 and 2007 was caused by a variety of factors. About half of the change was caused by increases in non-labor income, including transfers such as the BFP.

The other half came from social changes such as increases in access to education and the expansion of the formal sector labor market (Barros et al., 2010). The steady increase in the real value of the minimum wage was also significant.

Brazil's recent performance with regard to poverty and inequality look attractive in comparative terms. In 1989, Brazil's income inequality as measured by the Gini index – a measure of income inequality in which 100 is the maximum and 0 absolute equality – was 63, the second highest in the world that year. By 2014, the Gini had reached 51, still high by global standards, but 19% lower than it had been in 1989 (World Bank Group, 2016, p. 103). Brazil achieved the first Millennium Development Goal – to reduce by half the proportion of the population living in extreme poverty – almost ten years in advance. This drew international attention to the Ministry for Social Development and Hunger Alleviation (*Ministério do Desenvolvimento Social e Combate à Fome*), the Federal agency with primary responsibility for the BFP. The Ministry has received 131 delegations from 21 countries interested in learning more about *Bolsa Família* since 2003. It has also signed technical cooperation agreements, dealing with some aspects of CCT programs, with 11 countries. Most of these countries have human development indices lower than Brazil's (Campello and Neri, 2014, p. 65).

The Brazilian government has also worked with the UK Department for International Development (DFID) to share knowledge of Brazilian social policies with African partners (Hall, 2013, pp. 178–179). The Ministry of Social Development has worked with another Brazilian Federal agency, the Institute of Applied Economic Research (*Instituto de Pesquisa Econômica Aplicada*, IPEA) and two multilateral organizations, the United Nations Development Programme (UNDP) and the World Bank, in a global anti-poverty initiative in which the Brazilian experience features prominently.[9] The Brazilian government has, therefore, been active in "exporting" the BFP, or at least sharing information about it with other interested governments and multilateral organizations.

Its implementation may be the least controversial aspect of *Bolsa Família*. Despite occasional grumblings about its generation of a "culture of dependence," there are relatively few criticisms about how the program has been carried out (Hall, 2013, p. 174). A high degree of technical competence, uniformity, and impartiality seem to characterize the BFP. In many ways the program's implementation is better than, and avoids many of the distortions of, the wider political system (Melo and Pereira, 2013).

For every *real* spent on the BFP, economic activity increases by R$1.78 (Campello and Neri, 2014, p. 36). Especially in small towns in poor regions, the BFP strengthens local economies by boosting demand at local shops and markets. Inequality has many dimensions, including region (Garmany, 2016). The BFP appears to have contributed to a drop in regional inequality that is part of the story of poverty and inequality reduction in Brazil (Barros, 2011). The majority of recipients (50.2%) live in the Northeast (Campello and Neri, 2014,

p. 31). There is also a gender and racial dimension to the impact of the BFP. As we have seen, a huge majority of recipients are women, and the majority is non-white (self-identifying as *pardo*, brown, or *preto*, black).

Women's empowerment has been touted as an outcome of *Bolsa Família*. Without detailed household studies and ethnography, it is difficult to know whether the cash transfer, in and of itself, provides the basis for greater female autonomy in decision-making. For example, researchers studying the gendered impacts of CCTs in other Latin American countries have reported *increased* burdens on women (Cookson, 2016; Corboz, 2013). Still, in Brazil, at least in some cases, gender empowerment seems plausible. One study showed that participation in the BFP increases the likelihood of a woman reporting exclusive control over contraception by ten percentage points (Hunter and Sugiyama, 2017, p. 146).

The Brazilian economist Lena Lavinas criticizes the BFP and other CCT programs and compares them unfavorably to social protection programs of the late nineteenth and twentieth centuries. The latter, she argues, developed in parallel with workers' movements, aimed to "protect and equalize access and opportunities, irrespective of income level and social status," and succeeded in promoting "equity and convergence" through what Karl Polanyi (2002) calls "de-commodification" of, for example, health services, education, and housing (Lavinas, 2013, p. 40). In contrast, twenty-first century social protection, argues Lavinas, is based primarily on market mechanisms. For her, "cash transfers and expanded household debt, the latter underwritten by the former, are key elements in this framework, in which decommodified provision is to be pared to the barest bones." Lavinas calls this the "downsizing of social protection in the name of the poor," and worries that CCTs in the developing world may not be sustainable (Lavinas, 2013, p. 40).

This critique is interesting at the global level and particularly relevant to the brutal austerity and squeeze on the welfare state and previous social contract in Europe, which has been particularly damaging in Greece, Portugal, and Spain. It is also relevant to Brazil, where, according to Lavinas, the increase in the poor's disposable income has not been matched by a corresponding increase in the quality of public goods that could make their lives better, such as health services, education, public transportation, and public security. Thus, while the poor in Brazil are likely to have experienced the BFP as an unambiguous enhancement of their well-being and agency (Hunter and Sugiyama, 2017; Rego and Pinzani, 2013), more cash alone will not fulfill all of their expectations of an improvement in living standards and the prospects for social mobility of their children. The latter depend crucially on public services, which, in turn, rely on an improvement in the state's fiscal and administrative capacity.

The recession of 2015–2016: challenges in fiscal and social policy

President Lula finished his term in 2010 as one of the most popular presidents in Brazil's recent history. Brazil had weathered the global 2008–2009 financial crisis in robust fashion, experiencing a mild recession in 2009 and then bouncing back. Growth was an unusual 7.5% in 2010, and several observers hailed Brazil's "rise" and "arrival" on the world stage as an influential country with an attractive, socially inclusive model of growth and a robust democracy (see, for example, Roett, 2010; Rohter, 2010). President Lula succeeded in getting his hand-picked successor, Dilma Rousseff, elected president in 2010, for a third consecutive term of Workers' Party rule at the federal level. Brazil's positive trajectory, however, was not maintained. The Brazilian economy slowed down, along with the commodity cycle in the world economy. While President Rousseff narrowly won her re-election bid in 2014, the country was plunged thereafter into a political and economic crisis. In 2015 and 2016, Brazil experienced its worst economic recession in more than 100 years, shrinking 3.8% and 3.6%, respectively, as inflation crept over the 6.5% ceiling and unemployment soared to over ten percent.

The recession put a stop to the gradual reduction of poverty that had occurred from the mid-1990s to the mid-2010s. President Rousseff was impeached in 2016 and replaced by a government led by her Vice President, Michel Temer. The Temer government (2016–2018) turned government policy in a liberal direction, ending Petrobras' monopoly on offshore oil production, opening the way for greater participation by multinationals, initiating a large privatization program, and making labor laws flexible. At the end of 2016, the government passed a constitutional amendment (Constitutional Amendment Number 95) freezing real government spending for 20 years. An age of austerity had begun.[10]

The spending freeze had the effect of curbing social spending, although its proponents would not necessarily have explicitly endorsed this. Advocates of the spending freeze argued that because tax revenue in Brazil is already at 37% percent of GDP, above the OECD average, there is no more room for increased taxation (Melo, 2016, p. 269). However, this interpretation of Brazil's "fiscal contract" is questionable. Taxation on wealth is extremely low. For example, inheritance tax is limited by the federal government to eight percent, and most states, which are responsible for the tax, levy about four percent. (In the UK, by contrast, the inheritance tax rate is 40% above the threshold of £325,000.) Taxes on land and property are also relatively low, and tax evasion widespread. About half of government revenues come from taxes on consumption (in the form of value added taxes). This is regressive. The poor can end up paying half of their income in tax – a far greater proportion than that paid by the well off – even if the absolute amounts they pay are low. Income tax, meanwhile, is capped at 27.5% (compared to 45% in the UK), while many independent professionals pay only 15%. Therefore, while the overall tax take of the Brazilian state is high, the distribution of the tax burden is extremely unequal, and this exacerbates the country's high income and wealth inequality.

This leaves Brazil with an important and contentious question. How can the recent reductions in poverty and inequality be sustained? And if they can, how will they be carried out, and who will bear the cost and reap the benefits of any changes in policy aimed at reducing poverty and inequality?

Conclusion

An active role for the state in coordinating economic activity is deeply rooted in Brazil. Beginning in the mid-twentieth century, a panoply of institutions was created to regulate private business activity in a variety of ways. These activities go beyond state ownership of strategic enterprises and include macroeconomic policy, fiscal instruments, taxation, labor, and social policies. "Developmentalism", with its statist variety of capitalism, has endured the transition to democracy in the 1980s and is still dominant in Brazil, despite critiques by liberals and post-developmentalists, and some changes in a more liberal direction in recent years. Compared to many other economies in the world today, the Brazilian economy is still relatively closed.

There are limits, however, to developmentalism in Brazil. Brazil's savings rate is low and it has been compelled to seek foreign investment to make up this gap. This, in turn, makes it dependent on capital from abroad. Brazilian policymakers fear straying too far from market orthodoxy. They do not want to drive away foreign investors or return to the (bad) old days of high inflation of the late 1980s and early 1990s. Brazil's developmentalism, therefore, tends to be timid and sporadic, co-existing with liberal measures and institutions and limited by a stop-and-go pattern, in which innovation in developmentalism is followed by sharp turns towards liberalism, as has been seen in the government of Michel Temer (2016–2018).

It remains to be seen whether the dramatic change advocated by liberals or post-developmentalists occurs in Brazil. If Brazil does join the OECD and adopts the regulatory and corporate governance reforms that it requires, this could stimulate a further move towards liberalism and the competitive shock, as well as the downsizing of the state, which liberals desire. While less likely, a post-developmental shift is also possible, moving Brazil towards a low-carbon, socially inclusive model of development. The most likely scenario, however, is that some form of developmentalism will endure in Brazil. The unique constellation of institutions and policies that characterize the Brazilian economy, including a large role for the public provision of credit, some degree of industrial policy, especially to protect manufacturing, a relatively closed economy, a highly regulated labor market, and a complicated and extensive set of social policies that is formally universalistic but in practice targeted, is likely to continue as the country moves towards the middle of the twenty-first century.

Notes

1 Note that Fernando Henrique Cardoso is listed twice: he is in the developmentalist camp for his work as an academic sociologist (e.g., Cardoso and Faletto, 1979), and he is in the liberal camp for his policies as President of Brazil (1995–2002), most notably his privatizations and lowering of tariff barriers.
2 See Kohn, R., 2012.

3 See World Wildlife Fund, 2017. The figure given on this site is that 17% of the forest cover in the whole of the Amazon (not just the Brazilian Amazon) has been lost in the past 50 years.

4 The Washington Consensus was a set of economic guidelines promoted by the international financial institutions such as the IMF and World Bank as well as the USA's Treasury. It reached the peak of its influence in the period from the mid-1980s to the mid-1990s, and is most clearly expressed in Williamson, 1990. Williamson's list of recommendations included fiscal discipline, moderate marginal tax rates, market-determined interest and exchange rates, trade liberalization, openness to foreign investment, privatization of state-owned enterprises, deregulation, and the guarantee of private property rights.

5 For these reasons Frei Betto, one of the creators of the Zero Hunger program, resigned from the Lula government after the program was incorporated into *Bolsa Família*. See Freire and Sydow, 2016, p. 335.

6 The information on the size of the PBF comes from Campello and Neri, 2014, pp. 9, 32. The information on the municipal coverage of the program comes from Campello and Neri, 2014, pp. 14, 18. See also Campello and Neri, 2013.

7 The exchange rate given is that of 2 June 2015.

8 The figure on total social spending comes from Montero, 2014, p. 139. Despite recent changes in the progressivity of government transfers, some 43% of tax revenue goes to fund the public pensions system (*previdência*). About 15% of revenue, or five percent of GDP, some R$220 billion *reais*, goes on interest on the public debt. According to the economist, Marcio Pochmann, much of these earnings go to Brazil's 20,000 richest families. See Allegrini, 2014, p. 17.

9 Interview with Mariana Hoffman, communications officer, International Policy Centre for Inclusive Growth (IPC-IG), Brasília, March 27, 2014. See www.wwp.org. br for more information on the World Without Poverty/Brazilian Learning Initiative.

10 The government that begins in 2019 will have to make a difficult decision about whether to preserve Constitutional Amendment Number 95, or to abolish it. The economist, Laura Carvalho, argues that it should be abolished in Heloisa Mendonça (2018) "Laura Carvalho: `Distribuir renda no Brasil sem mexer nos impostos é quixotesco'" in El País, 26 June 2018, accessed at: https://brasil.elpais.com/brasil/2018/06/15/economia/1529091114_614722.html on 2 July 2018 [accessed 1 July 2018].

Suggested English readings

Alston, L.J., Melo, M.A., Mueller, B., and Pereira, C. (2016). *Brazil in transition: Beliefs, leadership, and institutional change*. Princeton: Princeton University Press.

Furtado, C. (1976). *Economic development of Latin America*. Cambridge: Cambridge University Press.

Lavinas, L. (2013). 21st century welfare. *New Left Review*, 84, 5–40.

Pereira, A. (2015). Bolsa Família and democracy in Brazil. *Third World Quarterly*, 36(9), 1682–1699.

Pereira, A., and Mattei, L. (eds). (2015). *The Brazilian economy today: Towards a new socio-economic model?* London: Palgrave Macmillan.

Reid, M. (2014). *Brazil: The troubled rise of a global power*. New Haven: Yale University Press.

Saad-Filho, A. (2010). Neoliberalism, democracy, and development policy in Brazil. *Development and Society*, 39(1), 1–28.

Saad-Filho, A., and Morais, L. (2017). *Brazil: Neoliberalism vs democracy*. London: Pluto Press.

Taylor, M. (2015). The unchanging core of Brazilian state capitalism, 1985–2015. *American University School of International Service Research Paper Number 2015–8*. Posted 18 October 2015. Available at https://ssrn.com/astract=2674332 [accessed 13 November 2017]

References

Allegrini, G. (2014). Pobre é quem paga a conta. *Caros Amigos*, XVII(203), 14–17.

Alston, L.J., Melo, M.A., Mueller, B., and Pereira, C. (2016). *Brazil in transition: Beliefs, leadership, and institutional change*. Princeton: Princeton University Press.

Amsden, A. (1992). *Asia's next giant: South Korea and late industrialization*. New York: Oxford University Press.

Arbix, G., and Martin, S. (2012). Beyond developmentalism and market fundamentalism in Brazil: Inclusionary state activism without statism. In: LASA (Latin American Studies Association), *XXX International Congress: Toward a third century of independence in Latin America*. San Francisco, 23–26 May.

Barber, B. (2011). *Jihad vs McWorld*. London: Corgi.

Barros, A.R. (2011). *Desigualdades regionais no Brasil: Natureza, causas, origens e soluções*. Rio de Janeiro: Elsevier.

Barros, R., Carvalho, M. de, Franco, S., and Mendonça, R. (2010). Markets, the state and the dynamics of inequality in Brazil. In: L. López-Calva and N. Lustig (eds), *Declining inequality in Latin America: A decade of progress?* Washington DC: Brookings Institution Press, pp. 1–46.

Barzelay, M. (1992). *The politicized market economy: Alcohol in Brazil's energy strategy*. Berkeley: University of California Press.

Bastagli, F. (2009). From social safety net to social policy? The role of conditional cash transfers in welfare state development in Latin America. *Centre for Analysis of Social Exclusion, Working Paper Number 60*, December. London: London School of Economics.

Cardoso, F.H., and Faletto, E. (1979). *Dependency and development in Latin America*. Berkeley: University of California Press.

Campello, T., and Neri, M.C. (2013). *Programa Bolsa Família: uma década de inclusão e cidadania*. Brasília: IPEA.

Campello, T., and Neri, M.C. (2014). *Programa Bolsa Família: uma década de inclusão e cidadania: Sumário executivo*. Brasília: IPEA.

Chang, H. (2003). *Kicking away the ladder: Development strategy in historical perspective*. London: Anthem Press.

Chaui, M. (2013). On social classes: A new Brazilian working class. *Poverty in Focus*, 26, 21–24.

Chilcote, R. (2014). *Intellectuals and the search for national identity in twentieth-century Brazil*. New York: Cambridge University Press.

Cookson, T.P. (2016). Working for inclusion? Conditional cash transfers, rural women, and the reproduction of inequality. *Antipode*, 48(5), 1187–1205.

Corboz, J. (2013). Third-way neoliberalism and conditional cash transfers: the paradoxes of empowerment, participation and self-help among poor Uruguayan women. *Australian Journal of Anthropology*, 24(1), 64–80.

Doctor, M. (2017). *Business–State relations in Brazil: Challenges of the Port Reform Lobby.* New York: Routledge.

Eakin, M. (1998). *Brazil: The once and future country.* New York: Palgrave Macmillan.

Escobar, A. (1994). *Encountering development: The making and unmaking of the Third World.* Princeton: Princeton University Press.

Evans, P. (1979). *Dependent development: The alliance of multinational, state and local capital in Brazil.* Princeton: Princeton University Press.

Fausto, B. (1999). *A concise history of Brazil.* Cambridge: Cambridge University Press.

Ferreira, H.L.P. (2017). *Ideias e instituições econômicas: Uma introdução para o curso de direito.* Curitiba: Editora CRV.

Freire, A., and Sydow, E. (2016). *Frei Betto: Biografia.* Rio de Janeiro: Civilização Brasileira.

Furtado, C. (2007). *Formação econômica do Brasil.* São Paulo: Companhia das Letras.

Garmany, J. (2016). Neoliberalism, governance, and the geographies of conditional cash transfers. *Political Geography,* 50(1), 61–70.

Hall, A. (2013). Political dimensions of social protection in Brazil. In: J. Midgley and D. Piachaud (eds), *Social protection, economic growth and social change: Goals, issues and trajectories in China, India, Brazil and South Africa.* Cheltenham, UK: Edward Elgar, pp. 166–183.

Hall, A., and Branford, S. (2012). Development, dams and Dilma: The saga of Belo Monte. *Critical Sociology,* 38(6), 851–862.

Hemming, J. (2004). *Die if you must: Brazilian Indians in the twentieth century.* London: Pan Books.

Hochstetler, K., and Montero, A. (2012). Inertial statism and the new developmentalist state in Brazil. In: LASA (Latin American Studies Association), *XXX International Congress: Toward a third century of independence in Latin America.* San Francisco, 23–26 May.

Hunter, W., and Sugiyama, N.B. (2017). Assessing the Bolsa Família: Successes, shortcomings, and unknowns. In: P.R. Kingstone and T.J. Power (eds), *Democratic Brazil divided.* Pittsburgh: University of Pittsburgh Press, pp. 131–151.

Ioris, R. (2014). *Transforming Brazil: A history of national development in the postwar era.* New York: Routledge.

Johnson, C. (1982). *MITI and the Japanese miracle: The growth of industrial policy, 1925–1975.* Stanford: Stanford University Press.

Kohn, R. (2012). O que resta da Mata Atlântica do Brasil. *Sobre o Ambiente,* 9 December. Available at: https://rrupta.wordpress.com/2012/12/09/o-que-resta-da-mata-atlantica-no-brasil/ [accessed 27 February 2018].

Lavinas, L. (2013). 21st century welfare. *New Left Review,* 84, 5–40.

Melo, M.A. (2016). Political malaise and the new politics of accountability: Representation, taxation and the social contract. In: B. R. Schneider (ed.), *New order and progress: Development and democracy in Brazil.* New York: Oxford University Press, pp. 268–297.

Melo, M.A., and Pereira, C. (2013). *Making Brazil work: Checking the President in a multiparty system.* New York: Palgrave Macmillan.

Montero, A. (2014). *Brazil: Reversal of fortune.* Malden, MA: Polity Press.

Morais, L., and Saad-Filho, A. (2012). Neo-developmentalism and the challenge of economic policymaking under Dilma Rousseff. *Critical Sociology,* 38(6), 789–798.

Neri, M. (2012). *A nova classe média: O lado brilhante da base da pirâmide.* São Paulo: Editora Saraiva.

Pereira, A. (2010). Brazil: Finally on the yellow BRIC road? *World Commerce Review,* 4(3), 12–15.

Pereira, A. (2015). Bolsa Família and democracy in Brazil. *Third World Quarterly*, 36(9), 1682–1699.

Pereira, A., and Mattei, L. (eds). (2015). *The Brazilian economy today: Towards a new socio-economic model?* London: Palgrave Macmillan.

Pereira, L.C.B. (1984). *Development and crisis in Brazil, 1930–1983*. Boulder, CO: Westview Press.

Pochmann, M. (2012). *Nova classe média? O trabalho na base da pirâmide social Brasileira*. São Paulo: Boitempo Editorial.

Pochmann, M. (2014). *O mito da grande classe média: Capitalismo e estrutura social*. São Paulo: Boitempo Editorial.

Polanyi, K. (2002). *The great transformation: The political and economic origins of our time*. 2nd ed. Boston: Beacon Press.

Power, T. (2016). The reduction of poverty and inequality in Brazil: Political causes, political consequences. In: B. R. Schneider (ed.), *New order and progress: Development and democracy in Brazil*. New York: Oxford University Press, pp. 212–237.

Prado, N. (2017). A Constituição de 1988 na visão de Roberto Campos. *O Estado de São Paulo*, 24 October. Available at: http://opiniao.estadao.com.br/noticias/geral,a-constituicao-de-1988-na-visao-de-roberto-campos,70002057765 [accessed 17 November 2017].

Prado Júnior, C. (1953). *História econômica do Brasil*. 3rd ed. São Paulo: Editora Brasiliense Limitada.

Ramos, A.R. (1998). *Indigenism: Ethnic politics in Brazil*. Madison: University of Wisconsin Press.

Rego, W.L., and Pinzani, A. (2013). *Vozes do Bolsa Família: Autonomia, dinheiro e cidadania*. São Paulo: Editora Unesp.

Reid, M. (2014). *Brazil: The troubled rise of a global power*. New Haven: Yale University Press.

Roett, R. (2010). *The new Brazil*. Washington DC: The Brookings Institution Press.

Rohter, L. (2010). *Brazil on the rise: The story of a country transformed*. New York: Palgrave Macmillan.

Sachs, W. (2009). *The development dictionary: A guide to knowledge as power*. London: Zed Books.

Santos, M.P.G. dos. (2013). The Brazilian social protection system: history and present configuration. In: J. Midgley and D. Piachaud (eds), *Social protection, economic growth and social change: Goals, issues and trajectories in China, India, Brazil and South Africa*. Cheltenham, UK: Edward Elgar, pp. 131–152.

Souza, A. de, and Lamounier, B. (2010). *A mlasse Média Brasileira: Ambições, valores e projetos de sociedade*. Rio de Janeiro/Brasília: Editora Elsevier/CNI.

Taylor, M. (2015). The unchanging core of Brazilian state capitalism, 1985–2015. *American University School of International Service Research Paper Number 2015–8*. Posted 18 October 2015. Available at: <https://ssrn.com/astract=2674332≥ [accessed 13 November 2017].

Valladão, A. (2013). Emergent Brazil and the curse of the 'hen's flight'. In: M. Emerson and R. Flôres (eds), *Enhancing the Brazil–EU strategic partnership – From the bilateral and the regional to the global*. Brussels: CEPS.

Vieira, V.R. (2017). Blended diplomacy: Institutional design and Brazil's national interest in trade. *Rising Powers Quarterly*, 2(2), 31–53.

Wade, R. (2004). *Governing the market: Economic theory and the role of government in East Asian industrialization*. Princeton: Princeton University Press.

Williamson, J. (1990). What Washington means by policy reform. In: J. Williamson (ed.), *Latin American adjustment: How much has happened?* Washington DC: Institute for International Economics. Available at: https://piie.com/commentary/speeches-papers/what-washington-means-policy-reform [accessed 17 November 2017].

World Bank Group (2016). *Taking on inequality: Poverty and shared prosperity 2016.* Washington, DC: International Bank for Reconstruction and Development. Available at: https://openknowledge.worldbank.org/bitstream/handle/10986/25078/9781464809583.pdf [accessed 23 August 2018].

World Wildlife Fund (2017). About the Amazon. Available at: http://wwf.panda.org/what_we_do/where_we_work/amazon/about_the_amazon/ [accessed 27 February 2018].

Wright, A., and Wolford, W. (2003). *To inherit the earth: The landless movement and the struggle for a New Brazil.* San Francisco: Food First Books.

5   Race and ethnicity in Brazil

Introduction

On 18 December 2017, the Brazilian pop star Anitta released the song and music video "Vai Malandra" to the public. The video "Vai Malandra", which can be loosely translated as "Go, Bad Girl",[1] had been shot in the Vidigal favela in Rio de Janeiro and featured 60 residents of Vidigal who had been hired as extras. Anitta wore her hair braided in the video, which received over 15 million views on YouTube in the first 24 hours after it was uploaded. While the video received predictable condemnations from some evangelical pastors, who objected to Anitta flaunting her body, the video also received criticism from more unexpected quarters. According to some observers, in braiding her hair, tanning her skin, and filming the video in Vidigal, Anitta was using "blackness" when it was convenient for her to do so. For the Afro-Brazilian journalist Stephanie Ribeiro, for example, Anitta had never self-identified as Afro-Brazilian before and was now "pretending" to be black in the video while at the same time benefiting from being perceived as non-black in her other public appearances (Ribeiro, 2017).[2]

The ensuing debate about Anitta's alleged "cultural appropriation" in "Vai Malandra" reveals something about how Brazilian race relations have changed over the past few decades. Whereas, in the past, a popular singer might have straightened her hair and lightened her skin in order to conform to prevailing white-centric stereotypes of beauty, in 2017 Anitta had adopted an Afro-Brazilian look and been criticized for it by some black activists. This, of course, is not to suggest that Afro-Brazilian cultural themes were not appropriated by white artists in the past (see, for example, Carmen Miranda), *or* that cultural appropriation is always the same, no matter which artists appropriate whatever themes. There are important imbalances of power to account for, as well as histories of marginalization and inequality that help to inform – albeit not without dispute – what forms of cultural appropriation are more or less acceptable. What, instead, draws attention in Anitta's case is how critiques of her cultural appropriation indicate that understandings of race, today in Brazil, are perhaps becoming more binary (i.e., one is either white *or* black), and that debates over white privilege may be changing how people see, talk about, and make sense of race on a daily basis.

This chapter reviews debates about race and ethnicity in Brazil, putting the controversy about Anitta in context. It first describes the racial and ethnic mix in Brazil, how these were changed by mass immigration in the nineteenth and early twentieth centuries, and the prevalence of pseudo-scientific racism during that period. It then analyses challenges to that racial status quo in the early twentieth century and how the spread of an ideology of "racial democracy" still maintained a pigmentocracy, or a racial hierarchy in which whites were on top, and darker-skinned people on the bottom. Finally, the chapter notes racial and ethnic mobilization of recent decades, their challenges to the ideology of racial democracy, the adoption of public policies aimed at furthering racial equality, such as affirmative action, and current debates about the desirability and efficacy of these policies.

Several questions animate this chapter. First, how different are Brazilian race relations from those of other countries in the Americas, including the USA? Second, to what extent was the ideology of racial democracy a challenge to, rather than an acceptance of, dominant ideas about race in Brazil and in the world? And third, to what extent have race-based mobilization and new public policies of racial inclusion broken down the old racial order or pigmentocracy?

Ethnic and racial mixture in Brazil

A few definitions are in order before we proceed to examine race and ethnicity in Brazil. By ethnic group, we mean a group of people that share social or cultural traits. These could include language, religion, regional or national origins, dress, customs (including food, music, dancing, literature, and festivals), lineage, or phenotype, and aspects of physical appearance (Stephens, 1989, p. 3). Ethnic groups are sometimes minorities within nation-states. Within Brazil there are the Yanomami and Xingu indigenous people, for example, and also descendants of Germans, Lebanese, and Japanese. Unlike in some other countries of the Americas, such as the USA, however, where many people still identify as "Italian-American" or "Irish-American" (even though their families have lived in the US for generations), Brazilians *today* rarely link their ethnicity with their ancestral origins.[3] They are more likely to associate their ethnicity with the state or region where they were born, or identify as simply "Brazilian." Nevertheless, some people do identify ethnically, and, in the history of nationalism and nation-building, we know that ethnicity has been hugely important to such processes (Hobsbawm, 1992).

Race, on the other hand, is mainly about phenotypical variation or the physical characteristics that people have. It can also relate to genealogy, descent, or "blood". An example of this difference can be seen in the comparison of blackness in the USA and Brazil. In the USA, it was said to have been defined by descent, by whether one had a single "drop" of African "blood", whereas, in Brazil, it was about phenotype, or how one looked, and also about one's social condition. Racial groups are groups that are distinguished on the basis of their physical appearance or lineage. Despite their supposed natural and/or scientific basis, racial categories are also fluid and determined by numerous cultural factors. Similarly, race and skin color are not necessarily the same, even though they are often used synonymously. For example, in the Brazilian census one finds white (*branco*), brown (*pardo*), black (*preto*), yellow (*amarelo*), and indigenous (*indígena*) as discrete racial categories. However, if you ask people what color they are, they might come up with one of more than one hundred terms for color, some of which – like *moreno* (brown or dark) – can be very ambiguous. In brief, ethnic categories largely refer to cultural differences; racial categories largely refer to physical differences; and skin color largely refers to skin tone and coloration (which, of course, can change due to factors such as sun exposure, etc.).

Both ethnic and racial categories are socially constructed. They are "partial, unstable, contextual, fragmentary" (Wade, 1997, p. 20; see also Weinstein, 2015, p. 18). They are not mutually exclusive: anyone can have both a racial and an ethnic identity (Wade, 1997, p. 21). Such an assertion is not a denial of biology. Racial differences exist, but the categories we use to discuss race are arbitrary: so-called "white" people are not really white, and they are not the same from country to country. Racial categories also change over time and are shaped by history, and they often develop in opposition to other groups (e.g., people who are not part of the in-group). There is no genetic or scientific basis for the racial categories we tend to use, yet both race and ethnicity "involve a discourse about origins and about the transmission of essences across generations" (Wade, 1997, p. 21). In the Americas, histories of ethnicity and race reflect, in many ways, the socio-political hierarchies in which they were produced. As Stephens writes (1989, p. 5), terms for race and ethnicity "are imbued with the function of maintaining order in the social structure through the linguistic manifestations, often in the form of biases, of the Latin Americans who use them."

The Portuguese of the sixteenth century, Brazil's colonizers, had their own obsessions with race, purity of blood (*pureza de sangue*), and so-called contaminated races (*raças infectadas*) (Boxer, 1969, p. 251; see also Bethencourt and Pearce, 2012). They had overturned Moorish rule in Portugal and were concerned, on the one hand, with differences between people with Old Christian, aristocratic blood and legitimate birth, and, on the other hand, Moors, Jews, Africans, and indigenous people (Boxer, 1969, p. 264). In 1497, King Manuel of Portugal decreed that all Jews had to convert to Christianity or leave the country (Hatton, 2011, p. 99). This led to the conversion, genuine or otherwise, of many Jewish people to Catholicism.

The Portuguese Inquisition was established in 1536 and eventually expanded within the Portuguese Empire, targeting so-called New Christians (converts from Judaism, *conversos* or *marranos*) (Hatton, 2011, p. 95). As a result of this repression, thousands of Jews fled Portugal and went to Amsterdam, London, and other European cities, as well as the New World. The first synagogue in the Americas was established in Recife in 1636 when the Dutch were ruling Pernambuco (see Figure 5.1). After the Dutch were expelled from the area in 1654, 23 immigrants from this group went to the Caribbean and then New Amsterdam, establishing the first Jewish settlement in what became New York City.

Figure 5.1 Synagogue Kahal Zur Israel in Recife, Pernambuco. First established in 1636, the building today functions as a museum.

Source: Ricardo André Frantz, Wikimedia commons: https://commons.wikimedia.org/wiki/File:Sina goga-kahal-zur-israel-recife.jpg

There were also millions of indigenous people in what is now Brazil in the sixteenth century, scattered among hundreds of different ethnic groups. This number quickly began to decline, however, mainly due to the spread of European and African diseases for which the indigenous people had no genetic defenses (Hemming, 1978, p. xv).[4] Attempts to enslave the indigenous and use them as a labor force were largely unsuccessful. Most indigenous groups ran away from, resisted, or perished under European occupation, so the Portuguese turned to the large-scale importation of African slaves. Millions of slaves went to Brazil in the colonial and imperial periods from the mid-sixteenth to the mid-nineteenth centuries. A relatively small cadre of white Portuguese, most of them men who had emigrated to Brazil without families, sat at the summit of a society with a large number of indigenous and Afro-Brazilians. In this society, racial mixture was common. Notes Holston, "in Brazil, the encouragement of integration through mixed-race settlement and marriage had been official, legislated policy since colonial times" (Holston, 2009, p. 69).

In fact, racial mixture first began with the arrival of Pedro Álvares Cabral in Brazil in 1500. Cabral brought with him two convicts who had been sentenced to death. He abandoned them in the New World, leaving them with an indigenous group with whom they were expected to settle and have children (Hemming, 1978, p. 6).[5]

This does not mean, however, that Brazil's history of miscegenation necessarily led to more egalitarian racial and social relations. To the contrary, much academic scholarship highlights the ways differentiated racial categories continued to persist, and how racism intertwined with cultures of chauvinism and hypermasculinism, working to hypersexualize non-white Brazilian women (*and* men) (Chaui, 2017; Goldstein, 2003). Related to this, sociologist Jessé Souza (2017) argues that in order to explain ongoing inequalities, political corruption, and the misrule of law in Brazil, one must place Brazil's history of slavery at the center of debates. Like others before him seeking to explain Brazil's culture of elite privilege and patrimony (e.g., Sérgio Buarque de Holanda, Gilberto Freyre, Raymundo Faoro), Souza returns to the roots of Brazil's colonial history. But, differently from others, Souza argues that contemporary Brazil's enduring traditions of elite privilege and political corruption connect directly to slavery, and that, among several factors, what helps to explain the not-so-democratic rule of law in Brazil (e.g., corruption and authoritarianism) is stigma and fear of the lower, non-white classes. As such, Souza draws attention to the (perversely) functional roles of racism, stigma, and inequality in contemporary Brazilian society – for example, how fear of non-white (often poor) people diverts attention away from the corrupt practices of elites – and how these processes connect Brazil's colonial past with its political present.

For much of its colonial and imperial history, Brazil was dominated by the idea of "racial pessimism." This pessimism was heightened by the pseudo-scientific racism of the nineteenth century and epitomized by theorists such as the French intellectual and diplomat Joseph Arthur de Gobineau (Weinstein, 2015, p. 6). Because it was a mixed-race country where many people were of indigenous and African descent, Brazil was destined to be inferior, according to theorists like Gobineau, and incapable of living up to the standards of the "civilized" European and North American countries that were the rich, imperial powers in the world at that time. To counter this pessimism, authorities in Brazil encouraged the migration of Europeans, not only to fulfill the labor needs of the growing country, but also to "whiten" the population. Immigration increased after the abolition of slavery in 1888.[6] This immigration was often subsidized by state governments. For example, the government of São Paulo encouraged immigrants to come to work in the coffee plantations by loaning them the cost of their passage. Most European immigrants from Italy, Spain, and Portugal went to these states in the more temperate parts of the country (in the Southeast and South).

The idea of "whitening" cemented what could be called a "pigmentocracy" in Brazil. Whites were clearly at the top of the pigmentocracy's social pyramid, with the darkest-skinned Afro-Brazilians at the bottom. The indigenous people had a slightly ambiguous position in this hierarchy because they were often used as symbols of national identity and sovereignty even while, in practice, they were discriminated against. The Brazilian government never considered the indigenous as separate nations, as did the USA's government (Holston, 2009, pp. 54, 63), but it did consider them wards of the state (Ramos, 1998, pp. 18–19). Whitening, within the pigmentocracy, offered the chance of social mobility to future generations of non-white Brazilians. The idea can be seen in a painting by Modesto Brocos from 1895 called "Redenção de Ham" (Ham's Redemption) (see Figure 5.2). In the painting, which is exhibited in the Museu Nacional de Belas Artes in Rio de Janeiro, a black grandmother stands and exults at seeing her light-skinned grandchild, held by her mixed-race daughter and observed by her white son-in-law. This is a graphic depiction of the ideal of whitening which,

Figure 5.2 Redenção de Ham (Ham's Redemption), painted by Modesto Brocos in 1895 and currently displayed at the Museu Nacional de Belas Artes in Rio de Janeiro.

Source: Photographic reproduction of original painting, Wikimedia commons: https://commons. wikimedia.org/wiki/File:Redenção.jpg

according to some observers such as the intellectual and diplomat, Oliveira Lima, would lead eventually to the elimination of Brazil's black population (Pereira, 2012, p. 12).[7]

The notion of whitening also had regional implications for Brazil. The South and southeastern regions were whiter regions than the Northeast, which had more Afro-Brazilian influence, and the North, where the indigenous presence was stronger. For some Brazilian elites, this brought the South and the Southeast closer to the standard by which they were measuring themselves: the "civilized", imperial nations of Europe and the rising power, the USA (Weinstein, 2015, p. 6).[8] In the first part of the twentieth century, however, Brazil's racial and ethnic profile was further diversified by new migrations: the Japanese, the so-called "Turks" from the former Ottoman Empire, and eastern European Jews (Lesser, 2013, p. 2). These groups presented a challenge to "whiteness" in Brazil, as understandings of race and skin color were further complicated by the ethnic and cultural differences of these new migrants. For example, could "white" mean non-Christian and non-European, or was whiteness bound exclusively to European cultural and ethnic traits? These questions were bound within arguments over Brazilian national identity, and, to be fair, Brazil was by no means the only country engaging in these (often racist) debates.

Challenging pseudo-scientific racism: the advances and silences of "racial democracy"

Brazilian conceptions of race were further challenged in 1933 with the publication of Gilberto Freyre's *Casa Grande e Senzala* (literally, The Big House and the Slave Quarters, but translated as *The Masters and the Slaves* and published in English in 1946). Freyre was born on a sugar plantation in Apipucos, now part of greater Recife, the capital of the state of Pernambuco in northeastern Brazil. He was a Baptist and went to study at Baylor University in Texas before starting a PhD under the anthropologist, Franz Boas, at Columbia University in New York City. Boas recommended that he not try to get the PhD and Freyre left Columbia without finishing, instead publishing his research as a book (Freyre, 1946).

In the book, Freyre flipped pseudo-scientific racism on its head and painted a positive portrait of Brazil's racial mixture. For Freyre, each of the three central elements of Brazil's racial hybridity had played a part in the development of Brazilian civilization. This new world, or what he later called luso-tropical civilization, was formed from the unique contributions of the indigenous, the Portuguese colonizer, and the Afro-Brazilian slave. Rather than racial mixture being something that despoiled the nation, he said that this was its genius; it could bring a harmonious whole out of these three disparate, very different elements. Rather than be ashamed of its large non-white population, Brazil should celebrate it and appreciate and recognize the contributions of the indigenous and Afro-Brazilians to the formation of Brazilian national culture, which has many non-European elements. Freyre even once said that he deliberately chose words that came from indigenous or African languages while writing *Casa Grande e Senzala*, in order to emphasize the originality of Brazilian Portuguese and its fusion of different influences.

In many ways, Freyre's book was ahead of its time. It was what we would now call social history. Nothing was too intimate or small scale to escape his attention. For example, in *Casa Grande e Senzala*, he describes recipes, everyday expressions, household routines, diary excerpts, and popular songs, the kinds of domestic details that many scholars of that time ignored in favor of analyses of the great leaders of the day.[9] The publication date is also significant, as, in 1933, the Nazis came to power in Germany through an election, and ethno-nationalist ideas were taking hold in Europe and beyond. Freyre's book was important in its rejection of racial pessimism and in its acceptance of racial mixture as a positive fact of Brazilian life (Eakin, 2017, p. 251; Pallares-Burke, 2012; Weinstein, 2015, p. 13).

Over the years, however, criticisms of Freyre's book have outweighed the appreciation. Critics point to the sentimental and patriarchal portrait of plantation life painted by Freyre, and its over-generous assessment of the achievement of racial harmony in Brazil. Freyre's vision also soft-pedaled the violence meted out to Afro-Brazilians and the indigenous and downplayed the inequalities of the pigmentocracy, the racial hierarchy that came out of race mixture in Brazil. The book also relied on a strong dose of essentialism about the character of each of the three major racial groups that were said to make up Brazil, with the Portuguese seen as rational and calculating, the Africans sensuous and joyful, and the indigenous melancholy and undisciplined. As philosopher Marilena Chaui points out, to praise Afro-Brazilian sensuality in a white, Western, Christian culture "that values the spirit over the flesh, the intellect over sensibility, reason over emotions is not to eulogize but to devalue the 'inferior others'" (Chaui, 2017, p. 76). Critics at the University of São Paulo coined a phrase that Freyre did not use in *Casa Grande e Senzala* – racial democracy – to suggest that the book was a whitewash of Brazilian history. They argued that the book painted a false picture of Brazil as an essentially colorblind society in which racial equality was a real achievement rather than an aspiration (see also Souza, 2017, p. 28).

Freyre's was a uniquely Brazilian spin on an affirmation of identity that took place throughout Latin America in the 1920s and 1930s. In Mexico, to give one example, José Vasconcelos, a philosopher, Minister of Education, and future presidential candidate, published *La Raza Cosmica* (The Cosmic Race) in 1925. In that book, Vasconcelos wrote about *mestizaje*, the mixture of the Spaniards and the indigenous that created what he called a "bronze race." Because it had elements of all the world's races, he said it was universal, or "cosmic," and it could transcend social Darwinism (Vasconcelos, 1997). Vasconcelos even coined the motto of the National University of Mexico: "through my race the spirit will speak." Freyre's positive vision of Brazilian *mestiçagem* had clear affinities with that of Vasconcelos.

As years passed following the publication of *Casa Grande e Senzala*, it became clear that Brazil's racial order had distinctive characteristics. Unlike the racial order of the USA prior to the civil rights movement, or apartheid South Africa from 1948 to 1994, Brazil never legalized racial segregation (Marx, 1999; Telles, 2006). That does not mean, however, there was no race-based political mobilization. According to the historian, George Reid Andrews (2018), there were three race-based political parties in Latin America in the first part of the twentieth century. These were the *Partido Independiente de Color* (Independent Party of Color) founded in Cuba in 1908, the *Partido Autoctono Negro* (Autonomous Black Party) founded in Uruguay in 1936, and the *Frente Negra Brasileira* (Black Brazilian Front), founded in Brazil in 1931, with its directorate in São Paulo (Fernandes, 1969, p. 211). These parties are significant in that they evidence how racial inequality began to spur political mobilization even though racial segregation was not legalized, as in the USA or South Africa. Of these three parties, only the Uruguayan party was allowed by its government to continue to operate. The *Frente Negra Brasileira* was closed in 1937 by the *Estado Novo* regime headed by President Getúlio Vargas (Andrews, 2018; see also Fernandes, 1969, p. 221; Telles, 2006, p. 37).

In post-Second World War Brazil, the idea that the country was a racial democracy was still prevalent. The Austrian novelist, Stefan Zweig (2000), helped to popularize the idea of Brazil as a tolerant, racially harmonious country in his book *Brazil: A Land of the Future*, published in 1941.[10] Brazil's own literature often celebrated the ambiguity of race in the country, such as when the eponymous hero of Mario de Andrade's surrealistic comic novel *Macunaíma* takes a bath in enchanted waters and turns from an indigenous person into a white boy with blue eyes and blonde hair (Andrade, 1984). A common idea was that racial identity could be transcended by class, reflected in the Brazilian expressions "branco é quem tem dinheiro", or "he who has money is white" (Stephens, 1989, p. vii), and "dinheiro embranquece", or "money whitens" (Roth-Gordon, 2017, p. 42). The anthropologist, Darcy Ribeiro, tells the story of the Afro-Brazilian artist, Santa Rosa, who, while receiving an Afro-Brazilian friend who had become a diplomat, listened to his friend complain about racial prejudice and the barriers to his success. Santa Rosa empathized, replying, "I understand your case perfectly. I was also a negro once" (Ribeiro, 1995, p. 207).[11]

Important research by UNESCO in the post-Second World War period started with the presumption that Brazil was a racial democracy, but found, instead, structural racial inequalities. It also showed that the so-called "mulatto escape hatch" – that is, better life chances and outcomes for lighter-skinned Afro-Brazilians – did not appear to operate (Eakin, 2017, p. 238; Roth-Gordon, 2017, pp. 43–44). In 1951, Congress passed legislation that became the Afonso Arinos Law outlawing racial discrimination, but the legislation lacked the kind of detail that would have given it teeth and made it enforceable. Racial discrimination was part of everyday life, such as job advertisements in which employers asked for "boa aparência" (good appearance), a phrase that implicitly meant white looks or at least those of a light-skinned Afro-Brazilian (Roth-Gordon, 2017, p. 44).

Activism, public policies, and debates over race and ethnicity in Brazil

The 1970s, influenced by the USA's civil rights and Black Power movements, as well as decolonization in Africa, was a decade of racial reconsideration and Afro-Brazilian mobilization in Brazil (Dunn, 2016, p. 146; Gomes, 2017, p. 47; Turner, 1985, p. 73). As the Brazilian dictatorship liberalized, Afro-Brazilian organizations, along with other civil society entities, began to emerge. Perhaps the best known of them, the *Movimento Negro Unificado* (Unified Black Movement), was founded in São Paulo in 1978, when 2,000 Afro-Brazilians protested against racial discrimination in front of the Municipal Theater (Telles, 2006, p. 48; see also Dunn, 2016, p. 173; Eakin, 2017, p. 239). A new generation of intellectuals also began to develop new perspectives on Brazilian racism and race relations, challenging the ideology of racial democracy (Lehmann, 2018).

These debates about the nature of Brazilian race relations and the optimal policies by which to address racial inequality have continued into the twenty-first century. An example of different perspectives can be seen in the article published by the European sociologists, Pierre Bordieu and Loïc Wacquant (1999), and the strong reaction it elicited from the American historian, John French (2003). French argued that Bordieu and Wacquant had wrongly attacked the American political scientist Michael Hanchard's book *Orpheus and Power* (1998) for imposing an American model of race relations on Brazil. For French, the transnational dialogue on race in the USA and Brazil

> is far less unbalanced than in the past; indeed, one of the most fruitful and provocative developments has been the emergence of a clearly enunciated *Brazilian* articulation of the dialectics of similarity and differences between Brazil and the USA, especially in terms of identities and subjectivities.
>
> (French, 2003, p. 384, original emphasis)

In the early 2000s, policies designed to address racial inequality in Brazil began to be implemented. In 2001, the State University of Rio de Janeiro became the first Brazilian university to use quotas for Afro-Brazilians as part of its admissions policy (Kamel, 2007, p. 37). In 2002, under the presidency of Fernando Henrique Cardoso, the government launched a national program of affirmative actions (Kamel, 2007, p. 36). The promotion of affirmative actions, modeled on the experience of the USA but modified to fit Brazilian social circumstances, continued under the administrations of Presidents Lula (2003–2010) and Rousseff (2011–2016). This legislation, not surprisingly, generated plenty of controversy, and, in April 2012, the Brazilian Supreme Court finally ruled that race-based quotas for Afro-Brazilians and the indigenous in Brazilian universities were legal (Reid, 2014, p. 183). In August of the same year, President Dilma Rousseff signed a law requiring all federal universities to establish quotas for students from state schools, as well as Afro-Brazilians and the indigenous, in proportion to their presence in the state census (Reid, 2014, p. 183). As the Brazilian sociologist, Sergio Guimarães, pointed out, affirmative actions in Brazil modified the

US model, in that racial quotas were linked to social quotas (for public high school students). In this way, both radical class-based and race-based demands were defused (Guimarães, 2018, p. 14), resulting in a policy that is broadly popular, according to surveys (Telles, 2006, p. 260). The racial composition of Brazilian universities has, thus, begun to change, and this change has generated considerable commentary (Johnson, 2008).

Not all of the commentary, however, has been positive. For example, the anthropologist, Peter Fry, born in Britain but a naturalized Brazilian, opposed race-based quotas in universities. He traced affirmative actions and other "multi-culturalist" policies back to indirect British rule in northern Nigeria and other British colonies, seeing them as a tactic of divide and rule that would inevitably spark opportunistic racial identification and mobilization that might even ignite white backlash. He argued that Brazil would be better off maintaining its officially colorblind policies (Fry, 2000). Another opponent of affirmative actions was the influential Globo journalist, Ali Kamel. Kamel argued that Brazil was not a "bicolor" nation such as the USA, but one in which race mixture was common and in which people identified themselves with a broad spectrum of colors. For Kamel, rather than affirmative actions, state investment in basic education was the best way to promote racial equality (2007, p. 40). For the historian, Marshall Eakin,

> the key question for those seeking to fight prejudice and discrimination is this: is it really necessary to have a binary system of racial classification to acknowledge and root out the injustice or can this be done while accepting the historical fluidity of color categories in Brazil?
>
> (Eakin, 2017, p. 265)

Such questions draw attention to the roots and effects of discrimination, as well as the ways racism persists – and even how race is fundamentally understood, as revealed in debates over Anitta's cultural/racial appropriation – in Brazil and countries elsewhere.

Affirmative actions in universities are today commonplace, and non-white Brazilians have become more visible and have established a stronger presence in universities. But this is a limited form of inclusion. Federal and state universities control access to elite professions such as engineering, law, and medicine, but affirmative actions at elite universities do little to alter deeply entrenched racial inequalities in the rest of Brazilian society. For example, in the 2010 census, 51% of Brazilians defined themselves as black or brown, yet the average income of this segment of the population is slightly less than *half* of those who describe themselves as white (Reid, 2014, p. 181). Related to this, some critics have turned to Brazil's violent policing, inegalitarian criminal justice system, and the steep increase in Brazil's prison population as fresh evidence of the high price non-whites pay for the inequalities of the social order (Alexander, 2017). These are issues that Marielle Franco, a rising municipal politician of humble origin (she was born and raised in the favela community Maré) in Rio de Janeiro frequently protested before she was assassinated in 2018. Franco not only drew attention to issues of racism and injustice, she experienced firsthand the sharp end of discrimination in Brazil. She was black, gay, became a mother at the age of 19, and came from a poor background. Her public critiques of racial inequality and police violence helped distinguish her career, and many believe she paid for it with her life (see Figure 5.3).

Despite mounting debates over race and the ways racism operates, many Brazilians continue to feel comfortable asserting, as did President Lula in 2009, that "We are not only a mixed people, but a people who like very much to be mixed; it is our identity" (quoted in Eakin, 2017, p. 253). According to anthropologist, Roberto DaMatta, "we [Brazilians], unlike the people of the USA, never say 'separate but equal'; instead we say 'different but united,' which is the golden rule of a hierarchical and relational universe such as ours" (DaMatta, 1991, p. 4). Brazilians often acknowledge that Brazil is not a racial democracy, and can see in the social hierarchy evidence of a pigmentocracy (Almeida, 2007, p. 232).[12] Does this mean, therefore, that Brazilians simply accept inequality as a fact of life, and/or that unity and cohesion are more important than social equality and justice? Or is it just the opposite; that *through* unity and social cohesion, greater equality might be realized and achieved?

Figure 5.3 Municipal council representative Marielle Franco at a political rally in Rio de Janeiro in 2016.

Source: Mídia NINJA, Wikimedia commons: https://commons.wikimedia.org/wiki/File:Marielle_Fran co_em_agosto_de_2016.jpg

These are the sorts of questions contemporary activists face, and they evidence how debates over social inequality in Brazil continue to gravitate around issues of race and ethnicity.

Conclusion

For many years, the scholarly consensus about Brazil's racial order was that it was not, as in the USA, a bipolar order reducible to black and white. This was a negative idea based partly on the abundant comparative analysis of USA and Brazilian race relations, and it emphasized what Brazil was *not* rather than what it was. Inside Brazil, successive waves of scholars attacked the Freyrian idea of a harmonious mixture of the indigenous, the European, and the African as misleading. Most rejected the notion of a racial democracy, but sometimes disagreed over how best to characterize Brazil's racial and ethnic complexity, with its abundance of distinctive ethnic and racial identities, which were, in turn, linked to class, neighborhood, and regional identities.

Several simultaneous developments have complicated the picture of race relations painted by these two streams of literature. Brazil has adopted affirmative actions in federal universities, creating quotas for Afro-Brazilians, the indigenous, and students from publicly funded schools. At the same time, some Afro-Brazilian activists have advocated the self-conscious adoption of a "black" identity by those who are non-white. For these activists, hair and skin color have political connotations and the racial order looks increasingly more dualistic than it did in the past. This is reflected in Ribeiro's critique of Anitta (2017). In a complementary movement, scholars such as Hanchard (1998, 1999) have questioned whether Brazil, for all the complexity of its race relations, is really so different from the racial hierarchy found in the USA.

For comparativists, the nature of the USA' racial model has also been questioned. For some, the USA has moved away from its bipolar racial order and become more like Brazil (Eakin, 2017, p. 265), with more people of mixed race, the option of defining one's own race in the census, and states in which whites are a plurality, but not the majority of the population. The election of the first black president in the USA, Barack Obama, in 2008 and 2012, also indicated for some observers that the USA was finally making progress in breaking away from racial inequality. For others, the election of Donald J. Trump in 2016, and the Trump campaign's open courting of white nationalist movements, confirmed their worst suspicions of how entrenched white supremacy still is in the USA.

At present, two generalizations about Brazil endure in the literature: it has historically not had a USA-style bipolar racial order (although it may shift in that direction in the future), and it never implemented *de jure* segregation along the lines of Jim Crow in the southern USA or apartheid in South Africa. But the significance of the Freyrian rejection of pseudo-scientific racism, the scope for racial equality within the old racial order, and the desirability and efficacy of affirmative action remain topics of heated debate. What seems certain is that racial inequality and the exclusion of non-whites from the upper echelons of society will continue to be challenged. Race and ethnicity are likely to remain one of the most closely watched and controversial issues for observers of Brazil, both within and outside the country.

Notes

1 There are many other possible translations of *malandra* and *malandro*, the female and male characters who are bearers of *malandragem*. Artful dodger, rascal, rogue, and trickster are some of these translations, and the *malandro* is associated with informality, the Brazilian *jeitinho* (improvised short-cut, creative solution to a problem that may or may not be in keeping with the rules), street life, and non-white status. See DaMatta, 1991.

2 Ribeiro wrote that in a society marked by "colorism" (a social hierarchy based on skin color in which whites are on top), mixed-race individuals such as Anitta had a choice about whether to self-identify as Afro-Brazilian. Since Anitta had never done that previously, her appearance in the video, which Anitta herself described as "returning to her roots", was seen by Ribeiro as opportunistic and selective, causing discomfort to women such as Ribeiro who had always identified as black (*negra*) and who thereby regularly challenged and bore the brunt of the prejudices inherent in the colorist hierarchy. (Ribeiro's term colorism is equivalent to the pigmentocracy discussed in this chapter.) For more on colorism in a Brazilian context, see Costa 2018. For more on colorism in a USA context see Holmes, 2018, who describes it as a system that "places black people in an uncodified but nevertheless very real hierarchy, with the lighter-skinned among us at the top".

3 This has not always been the case. For example, prior to the *Estado Novo* government of Getúlio Vargas in the 1930s, plenty of Brazilians would have considered themselves ethnically Portuguese, Italian, German, and so on.

4 Hemming (1978, p. xiv) refers to "millions of natives living in the half of South America that is now Brazil".

5 Since we argued previously that ethnicity and race are socially constructed, it might seem incongruous to use the phrase "race mixture" in this context. If races do not exist in objective terms, then deciding what constitutes race mixture must be somewhat arbitrary. We mean mixing according to the racial categories used at that time, in this case European Portuguese and New World indigenous people. For a fascinating analysis of the construction of racial identities in contemporary Northeast Brazil, see French, 2009.

6 By some accounts the São Paulo coffee planters' success in inducing European immigrants to work in the fields was a crucial factor in them accepting the abolition of slavery in 1888.

7 The pioneering Afro-Brazilian activist and member of Congress Abdias do Nascimento called this ideology genocide by miscegenation, a fair description of the ultimate goal of whitening for many of its proponents. See Nascimento, 1990.

8 Weinstein (2015, p. 14) argues that in the period between the 1920s and the 1960s, the economic success of the state of São Paulo "cemented the widely assumed association between whiteness and civilization" and that "paulistas have routinely represented themselves as 'white' and *nordestinos* as 'nonwhite' regardless of genetics or physical appearance" (Weinstein, 2015, p. 10).

9 Freyre's book also seemed to be quite personal, drawing on the author's memories of his own experiences. For example, the chapter on Afro-Brazilians is entitled "The Negro Slave in the Sexual and Family Life of the Brazilian" and at the beginning of the chapter, Freyre writes, "Every Brazilian, even the light-skinned and fair-haired

one, carries about with him on his soul...the shadow, or at least the birthmark, of the aborigine or the Negro." He then goes on to eulogize "the mulatto girl...Who initiated us into physical love and, to the creaking of a canvas cot, gave us our first complete sensation of being a man" (Freyre, 1946, p. 278). According to Christopher Dunn (2016, p. 156), this type of nostalgia "reinforced cherished ideas about the power of sexuality, and specifically interracial sex, to overcome social barriers."

10 In his introduction, Zweig declares, "for centuries the Brazilian nation has been established on one principle alone, that of free and unrestrained intermixing, the total equality of black and white and brown and yellow" (Zweig, 2000, p. 10). And again, "the experiment we call Brazil, with its complete and conscious negation of all color and racial differences, is perhaps the most important contribution to doing away with a delusion that has brought more discord and disaster upon our world than any other" (Zweig, 2000, p. 12).

11 The original text is "Compreendo perfeitamente o seu caso, meu caro. Eu também ja fui negro."

12 Almeida shows through survey research that high status occupations are associated with whites, while low status occupations are associated with non-whites (Almeida, 2007, p. 232).

Suggested English readings

Eakin, M. (2017). *Becoming Brazilians: Race and national identity in twentieth-century Brazil.* Cambridge: Cambridge University Press.

Fernandes, F. (1969). *The negro in Brazilian society.* New York: Columbia University Press.

French, J.H. (2009). *Legalizing identities: Becoming Black or Indian in Brazil's northeast.* Chapel Hill: University of North Carolina Press.

Goldstein, D.M. (2003). *Laughter out of place: Race, class, violence, and sexuality in a Rio shantytown.* Berkeley: University of California Press.

Freyre, G. (1946). *The masters and the slaves.* Translated by Samuel Putnam. New York: Knopf.

Lehmann, D. (2018). *The prism of race.* Ann Arbor: University of Michigan Press.

Lesser, J. (2013). *Immigration, ethnicity and national identity in Brazil, 1808 to the present.* Cambridge: Cambridge University Press.

References

Alexander, M. (2017). *A nova segregação: Racismo e encarceramento em massa.* São Paulo: Boitempo.

Almeida, A.C. (2007). *A cabeça do Brasileiro.* Rio de Janeiro: Editora Record.

Andrade, M. de. (1984). *Macunaíma* [1928]. Translated by E.A. Goodland. New York: Random House.

Andrews, G.R. (2018). Afro-Uruguay: A brief history. *BlackPast.org.* Available at: http://www.blackpast.org/perspectives/afro-uruguay-brief-history [accessed 9 March 2017].

Bethencourt, F., and Pearce, A. (eds) (2012). *Racism and ethnic relations in the Portuguese-speaking world.* Oxford: Oxford University Press.

Bordieu, P., and Wacquant, L. (1999). On the cunning of imperialist reason. *Theory, Culture and Society,* 16(1), 41–58.

Boxer, C.R. (1969). *The Portuguese seaborne empire 1415–1825.* Harmondsworth, UK: Penguin.

Chaui, M. (2017). Nós, negros e mulatos. In: *Sobre a violência.* Belo Horizonte: Autêntica Editora, pp. 75–76.

Costa, N.L. (2018). Colorismo. *Raça*, 200, May.

DaMatta, R. (1991). *Carnivals, rogues and heroes: An interpretation of the Brazilian dilemma*. Translated by John Drury. South Bend: University of Notre Dame Press.

Dunn, C. (2016). *Contracultura: Alternative arts and social transformation in authoritarian Brazil*. Chapel Hill: University of North Carolina Press.

Eakin, M. (2017). *Becoming Brazilians: Race and national identity in twentieth-century Brazil*. Cambridge: Cambridge University Press.

Fernandes, F. (1969). *The negro in Brazilian society*. Translated by J. D. Skiles, A. Brunel, and A. Rothwell. New York: Columbia University Press.

French, J. (2003). Translation, diasporic dialogue, and the errors of Pierre Bordieu and Löic Wacquant. *Nepantla: Views from the South*, 4(2), 375–389.

French, J.H. (2009). *Legalizing identities: Becoming Black or Indian in Brazil's Northeast*. Chapel Hill: University of North Carolina Press.

Freyre, G. (1946). *The masters and the slaves*. Translated by Samuel Putnam. New York: Knopf.

Fry, P. (2000). Politics, nationality, and the meanings of `race' in Brazil. *Daedalus*, Spring, pp. 83–118.

Goldstein, D.M. (2003). *Laughter out of place: Race, class, violence, and sexuality in a Rio Sshantytown*. Berkeley: University of California Press.

Gomes, N.L. (2017). *O Movimento Negro Educador: Saberes construídos nas lutas por emancipação*. Petrópolis: Editora Vozes.

Guimarães, A.S.A. (2018). Foreword. In: D. Lehmann (ed.), *The prism of race*. Ann Arbor: University of Michigan Press, pp. 12–14.

Hanchard, M. (1998). *Orpheus and power: The "Movimento Negro" of Rio de Janeiro and São Paulo, Brazil 1945–1988*. Princeton: Princeton University Press.

Hanchard, M. (ed.). (1999). *Racial politics in contemporary Brazil*. Durham: Duke University Press.

Hatton, B. (2011). *The Portuguese: A modern history*. Northampton, MA: Interlink Books.

Hemming, J. (1978). *Red gold: The conquest of the Brazilian Indians, 1500–1760*. Cambridge, MA, Harvard University Press.

Hobsbawm, E. (1992). *Nations and nationalism since 1780: Programme, myth, reality*. Cambridge: Cambridge University Press.

Holmes, A. (2018). Black with (some) white privilege. *The New York Times*, 10 February. Available at: www.nytimes.com/2018/02/10/opinion/sunday/black-with-some-white-privilege.html?action=click&pgtype=Homepage& [accessed 11 February 2018].

Holston, J. (2009). *Insurgent citizenship: Disjunctions of democracy and modernity in Brazil*. Princeton: Princeton University Press.

Johnson, O. (2008). Afro-Brazilian politics: White supremacy, black struggle, and affirmative action. In: P. Kingstone and T. Power (eds), *Democratic Brazil Revisited*. Pittsburgh: University of Pittsburgh Press, pp. 209–230.

Kamel, A (2007). *Não somos racistas: Uma reação aos que querem nos transformar numa nação bicolor*. 7th ed. Rio de Janeiro: Editora Nova Fronteira.

Lehmann, D. (2018). *The prism of race*. Ann Arbor: University of Michigan Press.

Lesser, J. (2013). *Immigration, ethnicity and national identity in Brazil, 1808 to the present*. Cambridge: Cambridge University Press.

Marx, A. (1999). *Making race and nation: A comparison of the United States, South Africa and Brazil*. Cambridge: Cambridge University Press.

Nascimento, A. do. (1990). *Brazil: Mixture or massacre? Essays in the genocide of a Black people*. 2nd revised ed. Fitchburg, MA: Majority Press.

Pallares-Burke, M.L.G. (2012). Gilberto Freyre and Brazilian self-perception. In: F. Bethencourt and A. Pearce (eds), *Racism and ethnic relations in the Portuguese-speaking world*. Oxford: Oxford University Press, pp. 113–132.

Pereira, A. (2012). Brazilian studies then and now. *Brasiliana*, 1(1), 3–21.

Ramos, A.R. (1998). *Indigenism: Ethnic politics in Brazil*. Madison: University of Wisconsin Press.

Reid, M. (2014). *Brazil: The troubled rise of a global power*. New Haven: Yale University Press.

Ribeiro, D. (1995). *O povo Brasileiro: A formação e o sentido do Brasil*. São Paulo: Companhia de Bolso.

Ribeiro, S. (2017). Por que Anitta incomodou os negros com o clipe de "Vai Malandra". *Marie Claire*, 21 December 2017. Available at: https://revistamarieclaire.globo.com/Blogs/BlackGirlMagic/noticia/2017/12/stephanie-ribeiro-por-que-anitta-incomodou-os-negros-com-o-clipe-de-vai-malandra.html[accessed 4 March 2018].

Roth-Gordon, J. (2017). *Race and the Brazilian body: Blackness, whiteness, and everyday language in Rio de Janeiro*. Oakland: University of California Press.

Souza, J. (2017). *A elite do atraso: Da escravidão à Lava Jato*. Rio de Janeiro: LeYa.

Stephens, T. (1989). *Dictionary of Latin American racial and ethnic terminology*. Gainesville: University of Florida Press.

Telles, E. (2006). *Race in another America: The significance of skin color in Brazil*. Princeton: Princeton University Press.

Turner, J.M. (1985). Brown into black: Changing racial attitudes of Afro-Brazilian university students. In: P.-M. Fontaine (ed.), *Race, class and power in Brazil*. Los Angeles: University of California, Center for Afro-American Studies, pp. 73–94.

Vasconcelos, J. (1997). *The cosmic race/La raza cosmica: A bilingual edition*. Baltimore: Johns Hopkins University Press.

Wade, P. (1997). *Race and ethnicity in Latin America*. London: Pluto Press.

Weinstein, B. (2015). *The color of modernity: São Paulo and the making of race and nation in Brazil*. Durham: Duke University Press.

Zweig, S. (2000). *Brazil: A land of the future* [Brasilien: Ein Land der Zukunft (1941)]. Translated by Lowell A. Bangerter. Riverside, CA: Ariadne Press.

6 Urban Brazil today

Considering Brazilian cities

To say that Brazilian cities are often misunderstood would be an understatement. Brazilians themselves joke regularly about foreigners confusing Rio de Janeiro for the nation's capital or, even worse, for Buenos Aires. Included here would be widespread underappreciation of Brazil's size, and the ways non-Brazilians are often surprised to learn it has nearly 30 metropolitan regions with *at least* one million people (IBGE, 2017). Those who have little contact with Brazil tend to presume that, beyond the megacities of Rio and São Paulo, the country is mostly rural and/or populated by small cities and villages. Few are the foreigners who have visited other Brazilian metropolitan regions, and rare is it to find news articles, reports, or information regarding cities elsewhere in Brazil.

To be fair, there are clear reasons for why non-Brazilians – and even Brazilians themselves – are left to feel this way. The first is how Rio and São Paulo dominate Brazilian news media, entertainment, culture, etc., both in and outside of Brazil. While only about 15% of Brazil's total population lives in one of these two cities, they cast a massive shadow across the country (thanks in large part to the *Rede Globo* entertainment network). A second reason relates to the economic, political, and historic importance of these two cities, which again are significant factors not to be overlooked. A third reason, and one crucially important within the context of this chapter, is the way urban researchers both in *and* outside of Brazil focus overwhelmingly on Rio and São Paulo. To survey the academic literature on urban Brazil, whether from Brazilian or non-Brazilian authors, one finds the research dominated by studies of Rio and/or São Paulo (Garmany, 2011). It would even be fair to say that outside of southeastern Brazil, urban researchers confront several blind spots when it comes to Brazil's cities. It is not just *Rede Globo's* telenovelas that ignore Brazil's urban diversity: a quick look at Google Scholar shows how urban researchers also fixate on Rio and São Paulo.

There are several reasons for this, and perhaps most significant are academic resources, research money, and existing scholarly debates. For example, most of Brazil's top universities are located in the Southeast region, and since these states also have more robust economies and stronger tax bases, there is more research money in these areas for academics (São Paulo, in particular). As such, foreign researchers are drawn to these cities more so than others, and, consequently, academic debates about urban Brazil – whether from Brazilian or non-Brazilian researchers – focus disproportionately on Rio and São Paulo. Future researchers are apt to pick up on these same debates, and the cycle will likely continue as it has in the past.

All this is important for understanding contemporary academic scholarship in Brazil, as well as reasons for why Brazilian cities elsewhere are often misunderstood thanks to generalizations that lean heavily on findings from Rio and/or São Paulo. Again, Brazil's urban landscape is big, diverse, and distinguished by important bits of historical, cultural, geographic, and political economic nuance. Cities in different parts of the country are often distinct from one another, complicating generalizations that might be made. These are important lessons to keep in mind when reading this chapter. Related to this, it would, of course, be impossible to address *every* significant issue concerning Brazil's cities in one chapter, and instead we focus our attention on key issues faced by most large Brazilian cities today. Our goal is to provide background for understanding contemporary and future urban change in Brazil, as well as to draw attention to critical debates that confront both academic researchers *and* everyday urban residents.

We begin with a brief discussion of Brazil's urban growth and development, noting important geographic differences and the ways inequality and segregation have come to manifest in cities across Brazil. We then move on to address questions of urban informality, identifying reasons why, for example, favelas[1] are so common in Brazilian cities, including reasons for why they are unlikely to disappear in the near future. Part and parcel of this are questions of public security, and ongoing debates over crime, policing, and the increasing presence of private security providers. In the final section, we consider recent debates over housing, infrastructure, and urban growth strategies, as well as new development trends that include, among several characteristics, the rapid growth of 'new' cities in the Central West and North of Brazil.

Growth and urban infrastructure

Those with little background knowledge of Latin America tend to presume the region is mostly rural with many residents working in subsistence agriculture. They often assume that, like other regions in the 'Global South,' Latin America's reputation for underdevelopment also coincides with low levels of urbanization. While this sort of associative logic makes sense, it represents a major misconception about Latin America today: it is, in fact, one of the most highly urbanized regions in the world, with more than 75% of residents living in cities (Rodgers, Beall, and Kanbur, 2012). Brazil is no exception, where urban residents have outnumbered rural ones since the 1950s, and today the number of people living in cities is estimated at more than 85% of the total population (IBGE, 2017). Despite its reputation for raw materials and agricultural resources, Brazil, for decades, has been more urban than most countries in Europe and North America.[2]

Like other countries in the region, a host of historical factors help to explain this. For instance, long before Europeans arrived, there were indigenous groups in Latin America living in urban settings, complete with massive stone architecture, highly adapted infrastructural works, and widespread transportation networks (Cupples, 2013). Additionally, though colonization emphasized exploration and territorial expansion, many small cities and villages emerged in response to export needs and commodity chain networks (Weaver, 2000). Political independence did little to reverse this. Unlike some former colonies, such as the USA, where westward expansion helped to curb urban growth, Brazil's urban population climbed steadily through the nineteenth century. Contributing factors included the emancipation of slaves, the growth of capitalism, and the continued neglect of land reform policies. For example, while the US Homestead Act of 1862 encouraged settlers to move westward and claim land – at the direct expense of American indigenous populations – Brazil's 1850 Land Law (*Lei da Terra*) did just the opposite, requiring purchase of public land and terminating previous occupancy-based claims (*posse*) (Viotti da Costa 2000, pp. 78–79). In other words, lower-income people had little means or incentive to move westward or settle rural land, and urban populations continued to grow. Rural-to-urban migration then picked up as the twentieth century wore on, as, despite many hardships faced by the poor and working-classes in Brazilian cities, the countryside proved even more precarious (due to drought, starvation, etc.).

While cities in the Southeast of Brazil came to dominate the national landscape in the twentieth century, much of Brazil's urban history is rooted in the Northeast. This is where many of Brazil's oldest cities are located, and still today their landscapes reflect diverse cultural histories that combine African, indigenous, and multiple European influences (primarily Portuguese, Dutch, and French – see Figure 6.1). Well before coffee and gold from the Southeast came to dominate Brazil's colonial economy, sugarcane, cotton, timber, and tobacco exports drove urban growth in the Northeast. However, by the time Rio de Janeiro officially overtook Salvador as Brazil's capital city in 1763 – and sugarcane was no longer Brazil's most lucrative export – northeastern cities had long since lost their prominence. The Northeast remained tied to a declining primary export economy, and while no Brazilian city realized much industrial development until the twentieth century, from the mid-eighteenth century onward, the Southeast came to dominate export shipping, bureaucratic and banking operations, intellectual and cultural institutions, and nearly all other industries tethered to urban growth.

Perhaps surprisingly, though the states of São Paulo and Minas Gerais grew in the nineteenth century to rival Rio de Janeiro state in terms of political and economic power, neither of the present-day capitals of these two states were especially significant at the time. For example, Belo Horizonte, present-day capital of Minas Gerais and today one of Brazil's largest cities, was first established only in 1897. Likewise, the city of São Paulo, today one of the world's largest cities, would hardly be recognizable 100 years ago (e.g., Campos, 2010). It was not until the 1920s that these two cities began to expand

Figure 6.1 City of Recife, Pernambuco.

Source: Delma Paz (Marco zero – Recife – PE), Wikimedia commons: https://commons.wikimedia.
org/wiki/File:Recife-MarcoZero.jpg

substantially, and then once they did, they appeared to grow exponentially for the next several decades (some would say São Paulo continues this trend). One could certainly attribute today's urban infrastructure deficiencies and poor urban planning to such rapid growth and expansion, yet to lay blame for contemporary Brazil's urban problems squarely on overwhelming levels of growth would be shortsighted. Patterns of uneven development that characterize nearly every city in Brazil are rooted more often in unjust political economic and social processes, many of which can be traced all the way back to colonial times.

For example, though slavery finished in Brazil at the end of the nineteenth century, Brazil's reliance on cheap and overexploited human labor continued into the 1900s. Where Brazilian colonial cities were built on the backs of indigenous and African slaves, urban growth from the end of the nineteenth century was fueled by Brazil's massive population of destitute workers: millions of people that included former slaves and their offspring, peasants and indigenous groups with no land rights, and recently arrived immigrants from both Europe and Asia. Rural-to-urban migration was also a key factor. Large landowners expanded their holdings through privileged access to subsidized credit following the Second World War, squeezing out tenant farmers, sharecroppers, and day laborers (Pereira, 2003). In the Northeast, many peasants fled drought and starvation in the countryside for cities on the coast, and, finding little work there, migrated southward to Brazil's growing megacities. They built everything – homes, buildings, and roadways – and then stayed to work in these cities as domestic and professional servants. Their desperation, along with Brazilian elites, kept wages low, and cities in the Southeast grew enormously, if not also haphazardly. Extreme wealth grew alongside extreme poverty, each one fueling the other. The proximities of rich and poor in Brazilian cities became something of international legend by the late twentieth century, with few countries evidencing such peculiar patterns of urban segregation. For many urban researchers in Brazil, explaining the roots of this uneven development, the ways it persisted, and the mechanisms that maintained class (and also racial) segregation became central topics of debate (e.g., Kowarick, 1994; Marques, 2016; Rolnik, 1988).

To briefly summarize, different regions in Brazil have significantly different urban histories, making country-wide generalizations regarding processes of urban development difficult. Relatedly, to argue that Brazilian cities evidence striking patterns of urban informality, impoverishment, lacking infrastructure, etc., simply because they are poor would be a misnomer. There is, in fact, incredible wealth in most Brazilian cities, meaning that rather than a lack of resources *in general*, it is inequality that lies at the root of uneven and unjust processes of urban social and economic development. What fuels and sustains this perverse model of urban growth has, for decades, dominated academic debates in Brazil (as well as elsewhere in Latin America), and it is to these topics we now turn our attention.

Informality and segregation

Consider one of Brazil's most iconic (and infamous) urban landscape features: favela neighborhoods. Most famous are the ones sprawling along Rio de Janeiro's hillsides (see Figure 6.2). Communities like these are ubiquitous in Brazilian cities, though rarely are they located in such dramatic settings. Rio's topography and geographic setting are unique, often making it the exception instead of the norm in terms of urban growth. Nevertheless, when it comes to urban informality across Brazil, favelas tend to share similar origins of settlement and growth, including the roles they serve and the reasons they endure, as well as the conflicts they tend to face. Perhaps most misunderstood is the very existence of favelas in the first place: regularly conceptualized as 'problems' for urban development, or the result of poor urban planning and scarce resources, informal urban communities are, in fact, *solutions* to problems of urban growth and capitalist development. This is not to suggest they are good or socially just solutions, but rather to point out that instead of impeding urban growth in Brazil, favelas have actually *enabled* these processes for decades.

Political scientist, Lúcio Kowarick, is perhaps best known for developing this argument (1979). His notion of *espoliação urbana* (urban spoliation) has been important not only for researchers in Brazil, but also for social scientists around the world seeking to understand the relationships between urban growth,

Figure 6.2 Favela settlement Morro dos Prazeres in Rio de Janeiro.

Source: Tiago Celestino, Wikimedia commons: https://en.wikipedia.org/wiki/Morro_dos_Prazeres#/
media/File:Morro_dos_Prazeres_(RJ)_-_01.jpg

informality, and inequality. Briefly, what Kowarick argued is that urban informality in Brazil is by no means an aberrant feature, or somehow representative of
urban space that has been neglected by capital. Instead, urban informality is
produced by processes of capitalist development, allowing for an impoverished
labor force to socially reproduce itself at very little cost to the state or private
capital. In more simple terms, favelas provide housing solutions for a destitute
workforce so that wages, social services, and urban infrastructure can remain
poor, allowing wealth to stay concentrated and urban growth to continue, albeit
in ways that reflect extreme socio-economic inequality and a dilapidated urban
environment (hence, "urban spoliation").

Most cities around the world illustrate this trend to one degree or another, but
Brazil's continued negligence of public infrastructure has created something of a
unique context. For example, this is one reason why favelas are so often
centrally located in Brazilian cities, placing rich and poor in close proximity.
Due to poor transportation linkages, it would be untenable for the workforce
that lives in these communities to move to the urban periphery. They could not
get to work every day. This would be equally problematic for elites, as there
would be no one to see to the daily needs of domestic labor and childcare,
maintenance and construction work, security and grounds keeping, and pretty
much every other basic service sector job in the city. In more general terms,

without favelas, labor could not be joined with capital, bringing entire metro-politan regions to a standstill. In more recent years, scholars have pushed these ideas to consider urban growth more broadly in the Global South (e.g., Caldeira, 2017; Parnell and Robinson, 2012), with researchers like Ananya Roy succinctly arguing that urban informality provides a "a highly effective 'spatial fix'"[3] for capitalist development in emergent countries (2009, p. 8).

Important to remember here is that the overwhelming majority of favela residents are working-class families. Contrary to stigmatic accounts that depict favelas as places of unemployment, homelessness, and informal economic activity (i.e., drug trafficking), *most* favela residents actually have formal employment, most have retirement pensions, their children attend school, they have wireless internet at home, etc. (cf. McCann, 2014). With the exception of where they live and the extreme levels of inequality they face, their lives are not so different materially speaking from working-class families elsewhere in the world.[4] So why do favelas continue to endure and what are the origins of these informal communities?

Answers to these questions extend beyond the scope of this chapter, but here again it is useful to remember the contributions of Brazilian scholars like Kowarick (1979), Abreu (1987), and Bonduki and Rolnik (1979). Informal urban settle-ments and *cortiços* (slum tenements) grew steadily in Brazilian cities following abolition in 1888, providing housing for ex-slaves and other poor urban residents. This form of urban development allowed Brazil to move from a slave economy to a pre-capitalist one (and eventually a capitalist one) with little change to the broader socio-economic structure. People living in these communities were 'free workers', but the material conditions in which they lived had changed little since slavery. In short, informal urban settlements provided a *housing* solution for poor workers and a *social* solution for elites wanting to maintain Brazil's class hierarchy. Even today, the Brazilian constitution ostensibly allows for "squatter's rights" (Holston, 2008) – that is, possession rights based on occupancy and use rather than title or formal ownership – in theory on the grounds of social justice, but also because it would be impossible to expect Brazil's entire working-class population to live in formal housing. Favelas and *cortiços* continue to provide housing solutions without which the broader economies of most large Brazilian cities would collapse.

As they have grown across decades, Brazil's poor urban communities have changed massively, even displaying middle-class characteristics in many instances (see Figure 6.3). Almost never is this because middle-class residents have moved into favelas (i.e., gentrification), but, instead, because favela residents themselves have invested so much sweat equity into their homes. This, of course, raises questions of what makes a favela '*uma favela*' today in Brazil, particularly if poverty may no longer be a consistent identifying factor. Helpful here is the work of historian Bryan McCann, who argues, "favelas are not defined by a clear set of physical characteristics; rather, they are defined by their history [of informality]" (2014, p. 26). More than anything – for example, processes of occupation and auto-construction – this means most residents do

Figure 6.3 Community of Cristo Redentor in Fortaleza, Ceará, showing diversity of building structures and houses.

Source: the authors.

not have title of possession to their property. This also means that even as favelas grow and show improvements over time, "they continue to be recognized as nodes of difference within the surrounding city," never shedding the stigma of informality (McCann, 2014, p. 31).

So intense is prejudice against favelas that local residents confront discrimination in myriad ways both in and outside of their communities. Whether from the middle and upper classes, police, potential employers, universities, and even other working-class residents, those who live in the shadow of informality face a host of daily obstacles. One of the first to explore these processes was anthropologist Janice Perlman, who, starting in the 1970s, began to interrogate what she called "the myth of marginality" (1976). She argued favela residents were disadvantaged not because *they themselves* displayed characteristics typical of marginal groups (e.g., criminality, radicalism, social and cultural exclusion), but, instead, because of social, economic, political, and cultural barriers in Brazilian society. She also contested popular perceptions that favela residents were marginal to broader urban economies, showing how they provided vital skills and services. Perlman's work inspired a legion of favela ethnographies (e.g., Gay, 1993; Goldstein, 2003; Zaluar and Alvito, 1998), proving so popular in its methodological approach that, today, one can find social scientists poking around nearly every favela in Rio de Janeiro.

Noteworthy among this rich body of research are studies exploring the ways favelas continue to manifest as distinct (and marginalized) features of Brazilian cities, despite their ubiquity and embeddedness within urban landscapes (e.g.,

Almeida, D'Andrea, and De Lucca, 2008; Cavalcanti, 2014; Novaes, 2014). Beyond the work of those already mentioned in this chapter, researchers have also helped to understand the ways favela residents face historical and ongoing processes of exclusion and state violence (Fischer, 2008; Garmany, 2014; Vainer, 2011). Important also are environmental considerations and the risks poor residents confront with respect to natural hazards, which include, like poor people elsewhere in the world, increased vulnerability to processes like global climate change (Coates and Garmany, 2016; Maricato, 2003). To be sure, the urban poor have made significant political and material gains in recent years (Caldeira, 2017; Holston, 2008), yet the stigma of informality – as well as complex structures of discrimination and poverty – persists in cities across Brazil. Connected here are ongoing threats of violence and public insecurity, to which we direct our focus in the next section of this chapter.

Public security in Brazilian cities

Many Brazilian cities have long and tragic histories of violence, particularly state-based violence that include episodes of police repression and terror (cf. Caldeira, 2000). Violence of this sort, sadly, is not new to Brazil. When it comes to organized crime and international drug trafficking, however, such trends are more recent. Even Rio de Janeiro, notes Elizabeth Leeds (1996), saw little in the way of organized trafficking until the 1980s. According to legend, it was in Rio de Janeiro's infamous Ilha Grande prison in the 1970s where this first took root. Common criminals were housed with political prisoners during Brazil's military dictatorship, and the intellectuals taught the gang members organizational skills that were later put to work developing sophisticated crime networks throughout Rio.[5] As Brazil's cocaine trade skyrocketed in the 1980s and 1990s, organized crime became an increasingly powerful actor. These groups operated within Rio's favelas (as well as the prisons), where decades of state neglect allowed them to establish total control. As Leeds famously argued, these gangs came to exert sovereign-like authority over their territories, establishing what she called "parallel polities" that existed alongside (and in tension with) state actors such as the police (1996). In more simple terms, by the end of the 1990s, Rio's favelas were under the rule of drug traffickers, not the Brazilian state.

Like Perlman, Leeds helped to initiate a long series of debates concerning public security, crime, and governance in Brazilian cities. Crucial here has also been the work of Alba Zaluar, who perhaps more than anyone else worked to bridge the ethnographic perspectives of anthropologists with theoretical debates in other social science disciplines (e.g., Zaluar, 2004; Zaluar and Alvito, 1998). For example, questioning perceptions that young people in informal communities are flatly excluded from economic markets, Zaluar helped to show how they become "perversely integrated" through illicit activities (e.g., trafficking). The broader effects of this perverse integration include a host of jobs and services within their communities (many in the formal sector), as cash flows from drug sales induce far-reaching economic effects (2004). Such insights have been helpful for seeing the interconnectivities between formal and informal spaces and activities, and, more precisely, the ways legal and illegal markets are often two sides of the same coin in Latin American cities (e.g., Arias and Goldstein, 2010).

In the twenty-first century, researchers have continued to investigate the connections between legal and illegal actors, highlighting the ways Brazilian public security is precariously stitched together (e.g., Pereira, 2008). Noteworthy here is the work of Desmond Arias, who argues that, in contexts like Brazil, state power and authority (e.g., the law) are constituted differently than in places such as Europe and North America (2006). They include complex and usually informal networks between police, society, and criminal organizations, meaning that every-day urban governance is produced through a variety of processes that may or may not reflect the rule of law. Adding to these debates is Gabriel Feltran (2011), whose research in São Paulo draws attention to the porous, almost dialectical relationships between crime and the law, and how public security initiatives in many instances alienate low-income residents and work to fortify the authority of illicit actors. Feltran and others have also helped to shed light on the changing nature of organized crime in Brazilian cities, emphasizing the growing domination of the criminal organization known as the *Primeiro Comando da Capital* (First Capital Command, or PCC – see also Denyer Willis, 2015).

While problems of violence and safety are, indeed, more severe for the lower and working classes, they are not the only ones who confront public insecurity. In Brazil, most middle- and upper-class urban residents also live in fear, with little faith in public authorities to provide or even uphold the rule of law. Over the past several decades, they have increasingly taken matters into their own hands. Typical in Brazilian cities today are high walls with electrified fencing, sentinel posts staffed by armed security officers, heavily armored gates and doors, bullet-proof glass, and CCT cameras (see Figure 6.4). As Teresa Caldeira notes in her landmark work *City of Walls* (2000), such features, rather perversely, have become aesthetically chic in cities like São Paulo. Urban landscapes have grown so heavily fortified there exists little in the way of public space. Mounting numbers of middle- and upper-class residents live in gated communities, avoiding public space and preferring high surveillance environments like shopping malls and private clubs.

Such a dystopic urban environment poses the question of why elites and governing authorities in Brazil have let public security, like other bits of urban infrastructure, fall to such low levels. Reasons are again complex, but a basic explanation begins with a critical look towards policing. On the one hand is a notoriously dysfunctional police force, divided into several entities that have different roles and responsibilities. At the state level, police work is divided between the Military and Civil Police forces, where the former patrol the streets and respond to calls, and the latter carry out criminal investigation work. Many cities also have a Municipal Guard, whose role is to protect municipal property. In theory, these different police forces coordinate their efforts, but, in reality,

Figure 6.4 Private security for apartment residents in Fortaleza, Ceará.
Source: the authors.

there is poor communication between them and each is subordinate to a different political authority. Very often, there is tension among them and competition for resources. Few reforms have been made since Brazil's military dictatorship, and there exists little oversight to check the authoritarian ethos of the Military Police (Garmany, 2014). This is not even to mention problems of corruption, which stem, in large part, from poor leadership, low salaries, a lucrative and violent narco-trafficking industry, and a deeply rooted culture of bribery and theft among public officials.

On the other hand is the issue of socio-economic inequality. Again, it is often presumed that public security problems exist because Brazil is a poor country, yet this would be to overlook extreme levels of wealth in most cities. Rather than blaming poverty for Brazil's crime problems, it is much more useful to consider the over-accumulation of wealth by elites. In much the same way that favela settlements provide 'solutions' to urban development crises, so, too, does an under-resourced and corrupt public security apparatus benefit certain sectors of society. Such a police force has little credibility, weakening its authority and producing a context where elites are rarely subordinate to the rule of law.

Granted, this means the middle and upper classes often pay heavily for private security, but it also means they rarely face serious consequences should they overstep legal boundaries. Brazil's recent and ongoing political corruption scandal bears evidence of this – that is, the extent to which corruption remains deeply rooted and even ubiquitous in Brazilian politics – yet also shows (one hopes) how Brazil's culture of elite impunity is finally being challenged today.

The growth of urban private security is by no means restricted to wealthier areas. In the twenty-first century, private militias have sprung up in cities across Brazil. These militias tend to patrol lower-income areas, yet they can also take root in middle-class neighborhoods. Outwardly, they claim to provide residential security, but, in many cases, they simply extort local residents by requiring 'protection' fees, establishing protocol, collecting taxes, governing local businesses, and so on. They can be hard to disaggregate from local gangs, the police, and other security providers – not accidentally, the uniforms of private security personnel often look similar to those of the police (Zanetic, 2012) – and perhaps even more confusing are how their ranks are typically filled with off-duty or retired police officers (Zaular and Conceição, 2007). Like narco-trafficking gangs in the late twentieth century, militias have emerged from a context where public security and basic urban infrastructure have been shamefully neglected.

Such precarious, mismatched, and segregated urban environments show increasing signs of strain in the twenty-first century. Perhaps this stems from Brazil's growing consumer class (the 'C' class) and their frustrations with urban life, or maybe because old models of urban development are proving insufficient for ongoing economic crises in Brazilian cities. Whatever the roots of these problems, it appears historical solutions are increasingly untenable for contemporary and future contexts. Recent 'pacification' efforts by the Military Police in Rio de Janeiro show the state's increasing determination to insert itself into favela communities via a permanent police presence. As Tucker Landesman (2017) notes, this may have less to do with improving the lives of poor people, and more to do with middle- and upper-class cariocas growing tired of navigating so many 'no-go' zones within the city. Combined with this are also economic objectives: for example, integrating informal markets into formal ones creates new consumer markets out of favela communities. Such changes have, not surprisingly, induced a host of urban development growing pains, and it is to these issues we now turn in the penultimate section of the chapter.

Brazilian cities in the twenty-first century

Something rather remarkable took place in cities across Brazil during the early years of the twenty-first century. Over a span of roughly ten years, the number of auto-vehicles on Brazilian roads more than *tripled* (Jones and Azevedo, 2013). Thanks in large part to credit initiatives introduced by the Workers' Party, millions of people who had only dreamed of owning a car or motorbike suddenly found they could finance one through the federal savings bank. The effects were dramatic, if not also infuriating for urban commuters. Cities already facing gridlock were flooded with additional motorists. New construction and roadway maintenance could not keep pace, and, thus, cities today are increasingly clogged with round-the-clock traffic jams and slower commuting times. Even public transportation has been negatively affected in most cities, as buses and vans remain the only public transport option throughout most of Brazil. Like the Brazilian economy more generally, what began with a boom at the start the twenty-first century drew to a standstill less than a decade later.

Such changes have by no means been limited solely to auto vehicles. Brazil's market for durable consumer goods such as washing machines, microwaves, and computers has expanded massively since the start of the twenty-first century. Driving this has been a host of factors, including access to credit for the working and middle classes and, during the first decade of this century, robust economic growth. These changes have induced profound effects on cities across Brazil. As just one example, Brazilian patterns of urban segregation are beginning to change: rich and poor are more likely to bump into one another at shopping malls, restaurants, and airports (something almost unthinkable in the twentieth century), but the distances between where they live in the city are growing. This means that while some of urban Brazil's social barriers appear to be diminishing, in their place are new physical ones that can be every bit as segregative.

There is a host of factors that helps to explain this. On the one hand, durable consumer goods have made the middle and upper classes less dependent on cheap labor to carry out domestic work. For example, today washing machines do the work that, until recently, was undertaken by domestic servants. Combined with upward adjustments to Brazil's minimum wage (spurred mostly by the Workers' Party government between 2003 and 2016), these changes have helped transform labor markets. Where in the past it was common for middle-class families to have at least one full-time domestic servant, today they often contract someone for only one or two days each week. Hiring domestic servants has become more costly, and durable consumer goods have reduced the need for them.

On the other hand, now that so many working-class families are vehicle owners, they are more able and willing to move greater distances from their places of work. In the past, it was often necessary for the working classes to live near to their places of work due to insufficient public transportation. Again, this helps to explain why favelas are so ubiquitous in most Brazilian cities: historically, these neighborhoods were where the working classes lived. But today, with increased access to auto vehicles, the working classes are more willing – and often also *pushed* by state initiatives and rising costs of living – to move into formal, low-income housing further from urban centers and their traditional places of work. All told, these changing patterns of consumption, access to credit, labor markets, and growth in construction and housing have induced profound effects on processes of urban development in Brazilian cities.

In light of these changes, researchers are beginning to question whether processes like gentrification are becoming widespread in Brazilian cities (e.g., Betancur, 2014; Gaffney, 2016). While gentrification has long been observed and critiqued by social scientists in Europe and North America, until recently it was not thought especially prominent in Brazil or elsewhere in the Global South. There were numerous economic, political, social, and cultural factors preventing gentrification in countries like Brazil, including different processes of urban development already mentioned in this chapter (e.g., Caldeira, 2000; Kowarick, 1979; Marques, 2016). With recent changes to patterns of urban growth in Brazil, however, lower-income residents are increasingly moving to peripheral urban zones instead of occupying centrally located favela neighborhoods. And while the middle and upper classes have, for the most part, preferred to stay in their gated suburbs far from city centers, increasing urban transportation woes and new investment opportunities might one day draw them inward. This is to say that, for now, gentrification is not especially widespread in Brazilian cities, but this could change, and change rapidly, in years to come.

While gentrification might not yet be extensive in Brazil, Brazilian cities are still fraught by class conflict and unequal processes of urban redevelopment. The urban poor are not just being *pulled* from centrally located urban neighborhoods by new jobs and transportation options; they are also being *pushed* by urban planners, developers, state projects, businesses, and so forth. Examples of this come from cities all over Brazil, yet, once again, Rio and São Paulo tend to dominate both news media and academic discussion. The removal of hundreds of low-income families in preparation for the 2016 Olympics in Rio generated significant debate (e.g., Richmond and Garmany, 2017), as did the forced removal of residents of São Paulo's infamous *Cracolândia* near to the city center in 2017 (Valente, 2017). Such examples, argue some scholars, can hardly be called gentrification, as the logic, processes, and after effects of such cases reveal their own particularities more brutal and prejudiced than gentrification (cf. Ghertner, 2015; Malutas, 2011). As geographers Jeff Garmany and Matthew Richmond suggest, such instances are better described as processes of *higienização* (hygieneization), a Brazilian idea that emphasizes the central role of stigma and discrimination rather than 'market logic' when trying to make sense of how poor people are driven from central urban areas (Garmany and Richmond, 2017). As the Brazilian middle and upper classes have proven reluctant to move into gentrifiable areas, and banks and developers have also been wary of financing such investments, pathways for urban redevelopment in Brazilian inner cities are often different from cities in Europe and North America, and almost always involve a key role by the state.

Added to this are new social housing initiatives rolled out during the first two decades of the twenty-first century. Following the success of the Brazil's *Bolsa Família* conditional cash transfer program, the Workers' Party sought to address Brazil's housing deficit via a federally funded housing construction initiative. Called *Minha Casa, Minha Vida* ("My House, My Life"), this national program aims to address Brazil's lack of formal housing for low-income families (though not *only* low-income families; middle-class families can also access it). Since the program was launched in 2009, millions of homes have been built, and families resettled, thanks in large part to building contracts between the federal savings bank and major construction companies (see Figure 6.5). Not surprisingly, the program has also been criticized by academic researchers (Maricato, 2011; Rolnik et al., 2015). At one level are the government contracts for large construction companies, which have been scrutinized for their connections to bribery and payout scandals associated with the Workers' Party. Connected here is also the problematic role of investors in shaping the terms and conditions of the program. And at another level come concerns over the quality and location of the housing units themselves. Very often these homes are built near to the urban periphery where land is cheaper and more abundant, creating new problems of urban mobility and fragmented social networks for residents. Added to this are shoddy construction materials often used to build these homes, meaning that not only are residents facing longer commutes, new bills and expenses, the frequent presence of militias and drug traffickers, and so on, but, worst of all, their homes regularly start to fall apart shortly after they move in (e.g., Kolling, 2016).

By 2014, when Brazil hosted the World Cup in 12 cities nationwide, the national economy was no longer growing as it had for years beforehand. And by 2016, when Rio hosted the Olympic Games, it was in a free-fall. The benefits these mega-events were meant to induce in host cities have, rather famously, yet to materialize. So what does this mean for the future of Brazilian cities? Has

Figure 6.5 A Minha Casa, Minha Vida community in Rio de Janeiro.
Source: the authors.

urban growth stalled everywhere, with cities like Rio de Janeiro facing bleak futures with few economic prospects? Not necessarily. There are, in fact, plenty of cities in Brazil growing as fast as ever, with soaring rates of urban expansion. Most often they are situated in Brazil's Central West region, though the North and the Northeast are also home to some of these cities. The driving force behind their growth is Brazil's agro-industrial sector, though mining, energy, and even timber exports also play important roles. Notes Antonio Ioris (2017), cities in this oft-overlooked region of Brazil have mushroomed in recent years, and the social and environmental consequences of such rapid growth have yet to be grappled with.

Take, for example, the city of Sinop in the Central West of Brazil. Sinop is today one of the largest cities in the state of Mato Grosso, which, for several years, has seen steady economic growth thanks to a booming agricultural industry (soy, beef, cotton, etc.). While at first glance Sinop might not look impressive – in 2017 it had an estimated population of 135,874 according to the IBGE – one should bear in mind that until the mid 1970s, *no one* lived in Sinop. The city was established by a Brazilian construction firm only in 1974. Since then it has grown steadily, like other cities in the region, as Brazil's agribusiness sector continues to expand. This urban growth is fueled by agricultural production, the building of export infrastructure, urban and suburban construction, and, perhaps most importantly, international demand from countries such as China for non-durable goods. Whether or not this urban expansion will prove sustainable in the long run reflects a number of global economic and political factors, and not least environmental uncertainty brought on by deforestation and climate change. Such uncertainties are, of course, not unique to cities in Brazil's Central West region, but are, in fact, confronted by cities *everywhere* in the twenty-first century. We reflect on these issues, including the key takeaways from this chapter, in the brief conclusions that follow.

Conclusion

If we can say Rio de Janeiro appears to embody multiple characteristics from Brazil's urban development history, then so, too, might it represent in many ways Brazil's urban development future. Geographically, Rio is blessed in numerous ways, but such blessings offer little guarantee for long-term prosperity. During the twentieth century Rio ceded its banking and finance industry to São Paulo, and then lost many of its political operations to Brasília (though Rio still employs more federal civil servants than does Brasília). As Brazil's economy grew rapidly at the start of the twenty-first century, political and business elites in Rio lobbied to host several mega-events meant to spur long-term urban growth and development. By 2013, however, when protests erupted in cities all over Brazil, it was clear the Brazilian people were unconvinced by this strategy. And by 2016, when the Olympic Games finished and it became clear that both municipal and state coffers were empty, Rio was left to confront a very uncertain urban development future. What, for example, will drive Rio's economy in future years? And when, if ever, will Brazil's pre-salt offshore oil reserves begin producing revenue promised to sustain cities like Rio? Such questions are growing increasingly urgent for cariocas, and they are by no means unique to just the city of Rio de Janeiro.

Throughout this chapter, we have addressed a host of typical misunderstandings regarding Brazilian cities. For example, non-Brazilians are often surprised to learn that Brazil has, for decades, been a mostly urbanized country. Additionally, while most existing academic research comes from Rio and São Paulo, one must use caution when making broader generalizations about Brazilian cities elsewhere. Connected to this are misleading assumptions regarding Brazilian patterns of urban development. Features such as widespread informality are usually not the result of *under*development, *per se*, but, rather, alternative development models that mirror extreme socio-economic inequality. With this has come the growth and consolidation of organized crime in spaces long neglected by the state, leading to severe public security concerns in many Brazilian cities. Life for the working and middle classes is, thus, often characterized by limited urban mobility, private security measures, and little engagement with public space. Recent changes in patterns of urban development – and the growth of durable consumer goods such as auto vehicles and washing machines – have brought significant change, yet the future is perhaps more uncertain than ever for most urban residents.

This uncertainty is reflected in the growth of new cities in regions like the Amazon rainforest. States such as Mato Grosso, Goiás, and Pará have seen significant urban growth over the past few decades, but the sustainability of this growth is predicated upon a fragile balance between global political economic factors, environmental sustainability, and domestic policy-making. Such a delicate balance faces many cities around the world, and, while the future is almost certain to follow current trends of increasing urbanization, there are reasons to worry that historical cycles of urban boom and bust may grow ever more common. As the world grows more interconnected, and flows of capital and information continue to accelerate, it would seem that future patterns of urban growth – much like contemporary patterns of economic development – are likely to be volatile, temporary, and unmoored from specific countries or regions. Such urban uncertainty confronts countries everywhere, and, for countries like Brazil, where millions of people still struggle to secure their daily livelihoods, such a future could prove especially precarious.

Notes

1 In the most general sense, favelas are low-income urban communities characterized by informality (or, at least, a history of informality). Many of them also suffer poor basic services such as sewerage, healthcare, mail delivery, and so forth. As we argue in this chapter, however, the term is not as straightforward as it might appear.
2 It should be noted, however, that Brazil has a very liberal definition for urban settlements. Small towns that in other countries would not be defined as cities are, in Brazil, often classified as "urban."

3 Here Roy is drawing on David Harvey's notion of the "spatial fix" that is produced through relationships between uneven development and global capitalism. For more on this, please see Harvey (2007).
4 This is not to argue favela residents are surprisingly well off, but, rather, to suggest life has become increasingly precarious for working-class families worldwide.
5 Note how, in this account, the relationships between intellectuals and criminals seem suspiciously paternalistic and one-sided. This is perhaps not surprising, given that history is typically written by intellectuals.

Suggested English readings

Caldeira T. (2000). *City of walls: Crime, segregation and citizenship in São Paulo*. Berkeley: University of California Press.
Fischer, B. (2008). *A poverty of rights: Citizenship and inequality in twentieth-century Rio de Janeiro*. Sanford: Stanford University Press.
Goldstein, D.M. (2003). *Laughter out of place: Race, class, violence, and sexuality in a Rio shantytown*. Berkeley: University of California Press.
Holston, J. (2008). *Insurgent citizenship: Disjunctions of democracy and modernity in Brazil*. Princeton: Princeton University Press.
Kowarick, L. (ed.), (1994). *Social struggles and the city: The case of São Paulo*. New York: Monthly Review Press.
McCann, B. (2014). *Hard times in the marvelous city: From dictatorship to democracy in the favelas of Rio de Janeiro*. Durham, NC: Duke University Press.

References

Abreu, M.A. (1987). *Evolução urbana do Rio de Janeiro*. Rio de Janeiro: Iplanrio.
Almeida, R., D'Andrea, T., and De Lucca, D. (2008). Situações periféricas: Etnografia comparada de pobrezas urbanas. *Novos Estudos*, 82, 109–130.
Arias, E.D. (2006). *Drugs and democracy in Rio de Janeiro: Trafficking, social networks, and public security*. Chapel Hill: The University of North Carolina Press.
Arias, E.D., and Goldstein, D.M. (2010). *Violent democracies in Latin America*. Durham, NC: Duke University Press.
Betancur, J.J. (2014). Gentrification in Latin America: Overview and critical analysis *Urban Studies Research*, http://dx.doi.org/10.1155/2014/986961.
Bonduki, N., and Rolnik, R. (1979). *Periferias: Ocupação do espaço e reprodução da força de trabalho*. São Paulo: University of São Paulo.
Caldeira T. (2000). *City of walls: Crime, segregation and citizenship in São Paulo*. Berkeley: University of California Press.
Caldeira, T. (2017). Peripheral urbanization: Autoconstruction, transversal logics, and politics in cities of the global south. *Environment and Planning D: Society and Space*, 35(1), 3–20.
Campos, C. de, Oliveira, E.R., and Gitahey, M.L.C. (2010). *Território e cidades: Projetos e representações, 1870–1970*. São Paulo: Alameda.
Cavalcanti, M. (2014). Threshold markets: The production of real-estate value between the "favela" and the "pavement." In: B. Fischer, B. McCann, and J. Auyero (eds), *Cities from scratch: Poverty and informality in urban Latin America*. Durham: Duke University Press, pp. 208–237.

Coates, R., and Garmany, J. (2017). The ecology of citizenship: understanding vulnerability in urban Brazil. *International Development Planning Review*, 39(1), 37–56.

Cupples, J. (2013). *Latin American development*. London: Routledge.

Denyer Willis, G. (2015). *The killing consensus: Police, organized crime, and the regulation of life and death in urban Brazil*. Oakland: University of California Press.

Feltran, G.S. (2011). *Fronteiras de tensão: Política e violência nas periferias de São Paulo*. São Paulo: Editora UNESP.

Fischer, B. (2008). *A poverty of rights: Citizenship and inequality in twentieth-century Rio de Janeiro*. Stanford: Stanford University Press.

Gaffney, C. (2016). Gentrifications in pre-Olympic Rio de Janeiro. *Urban Geography*, 37(8), 1132–1153.

Garmany, J. (2011). Situating Fortaleza: Urban space and uneven development in northeastern Brazil. *Cities*, 28(1), 45–52.

Garmany, J. (2014). Space for the state? Police, violence, and urban poverty in Brazil. *The Annals of the Association of American Geographers*, 104(6), 1239–1255.

Garmany, J., and Richmond, M. (2017). Limits to gentrification in Brazil. Paper presented at American Association of Geographers Conference, 8 April, Boston, MA.

Gay, R. (1993). *Popular organization and democracy in Rio de Janeiro: A tale of two favelas*. Philadelphia: Temple University Press.

Ghertner, D.A. (2015). Why gentrification theory fails in "much of the world". *City*, 19(4), 552–563.

Goldstein, D.M. (2003). *Laughter out of place: Race, class, violence, and sexuality in a Rio shantytown*. Berkeley: University of California Press.

Harvey, D. (2007). *Limits to capital*. London: Verso.

Holston, J. (2008). *Insurgent citizenship: Disjunctions of democracy and modernity in Brazil*. Princeton: Princeton University Press.

IBGE (2017). Instituto Brasileiro de Geografia e Estatística. Available at: www.ibge.gov.br> [accessed 20 February 2018].

Ioris, A.A.R. (2017). *Agribusiness and the neoliberal food system in Brazil: Frontiers and fissures of agro-neoliberalism*. London: Routledge.

Jones, T., and Azevedo, L.N. (2013). Economic, social and cultural transformation and the role of the bicycle in Brazil. *Journal of Transport Geography*, 30, 208–219.

Kolling, M. (2016). New homes, new lives? Slum upgrading, consumptions dreams and debt in Brazil. PhD dissertation. University of Copenhagen.

Kowarick, L. (1979). *A espoliação urbana*. Rio de Janeiro: Paz e Terra.

Kowarick, L. (ed.). (1994). *Social struggles and the city: The case of São Paulo*. New York: Monthly Review Press.

Landesman, T. (2017). Remaking Rio de Janeiro through "favela integration": The politics of mobility and state space. PhD dissertation. London School of Economics and Political Science.

Leeds, E. (1996). Cocaine and parallel polities in the Brazilian urban periphery: Constraints on local-level democratization. *Latin American Research Review*, 31(3),47–83.

Maloutas, T. (2011). Contextual diversity in gentrification research. *Critical Sociology*, 38(1), 33–48.

Maricato, E. (2003). Metrópole, legislação e desigualdade. *Estudos Avançados*, 17, 151–166.

Maricato, E. (2011). *O impasse da política urbana no Brasil*. Petrópolis: Editora Vozes.

Marques, E. (2016). De volta aos capitais para melhor entender as políticas urbanas. *Novos Estudos CEBRAP*, 35(2), 15–33.

McCann, B. (2014). *Hard times in the marvelous city: from dictatorship to democracy in the favelas of Rio de Janeiro*. Durham NC: Duke University Press.

Novaes, A. (2014). Favelas and the divided city: Mapping silences and calculations in Rio de Janeiro's journalistic cartography. *Social and Cultural Geography*, 15(2), 201–225.

Parnell, S. and Robinson, J. (2012). (Re)theorizing cities from the global South: Looking beyond neoliberalism. *Urban Geography*, 33(4), 593–617.

Pereira, A. (2003). Brazil's agrarian reform: Democratic innovation or oligarchic exclusion redux? *Latin American Politics and Society*, 45(2), 41–65.

Pereira, A. (2008). Public security, private interests and police reform in Brazil. In: P. Kingstone and T. Power (eds), *Democratic Brazil revisited*. Pittsburgh: Pittsburgh University Press, pp. 185–208.

Perlman, J. (1976). *The myth of marginality: Urban poverty and politics in Rio de Janeiro*. Berkeley: University of California Press.

Richmond, M.A., and Garmany, J. (2016). 'Post-Third-World city' or neoliberal 'city of exception?' Rio de Janeiro in the Olympic Era. *International Journal of Urban and Regional Research*, 40(3),621–639.

Rodgers, D., Beall, J., and Kanbur, R. (2012). *Latin American development into the twenty-first century: Towards a renewed perspective on the city*. Basingstoke, UK: Palgrave MacMillan.

Rolnik, R. (1988). *O que é cidade*. São Paulo: Editora Brasiliense.

Rolnik, R., Pereira, A., Moreira, F., Oliveira Royer de, L., Iacovini, R., and Nisida, V. (2015). O programa Minha Casa Minha Vida nas regiões metropolitanas de São Paulo e Campinas: Aspectos socioespaciais e segregação. *Cadernos Metrópole, São Paulo*, 17(33), 127–154.

Roy, A. (2009). The twenty-first-century metropolis: New geographies of theory. *Regional Studies*, 43(6), 819–830.

Vainer, C. (2011). Cidade de exceção: Reflexões a partir do Rio de Janeiro. In: ANPUR (Associação Nacional de Pós-Graduação e Pesquisa em Planejamento Urbano e Regional), *XIV Encontro Nacional*. Rio de Janeiro. Available at: https://br.boell.org/sites/default/files/downloads/carlos_vainer_ippur_cidade_de_excecao_reflexoes_a_partir_do_rio_de_janeiro.pdf [accessed 20 February 2018].

Valente, F. (2017). Operação surpresa de guerra na Cracolândia choca entidades e recebe críticas. *Justificando*, 22 May. Available at: ",1,0,0>http://justificando.cartacapital.com.br/2017/05/22/operacao-surpresa-de-guerra-na-cracolandia-choca-entidades-e-recebe-cri tica> [accessed 20 February 2018].

Viotti da Costa, E. (2000). *The Brazilian empire: Myths and histories*. Chapel Hill: University of North Carolina Press, revised edition.

Weaver, F.S. (2000). *Latin America in the world economy: Mercantile colonialism to global capitalism*. Boulder: Westview Press.

Zaluar, A. (2004). *Integração perversa: Pobreza e tráfico de drogas*. Rio de Janeiro: Editora Fundação Getúlio Vargas.

Zaluar, A., and Alvito, M. (eds). (1998). *Um século de favela*. Rio de Janeiro: Editora Fundação Getúlio Vargas.

Zaluar, A., and Conceição, I.S. (2007). Favelas sob o controle das milícias no Rio de Janeiro: Que paz? *São Paulo em Perspectiva*, 21(2), 89–101.

Zanetic, A. (2012). Policiamento e segurança privada: Duas notas conceituais. *Estudos de Sociologia – Araraquara*, 17(33), 471–490.

7 Social movements and protest in Brazil

Introduction

When it comes to collective mobilization and public protest, 2013 was a momentous year in Brazil. During the month of June, when Brazil hosted the Confederations Cup international soccer tournament – an event *supposed* to dominate the national news media – something unprecedented happened. Millions of people in cities all over Brazil took to the streets (see Figure 7.1). Granted, Brazil had witnessed similar incidences of national protest in recent decades: the *Diretas Já!* campaign in 1984 for direct presidential elections is one example, as is the impeachment of President Fernando Collor in 1992. But these mobilizations coalesced around one, singular issue. In 2013, protestors came together over a seemingly infinite number of demands. Key issues were mismanaged public funds and spending initiatives, poor infrastructure and development priorities, lamentable public services such as healthcare, education, and transport, and, of course, widespread political corruption. Brazil captured headlines for weeks, with journalists unable to clarify the impetus and motivations for the protests. Virtually no one anticipated such a moment, and nearly everyone in the streets appeared to have their own reasons for being there. What was it, asked observers, that brought so many different people together, seemingly overnight?

While the "June Journeys," as some have called the protests of 2013, were indeed surprising (d'Andréa and Ziller, 2016), collective mobilization and public protest have deep roots in Brazil. Contrary to Brazil's reputation as a fun-loving, easy-going tropical country, acts of collective resistance are not uncommon in Brazilian cities. Case in point, what helped ignite the 2013 protests were efforts by the *Movimento Passe Livre* (MPL – the Free Fare Movement), a national social movement established in 2005. The MPL advocates free fares for mass transit, and, unhappy with rising costs for bus fares in Brazilian cities, they collaborated with others to organize a series of protests, first in Porto Alegre, beginning in January 2013 (Pereira, 2013). The protests soon spread, and within a few months the MPL was involved with demonstrations in several cities across Brazil. Activists suffered police violence in multiple locations, but, in early June, when journalists in São Paulo began to broadcast images of the military police

Figure 7.1 Protesters marching on Avenida Paulista in São Paulo, June 2013.

Source: Marcelo Camargo/ABr (Agência Brasil), Wikimedia commons: https://commons.wikimedia.org/wiki/File:ABr200613_MCA2268.jpg

assaulting peaceful protesters, public opinion swayed decisively towards the activists. Even conservative media outlets like *Rede Globo* and *Veja* sided with the protestors. Within days, millions of people were taking to the streets every night in cities throughout Brazil, united in their frustrations and defiant that the citizenry should not be ignored or mistreated. "*Vem pra Rua*" ("Come to the Street") and "*O Gigante Acordou*" ("The Giant Woke Up") became popular slogans of the time.

What distinguished this moment from any other in Brazilian history – or, for that matter, most countries around the world – was the way June 2013 saw the mass mobilization of diverse sectors of society that appeared to share little in common. People from virtually every sector of society participated in these nightly marches, with a surprisingly strong turnout from young, middle-class Brazilians. The number of different causes represented by protestors had almost no end. Moreover, political parties were sidelined, and as the protests caught fire, traditional organizational groups (e.g., labor unions, social movements, activist groups) ceased to play significant roles. Many of them even withdrew, like the MPL, once they realized the protests had grown to include groups on the far right. In previous decades, these protests would have taken weeks (if not months) to organize. In 2013, people connected over social media, and could then assemble nationwide within *hours*.

Scholars are still trying to make sense of the 2013 protests, with many suggesting they represent growing middle-class dissatisfaction that cuts across emerging countries such as Brazil, Turkey, Egypt, Spain, Chile, and so on. Linked to this are new communication technologies and social media that connect people instantly across space, facilitating new methods of organization and social networks (Gerbaudo, 2012, 2017). More to the point, in 2013, Brazil's protests may have been unprecedented, but there are good reasons to believe similar moments of mass mobilization will happen again, if not in Brazil then elsewhere (Conde and Jazeel, 2019). For example, as early as 2015 Brazil's streets filled again, but this time by those sharing common political and socio-economic interests, and with the clear goal of ousting President Dilma Rousseff's Workers' Party government (see Figure 7.2). These protests were different from the ones in 2013 – they were much more partisan – and they show how collective mobilization in Brazil is shifting in the twenty-first century. Today, there is increasing participation from groups that, historically, seldom participated in acts of public protest (viz., the middle and upper classes). Though difficult to predict what this spells for Brazil's future, what seems clear is that the *ways* in which people organize, and their *reasons* for mobilization, appear to be changing rapidly.

Figure 7.2 Protesters calling for the impeachment of President Dilma Rousseff in São Paulo, March 2016.

Source: Rovena Rosa (Agência Brasil), Wikimedia commons – https://commons.wikimedia.org/wiki/File:Manifestação_em_São_Paulo_contra_corrupção_e_o_governo_Dilma_em_13_de_mar ço_de_2016_(3).jpg

In this chapter, we attempt to make sense of this context. Our goal is to shed light on the roles and significance of social movements, collective mobilization, and public protest in contemporary Brazil. We begin by considering the roots of these traditions, starting with Brazil's long history of social resistance during colonial times and slavery. While most scholars would not connect these legacies with contemporary social movements – often because social movements are defined specifically by non-violent collective action (Tarrow, 1994) – we argue that these histories are important for understanding traditions of resistance and mobilization in contemporary Brazil.

We then move on to examine the roles of collective action in Brazil's fraught history with democracy and authoritarian leadership. Important here are theoretical perspectives of social movements, and we consider these ideas alongside Brazil's tradition of collective action. Though social movements were largely repressed until the end of the military dictatorship in 1985, important legacies and specific movements emerged in the mid-twentieth century. With Brazil's return to democracy in the 1980s, social movements began to surge, both in terms of numbers as well as accomplishments and socio-political significance. Marginalized groups and individuals mobilized around a host of issues (gender and racial inequality, homophobia, indigenous rights, housing, land reform, environmental concerns, etc.), and while Brazil remains one of the most unequal countries in the world, the victories won by these activist groups in recent decades should not be overlooked. Still, as noted above, new technologies and tactics of social organization are changing the ways social movements operate and collective action is achieved. We consider these questions in the second half of the chapter, exploring the possibilities and challenges for activist groups in the twenty-first century, in Brazil as well as elsewhere.

Roots: Brazil's legacy of resistance (1500–1930)

As in other postcolonial contexts, Brazil's legacy of social resistance begins with indigenous inhabitants. Little was recorded by Brazilian indigenous groups before the arrival of Europeans, but once colonization began in the sixteenth century, the story was similar to other regions in the Americas. Accounts were kept mostly by explorers and missionaries, and recount that indigenous people were sometimes friendly upon first contact but then quickly turned hostile (Skidmore, 2010). Reasons for this are today quite obvious: Europeans were looking for resources, territory, and souls, and when they encountered resistance – and even in some cases when they did not – the colonizers wanted indigenous people out of the way. Many indigenous groups fought back – tales of warfare and resistance bear evidence of this – but mostly they fled inland to escape disease, enslavement, and colonization. That today there are still autonomous tribes living in the Amazon region speaks to this history of resistance. Like other indigenous people in the Americas (as well as elsewhere in the world), the struggle against colonialism has been ongoing for centuries and has by no means disappeared.

When Brazil's indigenous population proved insufficient for colonial slave labor (due to high mortality rates and their ability to escape, along with the growing significance of the trans-Atlantic slave trade in the 1700s and the influence of the Catholic Church), the Portuguese turned to African slaves. Numbers vary, but recent research by the Trans-Atlantic Slave Database suggests almost five *million* people were brought to Brazil aboard slave ships and sold into slavery (slavevoyages.org). Though sociologist Gilberto Freyre famously argued that relations between slaves and slave owners in Brazil were more "fraternal" than in countries such as the USA (1964, p. xiii), historical evidence shows that Brazilian slavery was every bit as brutal and, thus, characterized by frequent acts of resistance. For example, already in the sixteenth century, *quilombo* settlements were forming throughout Brazil. *Quilombos* were communities of escaped slaves, sometimes numbering in the thousands. The largest was named Palmares, famously led by Ganga Zumba and then Zumbi, with an estimated population of nearly 20,000 when it fell to colonial forces in 1694 (Skidmore, 2010, p. 36). Palmares resisted attacks for decades before finally succumbing to a largescale military operation led by the *bandeirante* Domingos Jorge Velho.

While difficult to verify, historical evidence suggests there were hundreds (if not thousands) of *quilombos* throughout Brazil, and many of these communities remain continuously occupied until the present day. In fact, one of contemporary Brazil's most contentious debates involves the fight for national recognition by the descendants of *quilombo* communities (Bowen, 2010; French, 2009). According to Brazil's constitution, *quilombo* communities maintaining continuous residence may claim collective ownership over territory pertaining to the original *quilombo*. This legislation aims to address historical injustices, and for *quilombo* descendants – many of whom are poor and without land or capital to speak of – it provides significant socioeconomic opportunity (see Figure 7.3). The debate, however, typically involves proving the legitimacy of such claims: viz., whether current-day residents are, in fact, descendants of the original *quilombo*, or instead opportunists looking for free land. Establishing proof of these claims in the twenty-first century is hardly straightforward.

Brazil was also the site of multiple slave rebellions over the centuries, though none ever seriously threatened elites or Brazil's slave-holding society. The largest and most famous occurred in Salvador in 1835, an uprising led by *malês* (African Muslims) seeking to take control of the city (Reis, 1993). With slaves outnumbering slave owners in several parts of Brazil, regions like Bahia were especially vulnerable to such revolts. Elites in Salvador knew this, and, terrified by Haiti's recent and successful slave rebellion, acted quickly and forcefully to suppress the *malê* uprising. The revolt, despite careful planning and serious potential, lasted only a few hours.

The *malê* uprising was, in fact, one of several rebellions in nineteenth-century Brazil. These revolts involved a host of issues – for example, some were against Portuguese rule, while others for it – and participants were not always drawn from Brazil's lowest sectors of society. The most famous example comes from Minas

Figure 7.3 A present-day quilombo community near Fortaleza, Ceará.
Source: photo courtesy of Oélito Brandão.

Gerais in 1789, with the failed rebellion of a small group of elites known as the *Inconfidência Mineira* (the Minas Gerais conspiracy). Though Tiradentes, the one who ultimately lost his head (literally), was not an aristocrat, his co-conspirators were, and their social status almost certainly saved them the same fate as Tiradentes (Maxwell, 2004). As noted in Chapter 2, subsequent rebellions in the mid-1800s often involved resistance to Brazilian independence, or, at the very least, to governing authority in the nascent empire. These political, economic, and cultural battles continued throughout the nineteenth century, and while the abolition of slavery in 1888 and the declaration of the Brazilian republic one year later introduced profound societal changes, Brazil was still marked by severe inequality and underlying resistance (Fausto, 1999). The Canudos War and the ensuing massacre of rebel combatants in 1897 bears evidence of this, as well as the Brazilian state's ongoing tradition of authoritarian rule (cf. Chaui, 2000).

In the early years of the twentieth century, one can find plenty of examples of social resistance throughout Brazil, yet there was little formal organization or collective mobilization (e.g., Fausto, 1975; Meade, 1986). Several factors contributed to this, including low literacy levels, poor communication networks, vast distances across space, and cultural and ethnic divisions based on racial, geographic, and migration histories. The oligarchic state was also significant, outlawing labor unions and even policing everyday life through codes of public morality, family values, and gender roles (Caulfield, 2000). In both urban and rural Brazil, resentment of, and resistance to, social exclusion and exploitation grew, yet oppositional groups lacked the resources and political opportunities to organize themselves (Linhares and Silva, 1999; Wolfe, 1993). To be sure, some marginalized groups, such as Afro-Brazilians and women, slowly began to mobilize during this period (Butler, 1992; Rago, 1993), along with urban workers in southern Brazil who, in 1908, formed the Brazilian Workers' Confederation (*Confederação Operária Brasileira*) (Chilcote, 2014). Like movements elsewhere in the world, Brazilian labor unions were influenced by anarcho-syndicalism, and rallied for better working conditions and regular hours. Still, it was not until the 1930s and the end of the Old Republic that organized labor and what we today call *social movements* truly emerged (e.g., Tarrow, 1994). The rise of Getúlio Vargas opened new pathways for these groups, but they operated under heavy restriction from the Brazilian state.

Mobilization: political opportunities and resource mobilization (1930–1985)

While the 1930s was a time of significant political turmoil around the world, Brazil's Revolution of 1930 cannot be regarded as a radical, or even very democratic, regime change. In many Latin American countries, the oligarchies that had ruled for centuries were no longer able to maintain their grip on power after the worldwide economic crash of 1929. The classically liberal economic solutions they relied upon were no longer sufficient to address the growing crisis, and a host of combined factors – chiefly among them, a growing industrial working class – made it difficult for these governments to continue excluding the middle and lower classes from politics.

Brazilian elites faced similar problems, but, as Boris Fausto notes (1975), they took notice of what was happening in neighboring countries and moved quickly to maintain their political power. The Revolution of 1930 and the end of the Old Republic was brought about by a host of interconnected political and economic tensions, yet, in the most basic sense, it helped to stave off popular revolution and preserve Brazil's existing class structure. The name itself, the "Revolution," is misleading from a contemporary vantage point, suggesting deep-seated political change was carried out when, in actuality, little was done to alter Brazil's unequal balance of power. Getúlio Vargas came to head this new government and would not relinquish power for the next 15 years.

As noted in Chapter 2, Vargas recognized it was important to at least give the appearance of broadening political participation. For this reason, the 1930s were a significant moment for collective mobilization in Brazil. Though labor unions were sanctioned and regulated by the state (a system called *trabalhismo*, or, more pejoratively, *peleguismo*), they were no longer prohibited outright, and in industrial regions like São Paulo their ranks swelled. Strikes were also heavily regulated, yet they became more frequent (along with riots), and in both urban and rural sectors workers became better organized. Labor unions have long played important roles in Brazilian collective action, and their contributions were especially significant during the middle part of the twentieth century. 1943 even saw the establishment of consolidated and widely publicized labor laws.

In 1945, Vargas was ousted via a military coup, and soon after industrial workers began to mobilize in greater numbers and demand better wages and standardized labor practices. Voting rights were expanded to all literate adults under the 1946 constitution, and many workers voted for the first time in the 1950 elections. By the 1950s, these groups were building real political clout, even holding marches with hundreds of thousands in cities such as São Paulo. Again, the decisive role played by labor unions in Brazilian history bears iterating. These groups were crucial for establishing methods of collective action as well as pushing for real, participatory democracy. Vargas realized the changing times, and, as he campaigned for president in 1950, he began to champion workers' rights. He eventually won the ballot, returning to presidential office in 1951. Then, in a swooping turn of events – which *again* saw him staring down a military coup d'état in the face of political crisis – he committed suicide in 1954. His death brought hundreds of thousands of mourners to the streets in Rio de Janeiro, cementing his legacy, somewhat ironically, as a hero to the Brazilian working classes (McCann, 2003; Wolfe, 1993).

Land reform remained unaddressed, and it would be several years before rural labor unions were established. Still, the 1930s saw mobilization efforts that, several decades later, would play key roles in the formation of the *Movimento dos Trabalhadores Rurais Sem Terra* (The Landless Rural Workers Movement – the MST) (Linhares and Silva, 1999). At the same time, in 1932, women won the right to vote, and, according to Kim Butler (1992), this period also saw the rise of Afro-Brazilian political solidarity. The *Frente Negra Brasileira* (Black Brazilian Front), Brazil's first Afro-Brazilian political party, was officially established in 1931. This provided inspiration for subsequent groups, like TEN (O *Teatro Experimental do Negro*, the Black Experimental Theater), who formed in 1944 and used theater to critique Brazilian society and cultivate racial consciousness.

Though the roots of many contemporary Brazilian social movements can be traced to this period, it is important to remember the hurdles faced by activists and reasons for why widespread mobilization was slow to emerge. As sociologist Charles Tilly reminds us, social movements represent "a distinctive form of contentious politics – contentious in the sense that social movements involve collective making of claims that, if realized, would conflict with someone else's interests" (Tilly, 2004, p. 3). The "conflict" noted here by Tilly is especially relevant in Brazil's case, as, throughout history, Brazilian elites have been particularly resistant to changes that might compromise their privilege and class interests (e.g., Pastore, 1982; Santos, 1979). Additionally, returning to Chapter 2 and anthropologist Roberto DaMatta (1991), social conflict between different groups has long been anathema to narratives of Brazilian national identity. As such, any sort of identity-based political action (for example, rights for blacks, women, indigenous people, LGBTQ groups, and so on) have often been interpreted as sectarian, divisive, and, in many ways, 'anti-Brazilian.' Owing in large part to these two reasons – ongoing efforts by elites to maintain their class position and constructions of national identity that disavow prejudice and the mobilization efforts by marginalized groups – social movements in Brazil have consistently faced uphill battles.

Despite these obstacles, social activists continued to mobilize throughout the twentieth century, even during the most repressive years of Brazil's military dictatorship (1964–1985). Many social movement theorists, whether looking to Latin America or elsewhere, explain collective mobilization during this period through one (or both) of two frameworks: resource mobilization or political opportunity theory (Miller, 2000). According to the former, social movements typically form once their leaderships have attained sufficient resources (money, supplies, human capital, political victories, etc.) to mobilize broader participation with the movement. Political opportunity theory, on the other hand, emphasizes the ways social movements typically emerge thanks to political circumstances that, for example, open new space for protest (e.g., democracy), or, in other cases, might inspire collective mobilization due to political repression. In many cases these two perspectives work in tandem (rather than in tension) to make sense of social movement activism, especially in recent historical contexts. A closer look at Brazil's largest contemporary social movement, the MST – a social movement working for land reform in rural areas – helps to illustrate this.

As noted previously, though collective organization and labor unions were repressed under Vargas during the 1930s, non-landowning rural workers slowly began to mobilize during this time. When Vargas was removed via a coup in 1945, Cold War fears of communism began to grow, in many instances driven by the USA. This meant that socialist-leaning political parties and labor unions were heavily scrutinized, yet initiatives were also undertaken to reform exploitative models of agricultural production (viz., peasant agriculture based on sharecropping or tenant farming involving forced labor). The fear was that a communist uprising might sprout from Brazil's peasant population, as it had in Russia or China, and, thus, certain reforms were necessary to ward off full-scale revolution (Welch, 2006). This helps to explain the troubled existence of Brazil's Peasant Leagues (*As Ligas Camponesas*): first organized in 1945 to address the labor rights of landless rural workers, it was then outlawed in 1947 for connections with Brazil's communist party, and then re-emerged in 1954 to help appease restless rural workers. Over the next decade, the Peasant Leagues worked to mobilize Brazil's *camponês* population, forming the roots of what was to become, in the 1980s, the MST social movement.

Brazilian elites continued to grow more fearful of communism, particularly after the Cuban Revolution in 1959. When President Jânio Quadros unexpectedly resigned in 1961, Vice-President João Goulart assumed the presidency, increasing concerns among conservatives that Brazil was turning to the political left. Goulart maintained a centrist platform in many respects, but his support for rural worker unionization – among other proposed "base reforms" – proved too much: he was ousted in 1964 by a military coup. The military refused to relinquish power for more than two decades, and, during this time, Brazil was governed by a repressive and highly authoritarian dictatorship. Perceived oppositional groups such as the

Peasant Leagues were abolished by military leaders. Though some Brazilian *camponeses* continued to achieve modest political and economic gains during the dictatorship (e.g., formal pensions and health coverage – see Pereira, 1997), their leaderships went underground to escape arrest, torture, and assassination. As such, despite the fact that Brazil's repressive political landscape provided social movements with ammunition to mobilize their bases (i.e., political opportunities), activists had few resources to organize themselves.

It is here that Brazil's progressive Catholic Church enters the picture. Inspired by Liberation Theology (see Chapter 9), many clergy members provided cover for social activists during the military dictatorship (Wright and Wolford, 2003). The Church was one of very few institutions left mostly alone by the dictatorship, providing modest respite for left-leaning collectives during the 1960s and 1970s. Activist leaders from groups such as the Peasant Leagues often became involved with Ecclesiastical Base Communities (*Comunidades Eclesiais de Base* - CEBs), established by Catholic leaders in touch with Liberation Theology.

In this way, activists working for land reform found resources to continue mobilizing (or at least endure) during the most repressive years of the dictatorship. While the MST was not officially established until 1984 – when the military dictatorship drew to an end and restrictions on social movements and political parties were relaxed – land reform activists were already at work by the end of the 1970s. In fact, according to Sue Branford and Jan Rocha (2002), the first MST occupation was launched in 1979, as several families moved onto privately held land in Brazil's southernmost state of Rio Grande do Sul. Here, movement activists followed what would become the MST's signature strategy going forward: (1) occupy unused farmland; (2) petition the federal government to enforce constitutional laws emphasizing the landowner's social responsibility to make their land productive; and (3) hold out for land reform settlement, often for years, and frequently under serious threat from rural landowners (see Figure 7.4). Not without controversy and extreme danger, these tactics have today made the MST one of Latin America's largest and most successful social movements (Wright and Wolford, 2003).

By the time the military dictatorship gave way to civilian rule in the mid-1980s, the MST had sufficient resources to make the most of Brazil's new political landscape (i.e., mobilized resources *and* political opportunities). Over the next two decades, the MST grew quickly into the internationally renowned social movement it is today. In fact, Brazil's return to democracy was significant not only for largescale social movements like the MST: it was a watershed moment for activists across Brazil, leading to a surge in collective mobilization that spawned a new era in social activism (e.g., Green, 1994). As elsewhere around the world, many scholars distinguish this period from previous ones in Brazil thanks to the emergence of "new social movements" (Escobar and Alvarez, 1992). These groups are characterized by diverse forms of collective action, social resistance, and in-group solidarity, and, over the past few decades, they have established a formidable presence in Brazilian society. It is to these groups and their ongoing efforts we now turn our attention.

Figure 7.4 An MST settlement in rural Ceará.
Source: the authors.

Democracy: the rise of Brazil's 'new' social movements (1985–2013)

According to Sarah Radcliffe (2004), new social movement theory accounts for a significant shift in collective mobilization that occurred in the latter decades of the twentieth century. In Brazil and other Latin American countries, this shift was induced by two key political economic factors in the 1980s: a return to democracy after long periods of dictatorial rule, and the ensuing debt crisis that enveloped the region for more than a decade. From one perspective, political opportunity theory would seem to explain Brazil's social movement surge during this period, as the end of the military dictatorship and new constitution of 1988 generated a dynamic and progressive context for social activism. To explain these changes solely from this perspective, however, would be to overlook several factors. Included here were significant changes in the ways social movements began to organize, the diverse groups they quickly formed, changing engagements with political parties and the state, and new issues and identities forged by social movements. In particular, this included grassroots organizational tactics and a 'do-it-yourself' ethos that produced myriad social movements in short order. These characteristics are still very much alive today in Brazil, and they continue to be important for making sense of contemporary social activism.

What distinguishes new social movements (NSMs) from previous social movements in a country like Brazil is a host of combined factors. In the first instance, these groups often brought diverse sectors of society together that, in previous decades, were unlikely to forge alliances. This includes people from different socio-economic class backgrounds, and, in some cases, groups that were adversarial in previous years. What brought these different actors together were often localized and material issues related to housing, natural resource degradation, childcare, equal pay and opportunities, land rights, etc. In coming together around these issues, participants often formed new identities that, in some cases, were not especially relevant beforehand. For example, with the emergence of NSMs, people began to identify more often as environmentalists, feminists, Afro-Brazilians, LGBTQ, and so on.

This is importantly different from previous social movement identities, which more often emphasized political and/or class-based commonalities (e.g., labor unions and political parties). Related to this, and differently from Europe and North America, where researchers emphasize the 'post-material' objectives of NSMs (e.g., civil rights, anti-discrimination, environmental protection), in Brazil, NSMs more often came together over material concerns (e.g., housing, land rights, natural resources). As detailed in Chapter 8, the case of Chico Mendes and the rise of socio-environmentalism provides a clear illustration of this (Hecht and Cockburn, 1990).

Mendes himself never set out to be an environmentalist: he was a union organizer concerned with the livelihoods of other rubber tappers in the state of Acre. This led him to rally against deforestation in the region – because rubber tappers needed the trees to make a living – and this, in turn, led to new alliances with others in the region (e.g., indigenous communities along with transnational organizations such as the World Wildlife Fund). In many cases, these new alliances brought together actors that previously had few affinities, such as rubber tappers and indigenous groups. What linked them were similar environmental and natural resource concerns, leading to new and broader group identities that also connected them with likeminded activists around the world (e.g., the environmental movement).

This points to a second key characteristic of NSMs in Brazil: they have tended to draw on diverse organizational tactics, not working exclusively through labor unions and/or political parties, as social movements often did in previous decades. More generally, this represents a different mode of engagement with the state and political processes. NSMs have more often (though by no means exclusively) focused on immediate, material, and localized issues that affect them directly, steering away from the political networks and structural issues (e.g., class-based interests) addressed by previous social movements. This has helped organizers to form broader activist linkages that include participants from diverse socio-economic backgrounds, expanding the resources and human capital available to social movements. For example, by drawing attention to the connections between racial and gender inequality and socio-economic marginalization, NSMs have expanded their appeal to middle- and upper-class participants.

Finally, a third defining characteristic of NSMs in Brazil is a tradition of grassroots mobilization that has led them down different pathways from previous social movements (e.g., by not necessarily working through labor unions and/or political parties). This 'do-it-yourself' attitude helps to explain the rapid growth of NSMs, as well as the emergence of myriad nongovernmental organizations (NGOs). A poignant example was the surge of Brazilian neighborhood associations that took off in the 1980s and 1990s, and are today ubiquitous in low-income and working-class communities. These groups have played significant roles in securing land tenure, housing, social services, basic infrastructure, etc., though, in many instances, they have also fizzled out as participants lack resources, time, and professional skills necessary to maintain activist organizations (cf. Fischer, McCann, and Auyero, 2014).

Important to consider as well is the Latin American debt crisis of the 1980s, the ensuing growth of neoliberalism, and then the rise of the Brazilian Workers' Party in the twenty-first century. In Brazil, where insufficient state resources mixed with neoliberal discourses of individualism and entrepreneurship, social movements found fertile terrain in which to organize, yet simultaneously struggled to achieve their goals. Urban housing organizations such as the MNLM (O *Movimento Nacional de Luta pela Moradia* – The National Movement for the Fight for Housing) help to illustrate this.

Similar to the MST's tactics, housing movements like MNLM have carried out hundreds of occupations of abandoned buildings throughout Brazilian cities over the past few decades (see Figure 7.5). Why should people confront housing insecurity, they argue, when Brazilian cities have so many unused and abandoned buildings? They cite constitutional law – again, like the MST – acknowledging the social function of property and housing rights in Brazil. These groups have faced tremendous resistance throughout their existence, in part because they lack the resources and notoriety of groups like the MST, and also because of backlash from urban elites. Many activists were thusly encouraged in 2003 when the Workers' Party came to power, yet, in most cases, remain underwhelmed with reform measures carried out since then. As such, like many social movements, urban housing activists have continued their efforts in the twenty-first century, in some instances building even stronger public presences in cities such as São Paulo (Ferreira, 2012). These groups, however, remain wary of retaliation and backlash, and perhaps even more so after the impeachment of President Dilma Rousseff from the Workers' Party in 2016.

Related to urban housing movements and neighborhood associations, it is important to consider other NSMs that have changed significantly – and also changed *Brazil* significantly – since the 1980s. Key examples involve ongoing struggles for equal rights by women, Afro-Brazilians, LGBTQ groups, and indigenous Brazilians. While these groups have achieved significant victories in recent years – for example, federal laws addressing domestic violence and femicide; university quotas for students of color; the legalization of same-sex marriage; recognition of indigenous territories and land-use rights – they continue to face pushback in the public sphere. As already mentioned, two factors hindering their mobilization efforts are ongoing resistance from Brazilian elites and discourses of national unity that portray these groups as divisive. Added to this is outright societal prejudice – sexism, homophobia, racism, etc. (e.g., Alvarez, 1990; Hanchard, 1999; Mott, 1997) – and a lack of resources that confront these groups in pretty much every country.

Figure 7.5 An MNLM (*Movimento Nacional de Luta pela Moradia*) occupation in central
Rio de Janeiro.

Source: photo courtesy of Kayla Svoboda.

Finally, yet another hurdle faced by these movements involves what researchers
call issues of intersectionality: the ways different identities (e.g., class, race,
ethnicity, religion, sexual orientation, nationality, gender) do not exist indepen-
dently of one another, but are, in fact, interconnected in important and complex
ways. For example, presuming that *all* LGBTQ people share similar concerns and
priorities regarding civil rights and discrimination overlooks the fact LGBTQ
people are as diverse as any other group. Some face additional problems of racial or
ethnic discrimination, poverty, gender inequality, or discrimination based on their

religious beliefs. These points of intersection are crucial for understanding systems of oppression and marginalization, as well as the conflicts among *and within* different social movements over how best to address inequality and which inequalities are most worth addressing (Bernardino-Costa, 2014).

Consider, for example, tension between different social movements in Brazil as well as tension *within* these same groups. NSMs in Brazil have, in some cases, faced criticism from older social movements for individualizing their claims around race, gender, sexual orientation, and so on, and failing to emphasize the importance of class struggle and structural political change. The argument here is that by not connecting effectively with class-based political struggles (e.g., labor unions and political parties), NSMs have missed opportunities to produce broader, structural social change. Related to this are conflicts that exist between and within activist groups over intersecting issues of social inequality. For example, despite similar interests and social rights claims, not all movements are equally keen to link with others, for reasons that range from conflicts over ideology and practice, to more material struggles over resources and capital (cf. Bernardino-Costa, 2014).

Finally, there remains the issue of Brazil's contemporary political climate. Though more than a decade of Workers' Party leadership would seem favorable for many social movements – indeed, the twenty-first century has seen a host of important achievements, both through political legislation as well as collective action – activist groups continue to face uphill battles throughout Brazil. In addition to several factors already mentioned in this chapter, NSMs have been vulnerable to internal fissures as well as political co-optation by state actors. For example, perhaps because NSMs have tended not to make exclusive links with a singular political party, leaders within these movements have, in some cases, been wooed by elected officials seeking to expand their support bases, reach compromises, and make deals. Such alliances have understandably damaged the credibility of NSM leaders perceived to be 'selling out,' and helps to further explain the challenges confronting contemporary Brazilian social movements (cf. Gondim, 2004).

All this brings us to the present day, and very recent changes that characterize collective mobilization in Brazil. Returning to where this chapter began and considering newly established social movements such as the MPL, Brazil remains a hotbed for collective mobilization. Recent years have seen an explosion of social activism, as well as major changes to Brazil's social movement landscape. Political ruptures such as the impeachment of president Dilma Rousseff in 2016 and new organizational technologies such as social media are having profound effects on the ways people mobilize. We consider these changes in the penultimate section, trying to offer insight into what the future might hold for social activism in Brazil.

The twenty-first century: social movements going forward (2013 onward)

While there remains little consensus among scholars over *why* people came to the streets in 2013 – and *what*, precisely, were their reasons for being there – there is at least general agreement that it was an unprecedented moment in Brazil's history of social protest. As noted previously, many scholars suggest the protests were part of broader global trends that represent middle-class discontent in countries such as Brazil, Turkey, Spain, Egypt, Chile, and so on (Mendonça and Ercan, 2015). The argument is that, today, these countries have rapidly expanding middle-class populations who are growing restless with what they perceive as underwhelming opportunities and poor state governance. These are people that, since the rise of neoliberalism in the 1980s, were sold on the benefits of democracy and globalization, as well as promises that investing in education, homeownership, etc., would guarantee prosperity and financial security. Needless to say, these people feel misled, and, in recent years, their anger has begun to boil over.

These frustrations have, in many instances, been directed towards those who sold them on these ideas – for example, state actors – and not just because middle-class people feel swindled. The investment priorities of governments in countries such as Brazil, coupled with growing political corruption scandals, have left many people irate. As just one example, resources for public education and healthcare in Brazil are insufficient and/or unevenly distributed, even by standards of other Latin American countries. They are often funneled into projects and institutions privy to the upper classes. Brazilians are mostly aware of this, and, in 2013, as resources continued pouring into World Cup and Olympic preparations – and also into the personal bank accounts of political and economic elites – widespread anger swelled. As Alfredo Saad-Filho writes (2013), this context helps to explain, in part, the protests of 2013.

Equally significant here is the role of information technology and changes introduced by social media. Brazil's 2013 protests are a prime example of how new technologies are reshaping mass mobilizations today. People can communicate, organize, plan, and adjust in real time, coming together and/or adapting their efforts according to up-to-the-minute developments. Smartphones and social media have profoundly altered the coordination tools of mass mobilization. At the start of the twenty-first century, protests like those of 2013 were inconceivable in Brazil. One decade later, millions of people were marching in the streets. Communication and information technology will remain key to the future of collective mobilization, and not least because of preventative measures and increased surveillance by state actors (Joia, 2016).

Important to remember, however, is that largescale mobilizations such as the protests of 2013 can hardly be called organized social movements, at least not in the traditional sense of the term (e.g., Tilly, 2004). They represent moments of collective action, but they lack the focused goals and clear messages of past social movements. Granted, plenty of longtime social movements participated in the protests of 2013, even helping to lead and organize the nightly manifestations in the early stages. But, once in the street, the multitude became amorphous, a group constituted by affinity more so than common backgrounds, similar demands, or political affiliations. Such mobilizations have been criticized for lacking organization and a clear political message, with similar movements such as Occupy Wall Street said to have accomplished little (cf. Joia, 2016).

Yet, from another perspective, these very differences help to explain the strengths and potentialities of these new forms of collective action. By appealing to widespread and commonly shared frustrations rather than singular objectives or ideological motivations, these mobilizations connect with enormously broad participant bases. In an era when young people are often criticized for spending more time on their phones and computers than with other human beings, 'flash mob' protests have proven capable of bringing *millions* together in public space. Considering these changes – for example, the role of information technology and broad participation from diverse social groups – the protests of 2013 seem to indicate a new era for collective action, in Brazil as well as elsewhere. There are several factors that distinguish this period as a watershed moment, in the ways that social movements now organize as well as the potential for future mobilizations.

Consider, for example, how social movements are today able to connect globally, share information, pool resources, and articulate their messages without relying on traditional media sources. This, of course, can mean that individual social movements are drowned out by the online presence of so many groups, but the opportunities available to tech-savvy social movements are extraordinary. A few examples include the following: they can raise money from donors around the world; upload video showing their work as well as moments of social injustice; construct and adapt their message according to up-to-the-minute political and social change; learn from, and coordinate their efforts with, other social movements; and immediately call on and inform their participant bases when direct action is needed. These factors are potentially crucial for making sense of the 2013 protests in Brazil, as Brazilian social movements had access to groups in similar contexts (e.g., Egypt, Spain, Occupy Wall Street), could engage in real time solidarity with protestors elsewhere (e.g., Turkey), and then help to inspire and educate subsequent movements in other countries (cf. Joia, 2016). Such processes of international solidarity are, of course, not unprecedented, but the speed and direct connectivity offered by new technologies has profoundly altered the global landscape of collective mobilization.

Part and parcel of this are new questions regarding social movement organization, including the critical role of space in processes of collective mobilization. For example, in the past, social movements required physical space to meet and to organize. As noted previously, this helps to highlight the role of the progressive Catholic Church during Brazil's military dictatorship, as CEBs provided space for social movement leaderships to cultivate social resistance. Today, however, social movements can accomplish many of these organizational tasks online. Even protests and social resistance can be carried out online, whether to raise awareness, engage in public criticism, solicit financial support, or even hack and troll, as activist collectives such as Anonymous have proven effectively. The role of physical space is thus something that merits critical reflection. How significant is it, for example, for social movements to occupy public space as they have in the past, as well as for activists to continue interacting within these same spaces? Are there critical affinity bonds produced

Figure 7.6 Protestors in central Rio de Janeiro in 2018 calling for direct military intervention in Brazilian democracy.

Source: the authors.

in physical space that cannot be replicated in cyberspace? For those hoping to understand the future of social movements, whether in Brazil or elsewhere, these are important questions.

Also to be accounted for, especially when considering Brazil, are the ways changing societal relationships are likely to affect collective mobilization. Like many other countries, political and civil discourse in Brazil is growing more antagonistic, serving to normalize the messages of fringe and extremist groups. This helps to explain, on the one hand, recent calls by rightwing activists for the return of the military dictatorship (see Figure 7.6), as well as, on the other hand, the growing popularity of rightwing political figures like Jair Bolsonaro. This climate of growing hostility will almost certainly alter the ways social movements organize and take action, yet how this will happen, and what the effects are likely to be, are difficult to predict. These are pressing questions in the twenty-first century, and, for researchers concerned with the organizational tactics of social movements, the future of collective mobilization, and even calls for social justice more generally, understanding the relationships between these different processes remains a crucial area of analysis.

Conclusion

In this chapter, we have tried to make sense of contemporary Brazilian social movements and acts of ongoing popular resistance. Our goal has not been to address every individual social movement, but, instead, to help explain the origins of social resistance, the struggles still waged today, and questions important for the future of collective mobilization. We began by exploring the roots of social resistance in Brazil, starting with indigenous groups and African slaves. The nineteenth century saw continued acts of political and social rebellion, yet it was not until the 1930s that social movements truly took root in Brazil. Labor unions emerged during this time, women won the right to vote, and the first Afro-Brazilian political party was established (the *Frente Negra Brasileira* – the Black Brazilian Front). By the mid-twentieth century, the urban working classes were gaining force, yet land reform continued unaddressed, and for marginalized groups such as Afro-Brazilians, indigenous groups, gay, lesbian, and transgender Brazilians, and the rural poor, severe inequalities persisted. The context of the cold war further complicated organizational efforts by social movements, and when the military dictatorship came to power in the 1960s, many activists were forced underground.

Even then, during the military dictatorship, social movements continued to seek out political opportunities and mobilize resources available to them. When Brazil returned to democracy in 1985, there was an explosion of social movement activism, with groups such as the MST surging to international prominence in little more than a decade. This period saw the emergence of "new social movements," distinguished from their predecessors by alternative organizational structures and different methods of political engagement. This represented a new era for social activism, in Brazil and elsewhere, that continues, in many respects, to the present day. The protests of 2013 hailed yet another watershed moment for collective mobilization, if not for social movements, then at least for manifestations of popular protest. What these events made clear are the ways technology and social media are altering processes of collective mobilization, offering new tools as well as new challenges for contemporary social movements.

Going forward, there are several factors likely to alter the course of social activism in Brazil. Many of these are addressed in this chapter, and include such issues as diversifying participant bases, intersectional identities within and between different groups, and new technologies and social media platforms. Related here are challenges confronting social movements, including control and surveillance efforts by the state and private institutions, as well as alarmingly toxic political and civil discourses that threaten social activists, collective action, and democracy more generally. Future mobilization efforts will almost certainly continue to address discrimination, civil rights, social injustice, socioeconomic exclusion, political participation, environmental degradation, access to resources, and so on, yet new and unanticipated issues will likely reshape social activism in different ways (e.g., internet neutrality, privacy rights, migration and international cooperation, growing corporate governance, artificial intelligence). And, while social movements have historically been linked with progressive and left-leaning politics, it is possible that conservative and rightwing groups may become more involved with collective mobilization in the future. Brazil remains a dynamic and contested sociopolitical context, and, just as they have historically, social activists are sure to play important roles in future debates.

Suggested English readings

Alvarez, S. (1990). *Engendering democracy in Brazil: Women's movements in transition politics.* Princeton: Princeton University Press.

Carter, M. (2015). *Challenging social inequality: The Landless Rural Workers Movement and agrarian reform in Brazil.* Durham: Duke University Press.

Conde, M., and Jazeel, T. (2019). *Manifesting democracy? Urban protests and the politics of representation in Brazil post-2013.* London: Wiley-Blackwell.

Escobar, A., and Alvarez, S. (1992). *The making of social movements in Latin America: Identity, strategy, and democracy.* Boulder: Westview Press.

Green, J. (1994). The emergence of the Brazilian Gay Liberation Movement, 1977–1981. *Latin American Perspectives*, 21(1), 38–55.

Hanchard, M. (ed.). (1999). *Racial politics in contemporary Brazil.* Durham, NC: Duke University Press.

Holston, J. (2008). *Insurgent citizenship: Disjunctions of democracy and modernity in Brazil.* Princeton: Princeton University Press.

Mendes, C. (with Tony Gross). (1989). *Fight for the forest: Chico Mendes in his own words.* London: Latin American Bureau.

Reis, J.J. (1993). *Slave rebellion in Brazil: The Muslim uprising of 1835 in Bahia.* Baltimore: Johns Hopkins University Press.

Wolfe, J. (1993). *Working women, working men: São Paulo and the rise of Brazil's industrial working class, 1900–1955.* Durham, NC: Duke University Press.

Wright, A.L., and Wolford, W. (2003). *To inherit the earth: The landless movement and the struggle for a new Brazil.* Oakland: Food First Books.

References

Alvarez, S. (1990). *Engendering democracy in Brazil: Women's movements in transition politics.* Princeton: Princeton University Press.

Bernardino-Costa, J. (2014). Intersectionality and female domestic workers' unions in Brazil. *Women's Studies International Forum*, 46, 72–80.

Bowen, M. (2010). The struggle for black land rights in Brazil: An insider's view on *quilombos* and the *quilombo* land movement. *African and Black Diaspora: An International Journal*, 3(2), 147–168.

Branford, S., and Rocha, J. (2002). *Cutting the wire: The story of the landless movement in Brazil.* London: Latin American Bureau.

Butler, K.D. (1992). Up from slavery: Afro-Brazilian activism in São Paulo, 1888–1938. *The Americas*, 49(2), 179–206.

Caulfield, S. (2000). *In defense of honor: Sexual morality, modernity, and nation in early-twentieth-century Brazil.* Durham, NC: Duke University Press.

Chaui, M. (2000). *Brasil: Mito fundador e sociedade autoritária.* São Paulo: Fundação Perseu Abramo.

Chilcote, R.H. (2014). *Intellectuals and the search for national identity in twentieth-century Brazil.* Cambridge: Cambridge University Press.

Conde, M., and Jazeel, T. (2019). *Manifesting democracy? Urban protests and the politics of representation in Brazil post-2013*. London: Wiley-Blackwell.

DaMatta, R. (1991). *Carnivals, rogues, and heroes: An interpretation of the Brazilian dilemma*. Notre Dame, IN: University of Notre Dame Press.

d'Andréa, C., and Ziller, J. (2016). Violent scenes in Brazil's 2013 protests: The diversity of ordinary people's narratives. *Television and New Media*, 17(4), 324–334.

Escobar, A., and Alvarez, S. (1992). *The making of social movements in Latin America: Identity, strategy, and democracy*. Boulder: Westview Press.

Fausto, B. (1975). *A Revolução de 1930: Historiografia e história*. São Paulo: Brasiliense.

Fausto, B. (1999). *A concise history of Brazil*. Cambridge: Cambridge University Press.

Ferreira, R.F.C.F. (2012). Movimentos de moradia, autogestão e política habitacional no Brasil: Do acesso à moradia ao direito à cidade. *Segundo Fórum de Sociologia*, 1–4 August. Available at: www.observatoriodasmetropoles.net/download/01/artigo_reginaferreira_isa.pdf [accessed 4 March 2018].

Fischer, B., McCann, B., and Auyero, J. (eds). (2014). *Cities from scratch: Poverty and informality in urban Latin America*. Durham, NC: Duke University Press.

French, J.H. (2009). *Legalizing identities: Becoming Black or Indian in Brazil's northeast*. Chapel Hill: University of North Carolina Press.

Freyre, G. (1964). *The masters and the slaves: A study of the development of Brazilian civilization* [*Casa-Grande & Senzala: Formação da Família Brasileira sob o regime da economia patriarcal* (1933)]. Translated by Samuel Putnam. 4th ed. New York: Knopf.

Gerbaudo, P. (2012). *Tweets and the streets: Social media and contemporary activism*. London: Pluto Press.

Gerbaudo, P. (2017). *The mask and the flag: Populism, citizenism and global protest*. London: Hurst.

Gondim, L.M.P. (2004). Creating the image of a modern Fortaleza: Social inequalities, political change, and the impact of urban design. *Latin American Perspectives*, 135(2), 62–79.

Green, J. (1994). The emergence of the Brazilian Gay Liberation Movement, 1977–1981. *Latin American Perspectives*, 21(1), 38–55.

Hanchard, M. (ed.). (1999). *Racial politics in contemporary Brazil*. Durham, NC: Duke University Press.

Hecht, S.B., and Cockburn, A. (1990). *The fate of the forest: Developers, destroyers and defenders of the Amazon*. New York: Penguin.

Linhares, M.Y., and Silva, F.C.T. da, (1999). *Terra prometida: Uma história da questão agrária no Brasil*. Rio de Janeiro: Campus.

Joia, L.A. (2016). Social media and the "20 Cents Movements" in Brazil: What lessons can be learnt from this? *Information Technology for Development*, 22(3), 422–435.

Maxwell, M. (2004). *Conflicts and conspiracies: Brazil and Portugal 1750–1808*. London: Routledge.

McCann, B. (2003). Carlos Lacerda: The rise and fall of a middle-class populist in 1950s Brazil. *Hispanic American Historical Review*, 83(4), 661–696.

Meade, T. (1986). "Civilizing Rio de Janeiro": The public health campaign and the riot of 1904. *Journal of Social History*, 20(2), 301–322.

Mendonça, R.F., and Ercan, S. (2015). Deliberation and protest: strange bedfellows? Revealing the deliberative potential of 2013 protests in Turkey and Brazil. *Political Studies*, 36(3), 267–282.

Miller, B. (2000). *Geography and social movements: Comparing antinuclear activism in the Boston area*. Minneapolis: University of Minnesota Press.

Mott, L. (1997). *Homofobia: A violação dos direitos humanos dos gays, lésbicas e travestis no Brasil.* San Francisco: IGLRHC.

Pastore, J. (1982). *Inequality and social mobility in Brazil.* Madison: University of Wisconsin Press.

Pereira, A.W. (1997). *The end of the peasantry: The rural labor movement in Northeast Brazil, 1961–1988.* Pittsburgh: University of Pittsburgh Press.

Pereira, C. (2013). Inspirados em Porto Alegre, protestos em série contra reajustes na tarifa de ônibus se espalham pelo país. *Zero Hora Notícias,* 15 June. Available at: https://gauchazh.clicrbs.com.br/geral/noticia/2013/06/inspirados–em–porto–alegre–protestos–em–serie–contra–reajustes–na–tarifa–de–onibus–se–espalham–pelo–pais–4171189.html [accessed 28 March 2018].

Radcliffe, S. (2004). Civil society, grassroots politics and livelihoods. In: R.N. Gwynne and C. Kay (eds), *Latin America transformed: Globalization and modernity.* 2nd ed. New York: Oxford University Press, pp. 193–209.

Rago, M. (1993). Prazer e sociabilidade no mundo da prostituição em São Paulo, 1890–1930. *Luso-Brazilian Review,* 30(1), 35–46.

Reis, J.J. (1993). *Slave rebellion in Brazil: The Muslim uprising of 1835 in Bahia.* Baltimore: Johns Hopkins University Press.

Saad-Filho, A. (2013). Mass protests under 'left neoliberalism': Brazil, June–July 2013. *Critical Sociology,* 39(5),657–659.

Santos, M. (1979). *The shared space: The two circuits of the urban economy in underdeveloped countries.* London: Methuen.

Skidmore, T.E. (2010). *Brazil: Five centuries of change.* 2nd ed. Oxford: Oxford University Press.

Tarrow, S. (1994). *Power in movement: Social movements, collective action and politics.* Cambridge: Cambridge University Press.

Tilly, C. (2004). *Social movements, 1768–2004.* Boulder: Paradigm.

Welch, C. (2006). Keeping communism down on the farm: The Brazilian rural labor movement during the cold war. *Latin American Perspectives,* 33(3), 28–50.

Wolfe, J. (1993). *Working women, working men: São Paulo and the rise of Brazil's industrial working class, 1900–1955.* Durham, NC: Duke University Press.

Wright, A.L., and Wolford, W. (2003). *To inherit the earth: The landless movement and the struggle for a new Brazil.* Oakland: Food First Books.

8 Environmental contexts and challenges

Introduction

Brazil is famously known as a country of contradictions (cf. Ribeiro, 2000). To be fair, every country has its contradictions, from glaring social inequalities, despite narratives of national unity, to discourses of freedom and opportunity in the face of political repression and mass incarceration. Consider environmental issues, for example: many countries celebrate their natural landscapes, commemorating them through artwork, patriotic symbols, national parks, and so on, yet they also heavily pollute these same environments. A country's natural environment is often important for constructions of national identity, and the natural features, flora, fauna, resources, etc., that exist within its borders are often celebrated with a sense of national pride. But these same environments and ecosystems are often overexploited, and regularly by the very same people and governments that celebrate them. Such contradictions appear hypocritical, and one would be hard pressed to identify a country without such problems.

Brazil, however, represents something of a special case. So numerous are Brazil's contradictions that it has earned an international reputation for bipolarity (Rhoter, 2012). Whether in terms of socio-economic inequality, legal protocol, historical memory, racial (in)equality, and so on, Brazil's contradictions are so ubiquitous that Brazilians themselves often make light of such issues. Culturally speaking, Brazilians love to laugh, but the humor can be quite dark, perhaps owing to the stark contradictions lived by so many on a daily basis (Goldstein, 2003). The environment and natural resources are no exception, with Brazil's forests, fauna, resources, and diverse ecosystems representing key features of national pride, yet also under serious threat from human degradation. To people outside Brazil, such contradictions can be puzzling. How can a country celebrate its natural environment while at the same time destroying it so rapidly? How do such conflicting realities coexist, at the same time and in the same spaces, without falling apart altogether? Do people not recognize these contradictions, become angry at the hypocrisy, and act to protect these resources important to them and the rest of the world?

The purpose of this chapter is to provide insight to these questions. By considering Brazil's environmental history and present-day paradoxes, this chapter seeks to explain why Brazil's environmental challenges are so complex, and how Brazil has changed – and continues to change – in the face of natural resource management and sustainability. One cannot unpack Brazil's environmental questions without also considering globalization and international engagement, along with important histories of colonialism and capitalist development. As such, this chapter is organized chronologically, starting with Brazil's colonization by the Portuguese and progressing through to the present day. To make sense of Brazil's contemporary environmental context, one must reflect on the country's ecological history, seeing how relationships between development, globalization, political economy, international diplomacy, and social and cultural conflict combine to produce the landscapes we see today. There are, of course, very few definitive answers to these questions, but by critically interrogating Brazil's environmental issues and their persisting contradictions, one can not only begin to make better sense of Brazil, but also other countries with similar histories and environmental contexts.

Colonization, exploitation, and globalization

Ever since humans first inhabited present-day Brazil, diverse cultural influences and processes of globalization have been at work. These humans came from elsewhere on the planet, arriving in Brazil through multiple entry points and at different times. Before the arrival of Europeans, there were hundreds (if not thousands) of different languages spoken in Brazil, and, no different from today, these people engaged one another through modes of production, trade, conquest, warfare, and so on (Dean, 1997). Contrary to Western-centric narratives that privilege European processes of colonialism and capitalist development, globalization has been at work – even thriving – since long before the present era.

Additionally, just as it is problematic to privilege Western/European perspectives of globalization, so, too, would it be wrong to overly romanticize the relationships between native Brazilians and their environments. Just like elsewhere in the world, indigenous people in the Americas harvested their local resources, sometimes to the point of overexploitation, without the aid of mechanized tools or capitalist modes of production. Exotic visions depicting indigenous people as 'noble savages' living in harmony with their surroundings are not only colonialist and inaccurate, they also infantilize and disrespect indigenous people, presuming they lacked the technological capability of Europeans who, through such means, came to spoil their own environments. Archaeological evidence suggests indigenous people in the Americas were certainly capable of environmental destruction (Denevan, 1992), but, unlike European colonizers, they recognized better the limits of resource extraction (i.e., they did not overdo it). Recent studies also point to the existence of large cities in Amazonia prior to European colonization (Mann, 2008), denting conventional wisdom that all indigenous people lived in small hunter-gatherer communities in pre-Colombian times.

Just as elsewhere in the Americas, European arrival in Brazil is a mostly tragic story of genocide, slavery, and environmental degradation. This again is not to suggest such processes were unheard of prior to European colonization, but with the arrival of the Portuguese in 1500, life changed irrevocably for people in Brazil. The human toll was enormous (Hemming, 1987), even if the economic effects were slow to emerge. The Portuguese were sluggish and decentralized in their colonization efforts, and it was not for several decades that Brazil's lucrative economic potential began to be realized.

In the mountains and forests, the colonizers sought Brazilwood, gold, and diamonds, and nearer to the coastline they grew sugar, coffee, cotton, and tobacco for export to Europe. It is significant that Brazil's name, in fact, comes from its first commodity export. At first, the Portuguese enslaved the native population, but indigenous Brazilians proved poorly suited to slave labor. They often died too quickly or simply ran away (Monteiro, 1994). It was not until the Atlantic slave trade was established in the sixteenth century that the colonial economy began to flourish. Millions of African slaves were eventually brought to Brazil, and by the seventeenth century their labor made the colony a crucial export hub for raw materials to the global economy (Skidmore, 2010). By the eighteenth century, gold replaced sugar as Brazil's primary export, and, unlike other European colonies in the Americas, Brazil's economic prominence far outweighed its colonial mother country (Barman, 1988). For the Portuguese and other European nations, Brazil appeared a vast, seemingly endless trove of natural resources waiting for extraction.

So why is this bit of colonial history so crucial for understanding Brazil's contemporary environmental context? At least two key processes that remain significant today are rooted in this period. The first relates to Brazil's role as a global resource for raw materials, both in the way the landscape was envisioned and understood, and also with respect to political economic development. One has to remember how large Brazil is, not just in actual space, but also in terms of biodiversity. The country is generally divided into six different biomes, all of which have significant agricultural, ranching, and/or resource extraction potential (see Figure 8.1). For the Portuguese, the territory and its resources appeared endless: like outer space, a never-ending frontier of expansion and possibilities (see Figure 8.2). Questions of sustainability or environmental limitations were irrelevant; the landscape and its resources seemed infinite (Dean, 1997). Rather than intensifying or making more efficient their extractive methods and modes of production, Brazil's colonizers simply expanded, drawing on more slave labor and new territory to increase economic growth. The real limit on production until the twentieth century was control over labor, not land, since the latter was so abundant.

Few efforts were made to industrialize or diversify, and the Portuguese discouraged such developments knowing it would only lead to greater autonomy and eventual independence for the colony. As many historians have noted, Brazil's expansive and resource-rich environment – coupled with slave labor – hindered industrial and technological innovation (e.g., Fausto, 1999). Brazil's

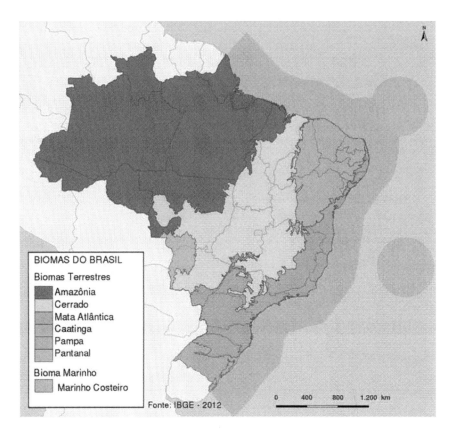

Figure 8.1 Map showing Brazil's six different biome regions.

Source: High source, Wikimedia commons: https://commons.wikimedia.org/wiki/File:Biomas_do_
Brasil.svg

comparative advantage was its landscape and abundance of natural resources, a narrative that has by no means disappeared today. Rather than national heroes, of whom Brazil has almost none, the natural environment exists as a key feature of national pride (e.g., Chaui, 2000). On the money are pictures of exotic animals rather than famous Brazilians, and the country's economic potential and future prospects continue to gravitate around abundant natural resources. Even the colors on the flag reflect this historical legacy. They were chosen during imperial times to honor the houses of Braganza (green) and Habsburg (yellow), yet today they are associated with Brazil's natural resources. The green is for the forests and the yellow for the gold, both depleted nowadays due to overexploitation.

Political economists have long debated the "curse" of Brazil's natural resources, and the ways environmental abundance may, in fact, impede economic development and industrialization (Furtado, 1959). Not to be overlooked

Figure 8.2 Painting by Frans Post showing Brazil's colonial landscape (c. 1649). Note how the natural environment is depicted as a bountiful and never-ending horizon.

Source: *Livre La Peinture romantique*, de Norbert Wolf, Taschen, 1999 (Wikimedia commons) – https://commons.wikimedia.org/wiki/File:Frans_Post_-_Paysage_brésilien.jpg

here are ongoing environmental issues, which, like current modes of economic production, are rooted in Brazil's colonial history and position within the global economy. This leads to the second of the two processes noted above, and again highlights ongoing legacies of Brazil's colonial history in contemporary environmental governance. As noted by Tiago Freitas and Augusto Mozine (2015), Brazil's inability (or perhaps unwillingness) to enforce contemporary environmental regulation stems in part from Portugal's subordinate relationship to Great Britain during colonial times. Though Portugal was extracting tremendous wealth from Brazil and its other colonies, it was also heavily in debt to Britain across several centuries, mostly for military protection. As such, the British held diplomatic sway over Portugal, influencing not only colonial trade and investment, but also international law and regulation. This boiled to head most famously in the early 1800s as Britain sought to ban the Atlantic slave trade, putting pressure on Portugal and, later, Brazil when it became independent. Officially, the Portuguese and Brazilians agreed to ban the slave trade, but in practice neither country enacted the laws.

No one knows for sure when the expression *para inglês ver* (meaning "for the English to see") first came about, but today it is often attributed to Portuguese and Brazilian noncompliance with British abolition efforts. Though agreements were signed and ratified, and, on paper and in political discourse, Portugal and Brazil claimed to enforce the regulations, in practice neither one followed the laws. For example, Brazil signed a treaty promising to end the slave trade in 1826, but then continued to import large numbers of slaves until the 1850s. The saying *para inglês ver* has since become a metaphor more generally in lusophone countries for laws that exist for the sake of appearances: a façade, constructed to please outsiders but not usually observed or upheld. For Freitas and Mozine, *para inglês ver* is today much more than just a metaphor,

> as it is both deeply embedded in the sensibilities of Portuguese language and culture (and specifically reflects a shared and subaltern way of dealing with external influences) and a useful analytical framework for investigation of human-environmental relations in lusophone countries.
>
> (2015, pp. 614–615)

More simply, the *para inglês ver* legacy continues to manifest in Brazilian environmental legislation – where laws are created for outward appearances and to make international actors happy – but on the ground, in Brazil, these regulations are rarely followed. Note Freitas and Mozine (2015), such contradictions have a long history in Portuguese-speaking countries, and are crucial for understanding how and why it is difficult to enforce environmental laws in Brazil.

From the time it was first inhabited, and particularly with the arrival of Europeans, Brazil's natural environment was shaped by processes of globalization and economic production. The colonial period brought tremendous change, turning the land and its people into objects for exploitation. Brazil became known as a base for raw materials, a reputation it continues to hold and project outwardly today. This history is important for understanding how the Brazilian landscape came to be imagined as an infinite frontier for natural resources (an imaginary that has not gone away today), and also why current efforts to enforce environmental regulation face an uphill battle. Important to remember is that Brazil, since it first became 'Brazil' in the sixteenth century, has always been connected to global relationships of political economic development and international engagement. Recognizing these connections, and seeing how they manifest in contemporary processes of environmental legislation and management, is crucial for making sense of present day contexts. Added to this is Brazil's legacy of slavery and socio-economic inequality, issues that are further explored in the next section as this chapter moves into the twentieth century.

'Valuing' the landscape

On 13 May, 1888, Brazil became the last country in the Western world to abolish slavery. Though slavery had been slowly fading in Brazil prior to then, with full abolition came a host of political, social, and economic changes. The final decade of the nineteenth century was a tumultuous one in Brazil's history. 1889 saw the overthrow of the monarchy and exile of Brazil's last emperor, Dom Pedro II. In that same year, the Old Republic replaced the Empire, and only a few years later, in 1897, the Canudos War came to an end, still today Brazil's bloodiest civil conflict. While in theory Brazil was fully united at the start of the twentieth century, with laws guaranteeing basic freedoms for everyone, in actuality the country had changed little since colonial times. It was still very decentralized politically, ruled by an oligarchy, and, for non-white Brazilians in particular, life was precarious and profoundly unequal.

The writer and engineer, Euclides da Cunha, is, of course, best known for his book *Os Sertões*, an epic account of the Canudos War in Northeast Brazil. Yet, according to political ecologist Susanna Hecht (2013), Da Cunha's most important contribution to Brazil may have been his diplomatic collaboration in Amazonia in 1904 with the Baron of Rio Branco, then Brazil's foreign minister. Notes Hecht, Da Cunha's written accounts of Brazil's northern frontier played a pivotal role in securing much of the Amazon region for Brazil, articulating national identity through the landscape and its people. Like all constructions of national identity, the logic was circular: the landscape was inherently Brazilian because Brazilians occupied it, and Brazilians occupied the landscape because it was inherently Brazilian. Such ideas resonated with environmentally determinist theories at the time (not to be overlooked here should be the influence of Positivism in Brazil), and even before samba, football, and feijoada, Brazil's natural landscape came to represent and evoke national identity.

Such ideas were further reified by Gilberto Freyre (1933), who by (unevenly) combining indigenous influences with Portuguese and African ones to construct Brazil's sociological DNA, conjured an almost transcendental connection between the population and the landscape. By 1937, when the Estado Novo was established, the natural environment had already become a key pillar of Brazil's "imagined community" (Anderson, 1983). This helped to further solidify the political rule of Getúlio Vargas, who, between 1930 and 1945, would do more to cultivate and essentialize Brazilian national identity than anyone before or since (Levine, 1998).

Though Brazil's landscape may have been crucial to the formation of national identity, by the mid-twentieth century, conceptions of the natural environment had, in fact, changed very little since colonial times. Like elsewhere in the Americas, the environment was a bountiful resource: perhaps not limitless as it had been for the colonizers, but still fruitful in its abundance. In literature, art, music, and so on, Brazil's environment was depicted along modernist lines as a generous provider (Philippou, 2005). No different from other countries, 'Nature' was imagined as something separate from humans (e.g., as an unadulterated space free from human influence), and the natural environment became a 'thing,' something conceivable, discrete, manageable, and understood by science. Brazil's growing capitalist economy required everything be made commensurable, from shelter and education to labor and natural resources. By the mid-twentieth century, the environment had become a commodity like any other, easily incorporated (at least on the surface) into global commodity chains and international development. Brazil's land was one of its greatest assets, an *invaluable* resource, though perversely commodifiable and understood through economic value.

Much as in Europe and North America, Brazil's first environmental movements began to appear around this same time. Kathryn Hochstetler and Margaret Keck (2007) note that Brazil's first environmental protection groups formed in the 1950s. These were small, nongovernmental collectives organized around conserving Brazil's natural resources. In line with then-popular developmentalist agendas that stressed step-by-step capitalist growth, a key objective for these groups was to guarantee and secure prolonged economic development by properly managing the environment. It was not until the 1970s and a second wave of environmental movements that activists began to articulate their demands through preservationist discourses (i.e., environmental protection for the sake of the planet, not just the economy), linking up with environmentalist groups in North America and Europe. Nevertheless, it should be noted that, in contrast to mainstream perceptions of environmental protection in Latin America, Brazil's history of environmental activism extends just as far back as countries in the Global North (Hochstetler and Keck, 2007).

Brazil's second wave of environmental protection groups launched around the same time as many other social movements were forming in Brazil: at the height of the repressive military dictatorship in the 1970s. According to Hochstetler and Keck (2007) these groups tended to organize around specific, localized issues of environmental degradation, championing such causes as water pollution, landfill problems, toxic seepage, exotic species protection, deforestation, and so on. This makes sense because, while many international observers believe that protecting the Amazon rain forest is Brazil's most important environmental challenge, for most Brazilians (i.e., those living in cities far to the south of the Amazon) the most important environmental problems they face are the degradation of the air, soil, and water where they live. Activists in the 1970s were influenced by writers like Rachel Carson, author of *Silent Spring*, and connected in many instances with environmental movements in North America. Like other Brazilian activist groups at the time, they were heavily suppressed by the dictatorship, and military leaders highlighted their connections with North American partners to link environmental activism with foreign influence and neocolonialism. Notwithstanding serious cases of environmental degradation they sought to address, along with centuries-old perceptions of 'limitless' environmental resources, environmentalists found themselves on the losing end of general public perceptions in Brazil.

At the same time that Brazilian environmentalists were fighting for political space, all over the country tens of millions of people were waging an everyday battle for survival. Though many outside of Brazil tend to associate poverty with urban areas – which makes sense, given high levels of informal housing (e.g., favelas) and homelessness in cities – impoverishment has long been much more severe in Brazil's rural areas. Reasons for this stem primarily from two inter-connected issues: (1) land ownership in Brazil is massively unequal, where, at the start of the twenty-first century, 45% of agricultural land was owned by only 1% of the population (Lerrer, 2003, p. 2), and (2) the salaries and living conditions for peasants (i.e., *camponeses*) and rural workers have improved little since the nineteenth century, where even today many people still work as sharecroppers or in similar forms of tenant farming (Garmany, 2008). There have been modest advancements over the past few decades thanks to social movements such as the MST (The Landless Rural Workers' Movement) and social welfare programs like *Bolsa Família*, but even now, well into the twenty-first century, Brazil's poverty remains most severe in rural areas.[1] Back in the 1970s, before Brazil's return to democracy and the legalization of social movements – *and* recent social welfare programs that have helped significantly to reduce hunger – rural Brazil looked much as it had in the nineteenth century. Millions of people lacked running water, electricity, education, or basic health-care, and many of them lived on the brink of starvation. The establishment of FUNRURAL provided modest relief – it was a social program launched by the federal government in 1971, giving rural workers a pension equivalent to the minimum wage, as well as medical care and legal assistance through the rural trade unions (Pereira, 1997) – yet still did little to change Brazil's unequal structure of land ownership.

Why is this context important for understanding contemporary environmental issues? As Hecht (2004) and several other researchers argue, the relationship between poverty and natural resource overexploitation is hugely important for those looking to address environmental degradation. Quite simply, and by way of an example, how can one realistically expect poor people not to practice deforestation if they have no other income opportunities; if either they cut down trees or their families will go hungry? Additionally, though poor people sometimes cause environmental degradation, the effects often pale in comparison to the damage of mining, logging, and agribusiness firms, some of which are multi-national. These were the issues facing Brazilian environmentalists in the 1970s, and, to be fair, these problems still persist. Environmental degradation in countries such as Brazil is deeply intertwined with socioeconomic inequality and poverty. One cannot hope to effectively protect the environment and natural resources without also addressing a host of political economic issues and the social welfare of poor populations.

Brazil's second wave of environmental activists certainly had their work cut out for them. They were up against nationalist discourses depicting the landscape and Brazil's natural resources as never ending; they faced a repressive military dictator-ship hostile towards any progressive social movement; most significantly, they confronted one of the world's most unequal societies. Impressively, however, significant change was to come over the next decade, and, with Brazil's return to democracy in 1985, environmentalists soon formed what seemed politically impossible only a few years earlier: Brazil's Green Party, officially established in 1986 (Hochstetler and Keck, 2007). Even more significant was the evolution of environmental activism in Brazil, which, in the 1980s, entered its third wave by addressing questions of poverty and socio-economic inequality. Called "socio-environmentalism," this new iteration of environmental activism called attention to the links between environmental degradation and social inequality, and, in so doing, made broader and more effective connections across Brazil and Latin America, even critiquing and pushing forward environmental debates in Europe and North America (Diegues, 2001). The movement even found an unlikely hero from the far-off state of Acre in northern Brazil: a caboclo rubber tapper named Chico Mendes.[2]

Socio-environmentalism, democracy, and twenty-first century legislation

Before the rise of Brazil's third wave of environmental protection groups in the 1980s, the solutions to environmental degradation seemed simple enough to activists: people just needed to stop polluting. Or killing endangered species. Or cutting down too many trees. The problem, of course, was that these solutions were impossible as well as hopelessly naïve. Environmentalists' hearts may have been in the right place, but they failed to recognize the broader social and political economic context of their fight. International groups such as Greenpeace leant their support to environmentalist efforts in countries such as Brazil, and, in many cases, their good intentions backfired. They could not just draw on experience from the Global North to fix problems in the Global South. For example, today in the USA it may be easy to imagine a national park as a 'natural' space free from human habitation. But in the Amazon, these same spaces are home to thousands of people. This, in fact, is where people fled centuries beforehand to escape European colonizers. Expecting already margin-alized people to cease harvesting their local resources is both unfair and unrealistic. How else are they to make a living? By addressing these realities, and showing also how they connect to issues of environmental sustainability, Brazilian activists provided a critical contribution to global environmental protection efforts beginning in the 1980s.

Chico Mendes never set out to be an environmental activist, and he almost certainly never imagined that one day he would be celebrated internationally for his efforts. He began collaborating with rural workers' unions in the 1970s, and, in 1980, he helped to establish a base for the Workers' Party (PT) in his home state of Acre. His motivation was to protect the livelihoods of fellow rubber tappers (*seringueiros*) in the Amazon region who were being marginalized by large-scale development projects and the expansion of agribusiness. The rubber tappers made their living by harvesting the latex from rubber trees (*Hevea brasiliensis*), and deforestation, caused primarily by cattle ranching, threatened to do away with their means of production. Mendes joined with other rubber tappers and rural workers in northwestern Brazil to help protect their own livelihoods, and, in so doing, began to team with diverse interest groups also working to protect the rainforest (Hecht and Cockburn, 1990). Perhaps more effectively than any social movement before or since, Mendes helped to articulate the necessary links between environmental conservation, sustainable economic practice, and social justice.

"Socio-environmentalism" is the term most often used to describe this third wave of Brazilian environmental activism, emerging in large part from the efforts of Mendes and other activists in the Amazon during the 1980s. The term is a broad one, encompassing multiple ideas related to socio-economic inequality and environmental degradation. According to Hochstetler and Keck, "it meant a belief that in the realm of development favoring the poor and protecting the environment were mutually reinforcing goals" (2007, p. 109). That socio-environmentalism took root in Brazil during this time was by no means coincidental, as several interrelated factors combined to change the course of environmental activism (Hochstetler and Keck, 2007). One was the end of the military dictatorship in 1985 and subsequent rise of social movements, particularly from the left. These social movements arose both out of political opportunity (i.e., they had been heavily regulated under the military dictatorship) as well as in response to societal need. The newly restored democratic government was ill prepared to handle all of Brazil's social dilemmas, and activists joined together to address socio-economic problems, environmental conservation, and a host of other concerns. A second contributing factor was the

Figure 8.3 Photo of Chico Mendes and his partner Ilzamar Mendes at their home in Xapuri, Acre.

Source: Miranda Smith, Miranda Productions, Inc., Wikimedia commons: https://en.wikipedia.org/wiki/Chico_Mendes#/media/File:Chico_%26_Ilsamar_Mendes_1988.png

assassination of Chico Mendes in 1988. He was shot by ranchers on his own doorstep. His murder was the 19th among rural activists that year alone in Brazil (Hall, 1997). A breaking point had been reached – perhaps Mendes was too well liked, both in Brazil and abroad – and diverse interest groups began banding together as never before (Hecht and Cockburn, 1990).

A third reason for why socio-environmentalism emerged in Brazil during this time relates to the UN Earth Summit in Rio de Janeiro in 1992 (Hochstetler and Keck, 2007). Even more important than the conference itself were preparations made by activists in the years leading up to it. Chico Mendes' murder galvanized groups in the Amazon, helping to unite rubber tappers, indigenous communities, and other forest residents who had formerly been antagonistic towards one another. Socio-environmentalist discourses provided an umbrella framework of social and environmental justice that helped connect many of these groups. One such example was the idea of an extractive reserve: a sustainable-use protected area owned and managed by the state, yet guaranteeing natural resource use rights to traditional inhabitants. Mendes himself had helped to conceptualize and lobby for the establishment of extractive reserves in Brazil, seeing them as a pragmatic way to pursue environmental protection without further marginalizing local communities whose livelihoods depended on these environments (Wright and Wolford, 2003). Today, there are dozens of extractive reserves in Brazil – along with similarly conceptualized 'indigenous reserves' for native Brazilian groups (most of which, like extractive reserves, lie in the North) – and, while not without controversy, they represent a key Brazilian policy initiative to help mitigate environmental degradation and social injustice.

In addition to bringing together environmental activists in Brazil, the 1992 Earth Summit in Rio also helped open Brazil to international environmental actors (Hochstetler and Keck, 2007). Beyond the UN, the World Bank, and foreign diplomats, international nongovernmental organizations (INGOs) such as Greenpeace began to establish a stronger presence there. Unlike diverse activist groups in Brazil, however, INGOs such as Greenpeace have historically struggled to build affinities with Brazilian environmentalists. Reasons for this are complex, and stem, on the one hand, from Brazilian (and Latin American) sensitivities to neocolonialism and questions of national sovereignty. Understandably, like most countries, they dislike foreigners telling them how they should manage their land and natural resources. And on the other hand, and more crucially, INGOs such as Greenpeace often failed to understand local socio-economic and cultural contexts in Brazil. Policy initiatives such as extractive reserves, along with the pro-poor, sometimes anti-capitalist ethos of socio-environmentalism rubbed awkwardly with INGOs accustomed to doing business in the Global North (e.g., they were concerned with environmental preservation, not poverty). The failure of international actors to understand the context of Brazilian environmental issues was especially problematic in the 1980s and 1990s, and stunted multilateral environmental protection efforts. Brazil developed a reputation, perhaps unfairly, for a lack of will to protect the environment, due in part to the resistance confronted by INGOs.

As the 1990s wore on, Brazil's environmental movements began to lose steam, but not without achieving several significant victories. Important legislation and policy measures had been achieved (for example, the creation of extractive reserves); environmental regulations and government agencies had been established; activists had created nationwide and international links; and efforts to protect the environment were producing results (e.g., rates of deforestation began to decrease). As noted by Hochstetler and Keck (2007), to understand the history, accomplishments, and challenges of environmental activism in Brazil, it is important to consider three key factors: the first relates to Brazil's political history, and, in particular, the shift from dictatorship to democracy in the 1980s. As described already in this chapter, this period saw the rise of numerous social movements and increased political activism, including environmental protection groups. The second factor is Brazil's federalist structure, with complicated linkages between individual states and the federal government. Political initiative for issues such as environmental protection can be significantly affected by bureaucratic protocol in Brazil, and trying to coordinate agencies and individuals at the municipal, state, and federal levels has consistently proven difficult for activists and policymakers alike.

The third key issue is a mixture between formal and informal institutions and practices in Brazil (Hochstetler and Keck, 2007). This can take many forms, and is perhaps best exemplified by mixtures of formal and informal economies in Brazil, or even between formal and informal (e.g., extralegal) governance. There are connections here with *para inglês ver*, as well as Brazilian *jeitinho* (e.g., creative ways for circumventing official protocol – see, for example, DaMatta, 1984). Related here are laws that fail to 'catch on' or take effect, considered in the next section. While often cast in a negative light – for example, attributing lax environmental governance to the influence of informality – such activities do not always have negative consequences. Brazil's history of informality is by no means to blame for widespread environmental destruction, and, in some cases, it can even help provide pragmatic, 'unofficial' solutions to bureaucratic headaches (Souza, 2017). By highlighting these three issues, Hochstetler and Keck (2007) help not only to unravel Brazil's history of environmental activism; they also shed crucial light on current and future concerns over environmental legislation. Nevertheless, to see what drives *and* limits Brazil's environmental governance and protection policies in the twenty-first century, one must consider three additional factors: Brazil's international and geopolitical ambitions; the realities of enforcing environmental legislation and the role of Brazil's Public Ministry; and, perhaps most importantly, the dominance of agribusiness in Brazil. These issues are explored in the final section of this chapter.

Brazil: environment of the future?

In the early part of the twenty-first century, something amazing began to happen in Brazil: rates of deforestation in the Amazon not only began to decrease; they dropped enormously in just a few years. Where, in the 1990s, many feared that rainforest destruction posed a serious threat to global environmental sustainability, all of a sudden, beginning around 2004, the problem seemed to be disappearing. Stranger still was that no one could explain exactly *what* was causing this change. So dramatic was the turnaround it could not be attributed to any single political initiative, economic shift, or change in environmental practice. Almost like magic, rates of deforestation began to reverse just one decade into the twenty-first century.

As Hecht (2011) explains, this change was facilitated by a wide range of political–ecological factors combining at certain times and in specific places. Involved here were issues of globalization and political decentralization in Brazil, providing social movements and civil society a stronger voice in public policy debates. Related to this were changing (or, more often, strengthened) environmental institutions in Brazil, along with social policies introduced by the Workers' Party during the first decade of the twenty-first century that helped reduce extreme poverty and promote sustainable land use practices (Castro, 2014). New monitoring and compliance mechanisms were also put in place, working alongside international environmental protection and payment schemes like REDD (reduced emissions from deforestation and forest degradation). Also important were changing peasant economies and increased levels of urbanization in the Amazon, leading to fewer clear cutting activities and smaller ecological footprints for local populations. Though alterations to Brazil's Forest Code (i.e., federal environmental protection legislation) in 2012 worked to reverse this trend slightly, the overall change was astonishing. In less than a decade, Brazil's deforestation crisis had been turned around. The catch, however, is that this change is by no means permanent, particularly when considering all the interrelated political ecological factors (Hecht, 2011).

To further understand these sorts of processes, it is important to recognize the changing roles of Brazilian political institutions in environmental management. For example, an increasingly significant actor in Brazilian politics – and, by extension, environmental legislation – is the Brazilian Public Ministry (*Ministério Público*), sometimes referred to in English as the Public Prosecutor's Office. The Public Ministry is made up of independent public prosecutors at both federal and state levels, and its purpose is to ensure that laws and constitutional measures are upheld. In a sense, the Public Ministry functions like a fourth branch of government, investigating both state and non-state actors when prosecutors suspect a violation of justice. Notes Lesley McAllister (2008), in recent years the Public Ministry has played a growing role in enforcing environmental law, even holding federal agencies such as the Brazilian Institute of Environmental and Renewable Nature Resources (*IBAMA*) to account for not fulfilling its responsibilities to protect Brazil's environment. Though Brazil historically is known as a weak enforcer of what are actually quite strong environmental laws, Public Ministry prosecutors have helped turn this around, boosting environmental regulation procedures and strengthening Brazilian environmental protection agencies.

Not to be overlooked is also the Brazilian Ministry of the Environment (*O Ministério do Meio Ambiente*). Officially established in 1985, it underwent frequent institutional change during the first decade of its existence. This constant reshuffling, note Hochstetler and Keck (2007), undermined many of the ministry's environmental protection goals. It was not until the 1990s, when it was promoted to cabinet level status, that many of its roles and institutional functions were more firmly solidified. With this stabilization came more effective legislation from the ministry, and, in 2003, it came under the direction of its to-date most famous minister, Marina Silva. Silva had already served as a federal senator for the state of Acre since 1994, and was a rising political star when she took control of the ministry. Her leadership was marked by several outspoken clashes with other politicians and business leaders (particularly from the agribusiness sector), and she famously resigned her post in 2008 when she felt her own political party (the PT) was more attuned to multinational interests than protecting Brazil's environment. In 2009, she joined the Green Party, ran for president in 2010, and finished an impressive third place with nearly 20% of the overall vote. She continues to remain a key political figure today, showing the growing importance of environmental issues to many Brazilian voters.

Connected to these domestic changes are also Brazil's larger geopolitical ambitions. Thus far in the twenty-first century, Brazil has shown a strong desire to take a more pronounced role in international diplomacy, even lobbying for permanent membership with the United Nations Security Council. Unlike other international heavyweights, however, Brazil does not have nuclear weapons, nor is it situated in a region of great international importance (viz., the Middle East). To compensate for this, Brazil increasingly has tried to build international credibility through other means, including participation with international peacekeeping efforts, hosting global mega-events such as the Olympics and the World Cup, and becoming a key actor in global climate change negotiations and carbon emissions reduction efforts (Hochstetler and Viola, 2012). A reputation for sustainable and pragmatic environmental stewardship is something Brazil's Ministry of Foreign Affairs (*Itamaraty*) is working to establish as part of the country's international image, anticipating that such a reputation will boost Brazil's clout in global decision-making processes. Often referred to as "soft power" – establishing international influence through cultural, political, and diplomatic measures rather than through force, coercion, or economic incentives (Nye, 2004) – Brazil's changing environmental management strategies represent not only a means to regulate domestic natural resources, they also reflect broader efforts to build international clout and significance.

Alongside these positive developments, however, Brazil continues to face several hurdles with respect to environmental protection and legislation in the twenty-first century. One important factor relates to Brazil's tradition for what might be called the 'inconsistent institution' of legal measures. More simply, not all laws in Brazil are actually put into practice. Strange as it may sound to someone unfamiliar with Brazil, the country has a long history of simply not following its own laws, a peculiarity often expressed in common vernacular as *uma lei que não pega* ("a law that does not catch on" – see, for example, Panizza and Brito, 1998). Much like *para inglês ver* (Mozine and Freitas, 2015), laws that do not catch on reflect historical and cultural legacies of colonialism and federalist governance, policies established for the sake of appearances both domestically and internationally, and, perhaps most importantly, weak institutions unable to enforce the law on more powerful private and political actors. Added to this is a history for law making which often incorporates new laws without revising or rescinding old ones, meaning not only is Brazilian law complicated and byzantine; many laws exist that appear to contradict one another (Holston, 2008). Such legacies greatly complicate environmental management legislation, meaning that, despite impressive headway made by institutions like Brazil's Public Ministry in recent years, environmentalists still face challenges when it comes to putting environmental protection laws into practice.

Finally, no discussion of Brazil's environmental dilemmas would be complete without considering the role of international and domestic capital, and, in particular, the influence of Brazil's agribusiness sector (see, for example, Ioris, 2017). Brazil is already one of the world's largest agricultural producers, with plans to significantly increase outputs and profits in coming decades. As such, the agribusiness industry is one of Brazil's most powerful lobby factions today, wielding heavy influence in matters of domestic policy and environmental legislation. This group is made up largely of land-owning elites involved with ranching and cash-crop farming, yet it also includes extended networks of businesses and firms connected to agricultural goods and services. Very bluntly, these are the people Chico Mendes was fighting against – at least in the Amazon region – and he paid for it with his life (Hecht and Cockburn, 1990). His murder is one among hundreds over the past few decades, showing how dangerous life is for Brazilian environmental activists still today (Hochstetler and Keck, 2007). Brazil's agribusiness sector is also tightly intertwined with international market demands, making it impossible to unpack Brazil's contemporary environmental dilemmas without accounting for processes of globalization and economic development. One cannot simply lay blame on transnational corporations like Monsanto, *or* on wealthy landed elites in Brazil. These interest groups are deeply interconnected, and they often represent powerful foes to environmentalists working to conserve land and natural resources (in Brazil as well as elsewhere).

Returning to where this chapter began, with the arrival of the Portuguese in 1500, Brazil's environmental issues remain steeped in questions of international development, trade, politics, and globalization. It is, of course, impossible to accurately predict Brazil's environmental future, but important features are likely to include increased multilateral approaches to issues of climate change and environmental governance (Cole and Liverman, 2011), along with continued expansion in the areas of mining, agriculture, and energy (see Figure 8.4). With a continuing wealth of natural resources, and, in particular, vast supplies of water and renewable energy resources, Brazil's energy production potential is

Figure 8.4 Environmental activists protest the construction of Belo Monte hydro-electrical dam in Pará. The signs read, from left to right, "Belo Monte de merda" ("Beautiful Pile of shit"), and "O Brasil precisa de energia, não de Belo Monte" ("Brazil needs energy, not Belo Monte").

Source: Roosewelt Pinheiro/Agência Brasil, Wikimedia commons: https://commons.wikimedia.org/wiki/File:Greenpeacebelomonte3.jpg

almost certain to draw increased international attention in coming years. Brazil is also likely to remain an important regional actor for decades to come, perhaps leading (or impeding) environmental protection efforts throughout Latin America. South–South cooperation has also been a priority for Brazilian international engagement in the twenty-first century (Hochstetler, 2013), and Brazil may likely continue to partner with countries in Africa and Asia to lobby internationally over issues of environmental conservation and sustainability. That Brazil appears keen to pursue international cooperation and diplomacy is probably a good sign, as today's environmental issues, due to their complexity and vast interconnectedness, increasingly require multi-partner engagement and global cooperation.

This chapter has sought to make better sense of the contradictions that characterize Brazil's relationship with its natural environment. For example, given links between environmental features, economic development, and understandings of national identity in Brazil, why do so many natural resources, landscapes, plant and animal life, and even human populations confront serious threats of environmental degradation? To provide insight to these questions, this chapter has explored Brazil's political ecological past, arguing that in order to understand present-day environmental contexts and paradoxes, one needs to consider complex histories of inequality and globalization. Brazil's legacies of colonialism, slavery, resource use and land ownership, capitalist development, democracy and federalism, and international engagement are crucial to debates of environmental protection and sustainability. Social movements have been shaped by these factors over time, and their successes and limitations reflect Brazil's social, political, economic, racial, gender, and cultural inequalities. Added to this is Brazil's complex legal structure, with mixtures of formal and informal practice, as well as historically weak institutions incapable of enforcing regulations over such vast and diverse landscapes. Yet, things are also changing in Brazil, and, despite the very real dangers still faced by environmental activists from sectors such as agribusiness, strengthening institutions like the Public Ministry and international collaborative efforts to address problems like climate change provide hope that Brazil's environmental future will be less destructive than its environmental past. Contradictions are certain to persist, just as they do in all countries, but it does not mean important headway cannot be made to address environmental degradation and inequality.

Notes

1 Though, as Antonio Ioris notes (2015), this can depend upon access to natural resources. For example, rural residents with good access to rich natural resources are less likely to suffer extreme poverty than rural residents who lack such access.
2 In Brazil, *caboclo* generally refers to someone of indigenous Brazilian and European ancestry.

Suggested English readings

Dean, W. (1997). *With broadax and firebrand: The destruction of the Brazilian Atlantic Forest.* Berkeley: University of California Press.

Hall, A.L. (1989). *Developing Amazonia: Deforestation and social conflict in Brazil's Carajás Programme.* Manchester: Manchester University Press.

Hecht, S.B. (2011). From eco-catastrophe to zero deforestation? Interdisciplinarities, politics, environmentalisms and reduced clearing in Amazonia. *Environmental Conservation* 39(1), 4–19.

Hecht, S., and Cockburn, A. (1990). *The fate of the forest: Developers, destroyers and defenders of the Amazon.* New York: Penguin.

Hemming, J. (1987). *Amazon frontier: The defeat of the Brazilian Indians.* London: Macmillan.

Hochstetler, K., and Keck, M.E. (2007). *Greening Brazil: Environmental activism in state and society.* Durham, NC: Duke University Press.

Mendes, C. (with Tony Gross). (1989). *Fight for the forest: Chico Mendes in his own words.* London: Latin American Bureau.

References

Anderson, B. (1983). *Imagined communities: Reflections on the origin and spread of nationalism.* London: Verso.

Barman, R.J. (1988). *Brazil: The forging of a nation.* Stanford: Stanford University Press.

Castro, F. de. (2014). Environmental policies in the Lula era: Accomplishments and contradictions. In F. de Castro et al. (eds), *Brazil under the Workers' Party: Continuity and change from Lula to Dilma.* Basingstoke, UK: Palgrave Macmillan, pp. 229–255.

Chaui, M. (2000). *Brasil: Mito fundador e sociedade autoritária.* São Paulo: Fundação Perseu Abramo.

Cole, J. C. and Liverman, D.M. (2011). Brazil's clean development mechanism governance in the context of Brazil's historical environment–development discourses. *Carbon Management*, 2(2), 145–160.

DaMatta, R. (1984). *O que faz o Brasil, Brasil?* Rio de Janeiro: Rocco.

Dean, W. (1997). *With broadax and firebrand: The destruction of the Brazilian Atlantic Forest.* Berkeley: University of California Press.

Denevan, W. (1992). The pristine myth: The landscape of the Americas in 1492. *Annals of the Association of American Geographers*, 82(3), 369–385.

Diegues, A.C. (2001). *O mito moderno da natureza intocada.* São Paulo: HUCITEC.

Fausto, B. (1999). *A concise history of Brazil.* Cambridge: Cambridge University Press.

Freitas, T.A.M., and Mozine, A.C.S. (2015). Towards a lusophone political ecology: Assessing "para inglês ver" environments. In: R. Bryant, (ed.), *International handbook of political ecology.* London: Edward Elgar, pp. 604–618.

Freyre, G. (1933). *Casa-Grande & senzala: Formação da Família Brasileira sob a regime da economia patriarchal.* Rio de Janeiro: Global Editora.

Furtado, C. (1959). *Formação econômica do Brasil.* Rio de Janeiro: Fundo de Cultura.

Garmany, J. (2008). The spaces of social movements: O Movimento dos Trabalhadores Rurais Sem Terra from a socio-spatial perspective. *Space and Polity*, 12(3), 311–328.

Goldstein, D. (2003). *Laughter out of place: Race, class, violence, and sexuality in a Rio shantytown.* Berkeley: University of California Press.

Hall, A. (1997). *Sustaining Amazonia: Grassroots action for productive conservation.* Manchester: Manchester University Press.

Hecht, S.B. (2004). Invisible forests. In: D. Peet and M. Watts (eds), *Liberation ecologies: Environment, development, and social movements.* London: Routledge, pp. 64–103.

Hecht, S.B. (2011). From eco-catastrophe to zero deforestation? Interdisciplinarities, politics, environmentalisms and reduced clearing in Amazonia. *Environmental Conservation*, 39(1), 4–19.

Hecht, S.B. (2013). *The scramble for the Amazon and the "Lost Paradise" of Euclides da Cunha.* Chicago: University of Chicago Press.

Hecht, S.B., and Cockburn, A. (1990). *The fate of the forest: Developers, destroyers and defenders of the Amazon.* New York: Penguin.

Hemming, J. (1987). *Amazon frontier: The defeat of the Brazilian Indians.* London: Macmillan.

Hochstetler, K. (2013). South–South trade and the environment: A Brazilian case study. *Global Environmental Politics*, 13(1), 30–48.

Hochstetler, K., and Keck, M.E. (2007). *Greening Brazil: Environmental activism in state and society.* Durham, NC: Duke University Press.

Hochstetler, K., and Viola, E. (2012). Brazil and the politics of climate change: Beyond the global commons. *Environmental Politics*, 21(5), 753–771.

Holston, J. (2008). *Insurgent citizenship: Disjunctions of democracy and modernity in Brazil.* Princeton: Princeton University Press.

Ioris, A.A.R. (2015). The production of poverty and the poverty of production in the Amazon: Reflections from those at the sharp end of development. *Capitalism Nature Socialism*, 26(4), 176–192.

Ioris, A.A.R. (2017). *Agribusiness and the neoliberal food system in Brazil: Frontiers and fissures of agro-neoliberalism*. London: Routledge.

Lerrer, D. (2003). *Reforma agrária: Os caminhos do impasse*. São Paulo: Editora Garçoni.

Levine, R.M. (1998). *Father of the poor? Vargas and his era*. Cambridge: Cambridge University Press.

Mann, C.C. (2008). Ancient earthmovers of the Amazon. *Science*, 321(5893), 1148–1152.

McAllister, L. (2008). *Making law matter: Environmental protection and legal institutions in Brazil*. Stanford: Stanford University Press.

Monteiro, J.M. (1994). *Negros da terra: Índios e bandeirantes nas origens de São Paulo*. São Paulo: Companhia das Letras.

Nye, J.S. 2004). *Soft power: The means to success in world politics*. New York: Public Affairs.

Panizza, F., and Brito, A.B. de. (1998). The politics of human rights in democratic Brazil: "A lei não pega". *Democratization*, 5(4), 20–51.

Pereira, A.W. (1997). *The end of the Peasantry: The emergence of the rural labor movement in northeast Brazil, 1961–1988*. Pittsburgh: University of Pittsburgh Press.

Philippou, S. (2005). Modernism and national identity in Brazil, or how to brew a Brazilian stew. *National Identities*, 7(3), 245–264.

Rhoter, L. (2012). *Brazil on the rise: The story of a country transformed*. Basingstoke, UK: Palgrave Macmillan.

Ribeiro, D. (2000). *The Brazilian people: The formation and meaning of Brazil*. Gainesville: University Press of Florida.

Souza, G.I. (2017). People, parks, and public policies in the 21st century: Human security and the political ecologies of the Brazilian Amazon. Reflections from the mosaic of protected areas of the lower River Negro, Amazonas. PhD dissertation. King's College London.

Skidmore, T.E. (2010). *Brazil: Five centuries of change*. 2nd ed. Oxford: Oxford University Press.

Wright, A.L., and Wolford, W. (2003). *To inherit the earth: The Landless Movement and the struggle for a new Brazil*. Oakland: Food First Books.

9 Culture and spirituality

Introduction

Along with soccer, beaches, and tremendous ecological diversity, Brazil is internationally renowned for its rich cultural attributes. Even those who struggle to identify Brazil on a map have usually at least heard tell of Rio de Janeiro's annual Carnival celebration. Reasons for this are largely twofold, and on the one hand include Brazil's astounding mixture of different cultural traditions. The diversity of indigenous, African, European, and Asian heritages in Brazil is truly remarkable. On the other hand, as mentioned in Chapter 2, is also the concerted effort by the Brazilian state to emphasize this diversity for reasons of national pride and unity. Granted, Brazil's cultural mix is, no doubt, special and unique, but a major reason for *why* this diversity is well known and celebrated has to do with specific nation building efforts (Philippou, 2005). That cultural and ethnic diversity is a key feature of Brazil's international reputation is not accidental: for nearly a century this has been a major trope of Brazilian national identity.

So, what are the roots of this cultural milieu, why is it significant today, and what does it mean for contemporary relationships and social struggle? Related to this, how is Brazil shifting culturally, and what are the roles of religious and spiritual change in these processes? As many researchers observe, Brazil has undergone significant religious transformation in recent years, with growing numbers of evangelical converts now shaping political and social debates (Schmidt and Engler, 2016). Where Brazil was overwhelmingly Catholic until the late twentieth century, today this *de facto* national spiritual identity is beginning to erode. What might this mean for Brazil's future, particularly as evangelical groups are taking more pronounced roles in national politics and social policy?

In this chapter we seek to address some of these questions, focusing particularly on academic and contemporary debates within Brazil. Like many of the topics in this book, we recognize that trying to address subjects such as contemporary Brazilian culture and spirituality in a single chapter might seem overly ambitious. As such, we focus on key contemporary cultural issues and emergent struggles, as well as addressing a host of scholarly debates useful for explaining cultural change in Brazil.

We begin by considering the origins of Brazil's cultural diversity, and the ways that different regions show distinct cultural attributes. These traits, of course, manifest themselves in different forms such as music and celebration, and we touch briefly on important differences that exist across Brazil regarding practices of cultural expression. Related to this are art forms such as literature and film, and the themes and struggles addressed by contemporary Brazilian artists. Also connected to these debates are questions of spirituality and religious change, and, in the second half of the chapter, we move on to consider Brazil's diverse spiritual mix and the role religion plays in contemporary society. Crucial here is the recent growth of evangelical faiths in Brazil, and their increasing prominence within national political and social debates. We address these issues in the penultimate section of the chapter, and question what these changing cultural practices might indicate for Brazil's future.

Origins and geographic differences

As discussed in Chapter 2, Brazil's cultural, ethnic, and regional diversity reflects, in many ways, histories of colonization and later patterns of international and internal migration. The first Brazilians, of course, were indigenous people, many of whom fled from colonial settlers and later settled in the hinterlands and the Amazon basin. Those who stayed were often killed by disease, warfare, or slavery. Perhaps for these reasons, Brazilian historical accounts make little mention of indigenous people beyond the early years of colonization (cf. Langfur, 2002). Already by the seventeenth century, indigenous populations had been so decimated by colonization that those who survived almost certainly avoided contact with European settlers. One of the few (relatively) safe havens for indigenous people in the Americas was the Amazon rainforest, as most European settlers steered clear of the region, believing it was uninhabitable. Vast numbers of people already living there were joined by those fleeing colonial intrusion elsewhere on the continent, producing a high concentration and diverse mix of indigenous groups in the heavily forested area (Hemming, 1987). This history of settlement and migration remains embodied within the region still today, as nowhere in Brazil has a higher percentage of indigenous people than the North and Central West regions connecting to the Amazon basin (IBGE, 2017).

Over the years, vast numbers of fortune seekers have sought gold, timber, rubber, and other natural resources in the Amazon, often bringing them into conflict with indigenous inhabitants. Despite these intrusions, the region remains largely unsettled, thanks in large part to ecological factors such as dense forests and swampy terrain, as well as Brazilian legislation helping to preserve large sections of forest. As of the early twenty-first century, there are even still some indigenous groups who have little or no contact with the outside world, continuing to live, for the most part, as they as they have for centuries (Bouchard, 2017).

Like many countries in the Americas, Brazil has incorporated indigenous cultures into national legacies in uneven, peculiar, and often troubling ways.

As discussed in Chapters 2 and 5, Brazilian indigeneity is important to the official narrative of national identity, but its presence is an anachronistic one, like an antiquated relic or an embodied historical presence. Culturally speaking, indigenous Brazilians are often celebrated as part of Brazil's history of miscegenation rather than acknowledged as a still present and marginalized collective of ethnic groups. Perhaps because Brazilian indigeneity is such a key and omnipresent feature of the nation's past – much like Aztecan identity in Mexico,[1] or Incan identity in Peru – there is little space for it in the cultural present. Indigenous people are more often cherished as part of Brazil's historical legacy rather than acknowledged as a living example of ongoing social injustice (cf. Bouchard, 2017; Ribeiro, 2000).

In similar fashion, so, too, are Afro-Brazilians bound within Brazil's cultural DNA. Over the past several decades, Brazil's African heritage has slowly garnered more national recognition, with increasing attention focused on the cultural contributions of African migrants (most of whom arrived in Brazil aboard slave ships). One might even say that Brazil's emphasis on Afro-Brazilian cultural influence draws attention away from other contributions by black Brazilians: most notably, slave labor that built the country. As just one example, many of Brazil's oldest cities such as Salvador, Recife, and Olinda are nationally celebrated for their 'culture', something for which northeasterners are often patted on the head paternalistically. But often this emphasis on 'culture' – for example, unique foods, architecture, music, dance, and so on – overlooks the brutal histories that produced it.

One of the clearest examples comes from Salvador da Bahia (see Figure 9.1). Each year millions of tourists flock to the historic Pelourinho district in central Salvador, a place widely advertised as Brazil's authentic homeland for African heritage (Romo, 2010). Yet, among the colorful buildings, lively rhythms, and exotic foods, little effort is made to emphasize how this was a place where, for centuries, *millions* of people came ashore and were sold into slavery. They were kept in chains, they were beaten, and regularly they were sold off with little regard for their families and loved ones. Children were taken from their mothers on these very streets. This is the history that produced the space where tourists now wander, haggling over souvenir prices and posting photos to social media. Even the word 'Pelourinho' is a perverse choice of names: in Portuguese, *pelourinho* means pillory, or whipping post, a place where slaves faced public torture and humiliation. The Pelourinho historic district takes its name from this object because, in colonial Salvador, *this* was where slaves endured acts of public torture. Today, all actual *pelourinhos* have been removed, presumably to keep tourists and *soteropolitanos* (residents of Salvador) from dwelling on ugly historical details. What one experiences instead is a crafted historical narrative emphasizing African *cultural* contributions to Brazilian society, and not their *material* contributions – that is, slave labor – that were responsible for building the country (*as well* as the culture).

Like other regions in the Americas with strong African cultural heritages (for example, the Caribbean, the southeastern USA, coastal Columbia), Brazil's

Figure 9.1 Pelourinho district in central Salvador da Bahia.
Source: UNESCO, Wikimedia commons: https://commons.wikimedia.org/wiki/File:Historic_Centre_of_
Salvador_de_Bahia-110101.jpg

Afro-Brazilian population tends to remain concentrated in areas where African slave labor was most prominent. States such as Bahia, Pernambuco, and Rio de Janeiro were primary shipping ports during colonial times, meaning this was where slave ships came to dock. Even today, Afro-Brazilian populations tend to be more numerous in these regions than elsewhere in Brazil. That said, it would be a misnomer to presume that Afro-Brazilians are underrepresented in newer cities such as Brasília and Belo Horizonte. On the contrary, these twentieth-century cities, like those before them, were mostly built by Brazil's poor and non-white populations, though the migration forces that brought them there were not so forceful as slavery. In fact, from the end of slavery in 1888, Brazil became a hotbed for both domestic and international migration (Skidmore, 2010). The Brazilian government encouraged migration from Europe, both to provide labor for Brazil's growing economy, and to 'whiten' Brazil's population following abolition (for more on this, see Chapters 2 and 5). As migrants have done for centuries, these people usually followed the footsteps of family and friends (what geographers call "chain migration"), meaning that different Brazilian regions tended to remain populated by specific cultural groups.

During the first half of the twentieth century, millions of new migrants poured into Brazil (Fausto, 1999). They settled primarily in the South and Southeast regions. Large numbers of Germans, Poles, Russians, and Romanians came to Brazil's southernmost states, while the Portuguese, Italians, Spanish, and Lebanese tended towards the Southeast. From the 1930s, Japanese migration became prominent, with families settling overwhelmingly in São Paulo (see Figure 9.2). During this time, internal migration also accelerated, with migrants from the Northeast going southward towards Brazil's industrializing urban centers. The cultural effects of northeastern chain migration are still easily observed: even today, *cearenses* and *pernambucanos* gravitate towards São Paulo, whereas *paraibanos* and *bahianos* tend towards Rio de Janeiro. This ongoing history of migration and cultural mixing is what produces contemporary Brazil's population and cultural diversity. And while Brazil's combination of people and cultures may be unique, there are, of course, other countries that share similar historical processes.

Despite ongoing internal migration and cultural mixing, regional and state identities remain significant in Brazil (cf. Ribeiro, 2000). Instead of placing much importance on ancestral origins (as in the USA), Brazilians tend to emphasize

Figure 9.2 A McDonald's restaurant in the neighborhood of Liberdade in central São Paulo.

Source: (WT-shared) Shoestring at wts wikivoyage, Wikimedia commons: https://commons.wikimedia.org/wiki/File:McDonald%27s_Liberdade_in_Sao_Paulo_002.JPG

their state heritages. Each state has particular cultural attributes that reveal themselves in language, foods, traditions, humor, holiday celebrations, music, dance, and so on. Such characteristics help to distinguish one state from another. These identities can also produce in-group solidarity, similar in many respects to ethnic or racial differences. Similarly, the states within a given Brazilian region – for example, the South – tend to share similar cultural and historical legacies, though here there exists considerable room for debate. For example, as Durval Muniz de Albuquerque Júnior argues (2009), what is today called the Northeast and northeastern culture is, in fact, a recent invention, something discursively produced by others (particularly in the Southeast) looking to distance and distinguish themselves from people who come from Bahia, Paraíba, Ceará, etc. Like the term Latin American (see Chapter 2), "the Northeast," argues Albuquerque Júnior, was invented from the outside, a process that reflects in many ways how racist tropes and ongoing discrimination persist in Brazil. Such debates are part of broader discussions about identity and culture, themes that have become ever more present in contemporary Brazilian art (e.g., Schwarz, 1992). We consider these questions in the next section, beginning with forms of cultural expression that include festivals and celebrations, and then move on to examine how writers, musicians, filmmakers, and artists have grown increasingly critical of Brazilian society in recent decades.

Forms of cultural expression

Just like Christmas, New Year's Day, and Easter, *Carnaval* celebrations are observed nationwide and are evidence of Brazil's strong Catholic/Christian roots. There are several other nationally observed holidays – Independence Day, Labor Day, *Tiradentes* Day, etc. – but all pale in comparison to *Carnaval*. While *Carnaval* celebrations almost always include music and dancing, there exist different types of music and dance throughout different parts of Brazil. What one sees in the Sambadrome of Rio de Janeiro is rarely what one experiences on the streets of Fortaleza, Porte Alegre, Belém, and so on. Though samba may be the official soundtrack to Rio's *Carnaval*, in a state like Pernambuco, *frevo* is the norm (see Figure 9.3). This is but one illustration of how Brazil's different states and regions show different cultural traditions, celebrations, foods, music, dance, and so forth.

These different cultural practices reflect the historical legacies and migrants who settled there, as well as the different geographies of these places. Take, for example, Brazil's *Festa Junina* celebrations. The origins of this holiday come from Europe; principally from Portugal and the commemoration of popular saints such as John, Anthony, Peter, and Paul. More interestingly, however, it also connects to pagan midsummer solstice celebrations – even though it falls in the middle of the Brazilian winter (at least for most of Brazil) – and, just as in Europe, it includes bonfires, dancing, and traditional foods. Even more curiously, the holiday is celebrated in a diversity of ways throughout different regions of Brazil. Perhaps most famous is the *quadrilha*, a sort of square dance practiced in

Figure 9.3 Frevo performers in Olinda, Pernambuco.

Source: Flickr, Prefeitura de Olinda, Wikimedia commons: https://commons.wikimedia.org/wiki/File: Frevo_dancers_-_Olinda,_Pernambuco,_Brazil.jpg

one form or another throughout most of Brazil during *Festa Junina*. But in addition to the *quadrilha* are other dancing celebrations, such as *Bumba meu boi*, most famous in the state of Maranhão. Even though *Bumba meu boi* is not widely practiced throughout all Brazil, one might call it the quintessential Brazilian celebration. It is extraordinarily syncretistic, blending African, indigenous, and European traditions, along with combining supernatural and animistic beliefs together with folkloric Catholicism.

In recent history, Brazil has come to celebrate this diversity as a point of national pride. Particularly under the Estado Novo and the first presidency of Getúlio Vargas (1937–1945), Brazil's unique cultural diversity was strategically woven into narratives of national identity (see also Chapter 2). Artists and writers who appeared to capture these traits – the 'essence' of Brazil, as it were – were exalted nationally as heroes of Brazilian culture (Philippou, 2005). One of Brazil's most famous was José de Alencar (1829–1877), a writer from the romantic period in the nineteenth century. Alencar helped pioneer Indianism in Brazilian art, a movement that iconized native Brazilians as 'noble savages' and has by no means disappeared today.

When it comes to identifying Brazil's most significant writer, however, there is little debate: nearly everyone agrees it is Joaquim Maria Machado de Assis (1838–1908). Famous for overcoming his humble origins – he was the grandson of slaves and mostly self-educated – Machado de Assis went on to become the first president of Brazil's highly regarded Academy of Letters literary society. Recognized as a titan during his own lifetime, his work continues to be highly influential today. In addition to his mastery of prose and creative use of language, Machado de Assis is perhaps best known for his irony and critiques of Brazilian society. One might call him a postmodern writer in a premodern era. So innovative was his work that Brazilian literature was never the same afterward. Without exaggeration, nearly *every* single major Brazilian writer since the beginning of the twentieth century shows his influence, particularly in the way they critique Brazilian society and make use of ambiguity and irony. Even classically modernist authors such as Jorge Amado – and certainly ones that defy categorization such as Clarice Lispector and Guimarães Rosa – are indebted to Machado de Assis. Drawing from his style, there continues in contemporary Brazilian literature a tense relationship with Brazilian society: a certain love that is fraught with frustration, yearning, and anger.[2]

At the risk of overstating Machado de Assis's importance, one can also see his influence in contemporary Brazilian film. The Brazilian cinema industry could not be called a major one, globally speaking, but among the handful of high budget films that are produced each year, one often sees critical engagement with Brazilian societal issues. Violence, in particular, draws attention, and the multiple and diverse ways in which violence undergirds contemporary Brazilian society (e.g., Hamburger, 2007). Social injustice and poverty are also regularly addressed by filmmakers, with growing attention paid to structures of inequality and Brazilian social class. Brazilian films are increasingly tackling more sensitive subjects such as racism and class privilege, with filmmakers such as Anna Muylaert and Kleber Mendonça Filho recognized internationally for finding sophisticated and vivid ways to address complex societal issues.

To be fair, however, Brazil's appetite for literature and domestic film has never been voracious. This is not to say Brazil lacks extraordinary writers and filmmakers (to the contrary!), but, rather, to point out that, for a country with over 200 million people, Brazil's literary and filmmaking industries are surprisingly small. There are a host of reasons for this. Starting with film, Brazilian moviegoers typically prefer big-budget Hollywood films, much as in countries elsewhere. Going to the cinema is also expensive, alienating a huge portion of the population. As such, Brazilian films, with their critical and often subversive themes, appeal mostly to middle and upper-class audiences looking for progressive and thought-provoking films. This, admittedly, is a small audience in *most* countries, let alone Brazil. Combined with other factors such as meager funding from state institutions, contemporary Brazilian film remains a niche industry in many respects. Turning to literature, one must remember that until recent decades, a huge portion of the population was illiterate. And among the middle and upper classes (i.e., those who *could* read), it could never be said that Brazil has had much of a 'book culture.' Again, there are various reasons for this, including, as mentioned in Chapter 2, Brazil's historical lack of university institutions. Add to this a small number of publishing companies, the scandalously high cost of books in Brazil, and the pitiful state of public libraries, what remains is a context in which most of the population does not have good access to literature.

Besides, as in most countries, today television is king, and before TV it was the radio (McCann, 1999; Sinclair and Straubhaar, 2013). As noted in other chapters, television has become ubiquitous in Brazilian homes over the last several decades, and, with it, Brazil's *Rede Globo* television network. It would be a mistake to underestimate the cultural influence of *Rede Globo*: from the way people talk, to their attitudes and beliefs, Globo programming has even been linked to declining birth rates in recent years (La Ferrara, Chong, and Duryea, 2008). The reason for this, it is argued, relates to the portrayal of young women on Brazil's telenovelas. Today, young female characters rarely have children and are more often depicted as career driven. Such is the influence of Brazilian telenovelas that young women may be emulating these behaviors, helping to explain Brazil's plummeting fertility rate over the past few decades. (Not to be overlooked here are also increasing education and employment levels for women, which are perhaps most significant when it comes to explaining declining birth rates.)

The above example is merely one case emphasizing the cultural significance of Brazilian telenovelas. Whether behavior, fashion, language, topics of conversation, and even attitudes and beliefs, telenovelas are probably the single most important cultural influence in Brazil today. The quality and production value of these programs is impressive, especially for *Globo*'s flagship "nine o'clock *novela*" (i.e., the telenovela that airs each evening at nine p.m. after the national news). This, of course, could change in future years as social media platforms and online content continue to expand, but, for now, the telenovelas, and TV more generally, continue to exert profound cultural influence over Brazilian society.

While television and its programming are, historically speaking, recent additions to Brazil's cultural milieu, music has been around for centuries and remains hugely significant. As mentioned previously, different regions of Brazil are home to diverse musical forms, each with its own style articulating the local culture(s) of specific regions. As in other countries, Brazilian music also reflects local histories, and the mixing of different cultural traditions across time. This is also to say that, for many Brazilians, music has for generations been a significant medium for expressing and sharing cultural moments. International music is also popular in Brazil – there is great love for The Beatles, Michael Jackson, Bob Marley, and so on – but, differently from Brazilian film, the domestic market for Brazilian music remains enormous. Sadly, few Brazilian musicians are well known outside of Brazil, but, much like Machado de Assis, many of them are hugely famous at home (and for good reason!).

Given its unique characteristics and often exceptional quality, it is puzzling that Brazilian music has not garnered more international attention. This can perhaps be explained by a few factors, the first of which is language. According to *Ethnologue* (2017), there are nearly 230 million Portuguese speakers world-wide (including native and non-native speakers), placing Portuguese slightly ahead of French as the ninth most commonly spoken language in the world (and well ahead of languages such as German, Japanese, and Italian). *However,* more than 90% of these speakers live in Brazil, meaning that, indeed, there exists a large market for Portuguese-language music, but this market is geographically concentrated in one country. A second reason relates to Brazil's unique rhythms, instrumentation, percussion, and so on, a direct reflection of Brazil's ethnic diversity. This is to say that while Brazilian music's unique sound can be attractive to some new listeners, it can also be alienating to others. Despite how people often say they like hearing new music, they tend to listen to what they are already familiar with. Turn on nearly any radio station for examples of this. Few are the people who are actually musically adventurous.

Finally, no discussion of Brazil's international cultural influence would be complete without mention of bossa nova music. Bossa nova is, of course, Brazil's most famous contribution to international audiences, even despite criticism that it reflects American smooth jazz more so than it does samba, *chorinho,* or other classic Brazilian genres. As much as anything, this perhaps reflects bossa nova's musical history and the commercial influence of North American consumer markets (Skidmore, 2010). Subsequently, while bossa nova enjoyed international success in the 1950s and 1960s, it is perhaps not surprising that contemporary audiences are turned off by Brazilian music after being subjected to bossa nova for long stints in cocktail lounges, reception halls, hotel lobbies, and elevators. In short, Brazilian music is often poorly recognized abroad, and among several contributing factors, maybe one can blame it on the bossa nova.[3]

Returning to common themes in contemporary Brazilian music, topics such as love, longing, heartbreak, and so on are just as common as they are in most countries. Related to this, much like Brazilian literature, music in Brazil has a long history of cultural subversion and social protest. This, in fact, is one of the reasons for why samba is so loved in Brazil (Vianna, 1999). Many of samba's roots can be traced to Brazilian slave culture, which, like capoeira, provided a subversive mode of communication and solidarity. This tradition merged into other musical genres, such as *Tropicália* and *Música Popular Brasileira* (Brazilian Popular Music), which helped convey subversive messages of social protest during the Military Dictatorship (1965–1984). Today, this tradition carries on, with music such as rap and hip-hop addressing issues of social injustice head on. This, however, is not to say that *most* Brazilians listen to this kind of music *most* of the time. On the contrary. Today, what is often called *sertanejo* music (sometimes *forró,* depending on local nomenclature) appears to be Brazil's most popular style, frequently played on radio stations, in public spaces, at restaurants, bars, and clubs. Similar to contemporary country music in North America, *sertanejo* appeals to a mass audience, usually steering away from politically charged subjects.

For some of Brazil's most truly radical art, one need look no further than contemporary public space; in particular, to Brazilian street art. This is one of Brazil's most controversial art forms, as plenty of Brazilians, not without reason, call it vandalism (see Figure 9.4). For example, there is graffiti artwork, for

Figure 9.4 Beco do Batman ("Batman Alley") in Vila Madalena, São Paulo.

Source: Diego Bravo (Somente Coisas Legais), Wikimedia commons: https://commons.wikimedia.org/wiki/File:Beco_do_Batman_-_Vila-Madalena,_São_Paulo_-_SP_07.jpg

which cities like São Paulo are today world famous. The history of this tradition is compelling, and, like the artwork itself, not without controversy. Whether the graffiti in a city such as São Paulo is driven by anger and social protest from those who feel excluded, or whether it simply represents widespread teenage vandalism, is hotly debated (e.g., Caldeira, 2012). There are even multiple words for graffiti in Brazil: *grafite*, recognized for its artistic qualities and legitimacy, and *pichação*, like tagging, often written off as vandalism. So marked up are São Paulo's walls and edifices that in 2016, Mayor João Doria initiated his "Beautiful City" campaign to paint over São Paulo's graffiti and *pichos*. Many paulistanos are divided over such initiatives, and not least because of Mayor Doria's broader conservative political agenda. Critics tend to argue that simply covering up (quite literally) São Paulo's problems in no way beautifies the city, and that the mayor's larger goal is to erase voices of dissent. Such debates between conservative and progressive viewpoints, or more generally what might be called right and left, have grown increasingly tense in recent years in Brazil. Connected to this are changing religious identities and the growing presence of Brazilian evangelicalism in national politics. These trends are proving hugely significant for Brazilian cultural, social, and political debates, and it is to these issues we shift our attention in the second half of this chapter.

Brazilian spirituality

Religious syncretism and diverse spiritualties are some of Brazil's richest cultural traits. This history is filled with complexity and geographic nuance, and our goal in this chapter is by no means to give an exhaustive account of these details. Instead, we focus on key processes that have helped produce Brazil's contemporary spiritual landscape, helping to make sense of why Brazilian religiosity looks the way it does today. As such, this section begins with the legacy of Portuguese colonization, and considers how this history facilitated syncretistic and diverse spiritual practices. This included a certain tolerance for, and tendency to incorporate, indigenous and African beliefs, as well as the growth of folkloric Catholicism. Throughout the twentieth century, Brazil continued to morph, as alternative religious faiths such as Spiritism became popular. This period in particular saw the growth of non-Catholic Christianity[4] (e.g., Pentecostal, Protestant, and evangelical faiths), which today is beginning to rival Catholicism in terms of total practitioners. The cultural significance of this shift, and the way it is affecting social and political debates in Brazil, is today a hot topic, and something we consider in the penultimate section of this chapter.

While Portuguese colonization in the Americas was every bit as catastrophic for indigenous groups as was Spanish colonization, there were important differences in the ways each country approached this process. The Portuguese were notoriously *laissez-faire*, helping to explain, in many respects, contemporary patterns of Brazilian governance. Religious conquest was no exception, where the Portuguese were less insistent than the Spanish when it came to conversion and adherence to Catholic protocol. Significant here were also missionary differences between Franciscans and Jesuits – the former more prominent in Spanish America and the latter more common in Brazil – and the ways Catholicism spread in the Americas, far from Vatican influence and therefore more fluid and attuned to folkloric elements. Importantly, this meant that unlike in most of Spanish America, Catholic missionaries in Brazil rarely sought to extinguish indigenous religions altogether. Over time, these factors helped establish a fertile landscape for religious syncretism, where multiple faiths were practiced alongside one another, and different spiritual traditions began to sample and borrow from one another (Page, 1995).

As the Atlantic slave trade brought increasing numbers of Africans to Brazil, the religious landscape continued to evolve. Again, like the original colonizers, Brazilian slave owners rarely insisted upon strict adherence to Catholic doctrine. Perhaps realizing they were outnumbered by slaves, or because in some cases they themselves were intrigued by African spirituality, slave owners regularly allowed for the continued practice of African faiths. In many instances they were satisfied if slaves gave the appearance of trying to practice Catholicism – a 'good faith' effort, so to speak – which, of course, led to even more religious syncretism. African faiths also found safe haven in Brazil's *quilombos*, communities of escaped slaves that numbered in the thousands throughout Brazil's interior (Reis and Gomes, 1996).

Passed on from generation to generation, these religions have endured over time, and still today there are tens of thousands in Brazil who observe African spiritual traditions. Several religious scholars identify Brazil as a key global center for the cultivation and preservation of these faiths (Mann and Bay, 2001). Included here are several traditions, including Umbanda and *Batuque*, but most common is candomblé, traditionally connected to Salvador da Bahia. These religions and their practitioners have consistently faced extreme prejudice, due in part to their geographic origins (i.e., racism) as well as general ignorance regarding their basic religious beliefs (e.g., calling them "voodoo"). As such, they have mixed and blended with Catholicism in multiple ways, and today Brazil is home to some of the world's most unique religious traditions and festivals. Perhaps best known is the *Lavagem do Bonfim* ceremony that happens annually as part of the *Festa do Bonfim* celebration in Salvador da Bahia. Here, the steps of the Nosso Senhor do Bonfim Catholic Church are ritually washed by candomblé practitioners (led by women in white dress called *baianas*) in a tradition that dates back hundreds of years (see Figure 9.5).

In addition to Christian, indigenous, and African religious influences, Brazil is also home to Islamic, Buddhist, and Jewish faiths. The twentieth century saw the arrival of Hinduism and the Bahá'í faith, as well as the growth of Spiritism that continues to attract large numbers today. Confusing for many outside of Brazil are

Figure 9.5 Lavagem do Bonfim ceremony in front of the Nosso Senhor do Bonfim Church in Salvador da Bahia.

Source: Adenilson Nunes/AGECOM - 14/01/10 Lavagem do Bomfim 2010, CC BY 2.0, Wikimedia Commons: https://commons.wikimedia.org/w/index.php?curid=19206808

the ways Brazilians frequently practice multiple religious faiths at the same time. This is to say that, for example, while most people identify with only one religion, they are not necessarily exclusive in their practice or belief in that one faith. In other words, in Brazil, one's identity as a Catholic is not necessarily compromised by ongoing observances of Spiritism or candomblé. This again reflects Brazil's legacy of syncretism and relative religious tolerance, as well as Brazil's intensely spiritual culture coupled with traditions of pragmatism (cf. Burdick, 1993).

In many respects, this helps to explain the recent growth of non-Catholic Christianity in Brazil, as well as some of the tensions unleashed by this religious shift. American Protestant missionaries inspired by the Second Great Awakening were already present in Brazil during the 1800s, but it was not until the twentieth century and the spread of Pentecostal faiths that non-Catholic Christianity became prominent. Pentecostal missionaries, most often from the USA, concentrated their efforts on the rural poor, and then shifted to urban centers as the century wore on (Stoll, 1990). Their promise of immediate salvation and a more personal, experiential relationship with god attracted believers put off by the monotony, abstraction, and hierarchy of the Catholic Church. Combined with this was their message of spiritual help for the challenges facing many low-income Brazilians (e.g., poverty, drug and alcohol abuse, unemployment, prostitution), and, seemingly overnight, non-Catholic Christian churches became ubiquitous in low-income communities. While the origins of this movement can be traced mostly to American missionaries (e.g., The Assemblies of God ministries), by the end of the twentieth century there were home-grown Brazilian denominations numbering in the millions (e.g., The Universal Church of the Kingdom of God). Brazil is today a mission *sending* country to many regions in the world, with some groups even proselytizing, somewhat ironically, in the USA (Garmany and Gerhardt, 2015).

Puzzling to many scholars about this trajectory is the way non-Catholic Christianity took off at the same time Liberation Theology was peaking in Brazil (Chestnut, 1997; Freston, 1994; Martin, 1990). Inspired by calls for social justice and questioning the roots of socio-economic inequality (viz., capitalism), Liberation Theology was a Catholic movement, most prominent in Latin America, which sought to address structural inequality faced by poor and marginalized people. Odd, however, was the way Liberation Theology appeared to coincide with Brazil's mass conversion to non-Catholic Christian faiths, particularly among the poor. Just when Catholic parishioners made a preferential option for the poor, the poor opted for evangelicalism. Explanations for this are multitude – not to be overlooked here were Vatican efforts to silence Catholic leaders considered too radical – yet some of the most compelling insights come from anthropologists like John Burdick (1993). Through extensive ethnographic work carried out in the 1990s, Burdick shows how, perhaps more than anything, Catholic ecclesiastical base communities (CEBs) failed to connect emotionally and experientially with poor people in the same ways as non-Catholic Christian churches. Simply put, the theological debates of CEBs had an alienating effect on many poor people, whereas evangelical and Pentecostal churches placed more emphasis on 'feeling' the Holy Spirit, focusing on personal change rather than structural and collective reform to address social problems. Liberation Theology was by no means a total failure – it had an enormous impact on social movements like the MST (Mariz, 1994; see also Chapter 7) – but the recent growth of non-Catholic Christianity illustrates a certain fissure between the Brazilian population and the Catholic Church.

According to the most recent census conducted in 2010 by the *Instituto Brasileiro de Geografía e Estatística* (IBGE – Brazilian Institute of Geography and Statistics), there still exists a significant gap between Catholics and non-Catholic Christians in Brazil. While non-Catholic Christianity has grown enormously in recent decades, now totaling more than 22% of the population, nearly 65% of Brazilians still identify as Catholic. These demographic figures, however, tell only part of the story. Non-Catholic Christian groups have effectively focused their efforts to establish a strong political and public presence in Brazilian society, using media technologies such as television and radio to communicate their messages, as well as linking directly with Brazilian political parties. Broadly speaking, these groups and their efforts make up what is called the *bancada evangélica* (literally, the "evangelical lobby," yet in practice a congressional lobby that includes representatives from several Christian faiths), one of contemporary Brazil's fastest growing and most polarizing political forces (Prandi and Santos, 2017). We consider their rise alongside broader societal changes in the penultimate section of this chapter, reflecting on current and future debates over religion, identity, and cultural conflict in twenty-first-century Brazil.

Religion's place in twenty-first-century Brazil

Turning on the TV or radio today in Brazil, one is sure to find several stations devoted entirely to evangelical broadcasting. Perhaps best known is *TV Universal*, an entire television station owned and operated by the Universal Church of the Kingdom of God. Established in 2011, *TV Universal* is a free-to-air, nationwide broadcast, bringing the message of the Universal Church to nearly every home in Brazil, 24 hours a day. Along with *TV Universal* are other channels, such as *Record TV*, one of Brazil's most significant stations that is today owned by Edir Macedo of the Universal Church. Switching on the radio, one encounters even more non-Catholic Christian stations. Judging by such a strong media presence, it might seem Brazil is a mostly evangelical country, or at least one where non-Catholic Christianity accounts for more than one quarter of the population. Though non-Catholic Christians remain a minority religious group in Brazil, they have a pronounced cultural presence, punching above their weight, as it were, in political and societal affairs. To understand this, and to make better sense of religious change today in Brazil, it is important to see how Brazilian non-Catholic Christianity has changed over time, and where, perhaps, it might be headed in the future.

In the 1990s, as academics began to take note of religious change in Latin America (Burdick, 1993; Chestnut, 1997; Freston, 1994), it was not far-fetched to speculate that non-Catholic Christianity could spell major social and political change for the region (Martin, 1990; Stoll, 1990). Many countries were emerging from long bouts of political turmoil (Brazil included), and these nascent democracies where being shaped by new and unpredictable forces. Perhaps even more significant at that time, in countries like Brazil, non-Catholic Christianity appeared strikingly fundamentalist. Converts often dressed in white and carried bibles in public, abstained from alcohol, tobacco, and other drugs, wore their hair in specific ways, refrained from using jewelry or make-up, avoided secular influences such as music, entertainment, and dance, and even steered clear of popular holidays and parties. Noted Virginia Garrand-Burnett (1993, p. 208), Latin American Protestants appeared "centrifugal and divisive," like religious fundamentalists intent on separating themselves from secular society. To be sure, Brazilian non-Catholic Christianity in the 1990s was a radical identity, appealing to those who *wanted* a clear break from their past and social surroundings (see, for example, Goldstein, 2003).

Fast forward to today and one finds a very different religious landscape from what one might have expected in the 1990s. Non-Catholic Christianity continues to attract large numbers of converts, but what it means to be non-Catholic Christian today in Brazil is different from what it was two or three decades ago. To begin, where evangelical and Pentecostal churches appealed overwhelmingly to lower-income people in the past, today these faiths are widely practiced among the middle and upper classes. In fact, though historically these churches placed little importance on material wealth, today many non-Catholic Christian faiths emphasize what is often called 'the gospel of prosperity' (i.e., the connection between Christian faith and personal wealth and success – cf. Lavalle and Castello, 2004). Equally significant are the ways non-Catholic Christians present and comport themselves in public space. Again, while in the past evangelical and Pentecostal practitioners were easily identified thanks to their style of dress and frequent proselytizing, today there is little to distinguish them from everyone else. While most still abstain from alcohol and other drugs, there is little else that clearly distinguishes them. Simply put, non-Catholic Christianity is no longer such a radical identity that signifies a decisive break with secular society. It has, without doubt, become mainstream. In bolder terms, one might argue non-Catholic Christianity has not significantly altered Brazilian society as many speculated in the 1990s, but, rather, Brazilian society has done much to change non-Catholic Christianity.

Related to this is non-Catholic Christianity's growing appeal to widespread and diverse sectors of society, as well as the continuing fluidity and syncretism of Brazilian spirituality. Despite non-Catholic Christianity's reputation for religious fanaticism and overzealous proselytizing, researchers consistently find little evidence of social segregation due to differences in religious faith (Garmany, 2013). Non-Catholic Christians are rarely marginalized, nor are they likely to sever relationships with others simply because of their beliefs. On the contrary, evangelical and Pentecostal faiths are proving just as dynamic as other religions in Brazil, even appealing to groups once thought anathema to non-Catholic

Christianity. Take, for example, an emergent group that one might jokingly call *trafi-crentes*: drug traffickers (*traficantes*) who are also non-Catholic Christians (*crentes* – "believers," common vernacular for non-Catholic Christians). Only a few years ago such an identity would seem impossible, an oxymoron, yet today such people exist (i.e., *trafi-crentes*), evidently secure in their roles as non-Catholic Christian drug traffickers. These sorts of fluid social dynamics point to Brazil's ongoing legacy of spiritual adaptation, and perhaps once again evidence Brazil's tradition for pragmatism over idealism.

Where key battle lines typically lie instead are in contemporary political debates. Much like in popular media, non-Catholic Christianity has established a strong presence in Brazilian politics. The aforementioned evangelical lobby has been successful in cultivating a strong support base, and, by focusing their efforts on specific, often high-profile issues, they have established a formidable presence in discussions over national policy. As in other countries, they have been especially successful in harnessing discourses of traditional family values – and combating the corrupt influences of modern society – in order to articulate their message to the general public. In doing this, the evangelical lobby has, of course, alienated large segments of society, but it would be a mistake to call them a fringe political actor. On the contrary, their platform has proven appealing to many in contemporary Brazil, including numerous Catholics drawn to their moralistic political discourse (Prandi and Santos, 2017).

Take, for example, incendiary issues like abortion and same-sex marriage. In Brazil, the former is illegal and carries potentially severe consequences (e.g., punishable by one to three years in prison for women who undertake abortions), while the latter was nationally legalized by the Supreme Court in 2013 (before that, only certain states recognized same-sex unions). Interesting here is that neither law very accurately reflects public opinion. While most Brazilians believe abortion laws should be modified (noteworthy here is that illegal abortions are relatively common in Brazil – Downie, 2010), according to a 2014 study by the Pew Research Center, a slight majority of Brazilians oppose same-sex marriage. Despite, for example, São Paulo's reputation for hosting one of the world's largest Gay Pride celebrations, many Brazilians still oppose equal rights for same-sex couples. These are political and social debates in which the evangelical lobby is heavily involved, perhaps reflecting the mismatch between legal precedent and public opinion, as well as the ambiguous distinction between church and state in countries like Brazil (consider also the USA). After all, hanging front and center in the main chamber of Brazil's federal supreme court is a crucifix, suggesting Christianity still plays an important role in Brazilian political, cultural, and juridical decision-making processes (Beechno, 2017).

Interesting to note, however, are current religious trends in Brazil. While non-Catholic Christianity continues to attract converts in large numbers, it is not the only rapidly expanding religious group. According to Marcelo Neri (2011), people under the age of 30 who today leave the Catholic Church are not necessarily converting to non-Catholic Christianity: they are more likely to identify as having "no religion." This is not to say they are atheists, but rather to

Figure 9.6 The main chamber of Brazil's federal supreme court in Brasília. Note the crucifix that hangs on the wall behind the desk of the chief justice.

Source: STF, Wikimedia commons: https://upload.wikimedia.org/wikipedia/commons/d/df/STF_Ple nario.jpg

point out that, as in many countries, Brazilians are growing increasingly skeptical of organized religion and established churches. Such trends reflect broader global patterns, with more and more people describing themselves as "spiritual" rather than "religious" (Rocha, 2017). What this spells for Brazil's future is, thus, increasingly hard to predict. While special interest groups such as the evangelical lobby continue to push for national laws that reflect distinctly Christian values, many Brazilians appear unsure what role organized religion should play in political decision making. As in many countries, these debates continue to intensify, with different sides appearing in many instances to drift further apart.

Conclusion

In this chapter, we have worked to address both cultural and spiritual debates in contemporary Brazil. Starting with the origins of Brazilian ethnic and cultural diversity – that is, colonization and slavery – Brazil has, from the beginning, been a place where indigenous, European, and African traditions mixed together. Over time, this came to manifest itself in distinct regional and state cultural identities, particularly as international and domestic migrants followed patterns of chain migration. These diverse cultural traits are made especially obvious in festivals and celebrations, and still today one can easily identify them in language, music, foods, and so on. This diversity and cultural mixture has long been important to constructions of Brazilian national identity, and, throughout the twentieth century, artists perceived to capture this spirit were nationally celebrated. Important to note, however, are strong subversive traditions in Brazilian literature, music, film, and other art forms that have long critiqued national myths of harmonious diversity. While mainstream cultural productions such as television and news media in Brazil are widely recognized for their conservative leanings, contemporary artists are frequently renowned for their insightful critiques of Brazilian society.

Connected to this legacy is Brazil's tradition for religious syncretism and spiritual diversity. Again, the roots of this can be traced to Portuguese colonization and the legacy of the Catholic Church in Brazil. Historically, the Church was more lenient in Brazil than in Spanish America. This permitted the ongoing practice of indigenous and African faiths, as well as the development of syncretistic religions like candomblé and folkloric Catholicism. Throughout the twentieth century, other religions such as Spiritism and Kardecism grew popular in Brazil, but it was not until later decades and the growth of non-Catholic Christianity that an alternative religious faith began to rival Catholicism in Brazil. Curiously, non-Catholic Christianity took off right when Liberation Theology was also peaking, indicating that the messages and religious practices of evangelicalism and Pentecostalism connected more effectively with many Brazilians than did those of Liberation Theology. Linked to this is non-Catholic Christianity's engagement with national politics (e.g., the *bancada evangélica*), as well as effective use of media technologies such as television and radio. With this, non-Catholic Christianity has continued to grow in the twenty-first century, due, in no small part, to changes in religious practice and doctrine that could be perceived as less radical and in alignment with ideologies of consumerism and wealth creation (i.e., capitalism). Today, however, more and more Brazilians are becoming skeptical of formal, institutionalized religions (particularly young people), casting uncertainty over the future of spiritual and cultural debates in Brazil.

To conclude this chapter, it is useful to remember that close study of Brazilian culture and spirituality, as in most postcolonial contexts, reveals in many ways the battle lines of social struggle, inequality, and contestations over national identity. Scholars of Brazil have long wrestled with these questions, returning often to debates over cultural authenticity, external influence, and specific traits that help to define and distinguish Brazil today (Buarque de Holanda, 2012; Chaui, 2000; DaMatta, 1986; Ribeiro, 2000). Despite yearnings for *inherently* Brazilian cultural characteristics, the eminent cultural theorist Roberto Schwarz (1988, p. 77) reminds us that the very nature of cultural life in countries such as Brazil often feels "artificial, inauthentic and imitative".[5] This, perhaps, is the fate of countries near to the periphery of globalization – if indeed not *all* countries – where the drive for cultural production is led not by intrinsic or essential cultural characteristics, but rather by a lack of, and a longing for, 'organic' cultural traits perceived as existing since time immemorial. Such insights are useful for making sense of contemporary cultural and spiritual debates in Brazil, where discourses of tradition, national identity, and authenticity often emerge to legitimize or silence arguments regarding public policy, social protest, and political rhetoric. As in many countries, tensions over cultural and ethnic identity are today running high in Brazil, and while historical precedent is useful for explaining present day contexts and future potentialities, ongoing and unpredictable processes of globalization will likely play key roles in future developments.

Notes

1 We are indebted to Bert Barickman for bringing this to our attention.
2 One of the most insightful works on Machado de Assis is Roberto Schwarz's, *A Master on the Periphery of Capitalism: Machado de Assis* (2001).
3 Sorry, that joke was too good to resist!
4 There are a host of non-Catholic, Christian-based churches today in Brazil, and they do not always fit neatly within categories such as 'evangelical,' 'Pentecostal,' 'Protestant,' etc. What they have in common, however, is that they are Christian-based faiths distinguished from Catholicism. To address this diversity, we refer to these as "non-Catholic Christian" churches and faiths.
5 We are indebted to Matthew A. Richmond for bringing this reference to our attention.

Suggested English readings

Burdick, J. (1993). *Looking for God in Brazil: The progressive Catholic Church in urban Brazil's religious arena.* Berkeley: University of California Press.
Ribeiro, D. (2000). *The Brazilian people: The formation and meaning of Brazil.* Gainesville: University Press of Florida.
Schwarz, R. (1992). *Misplaced ideas: Essays on Brazilian Culture.* London: Verso.
Sinclair, J., and Straubhaar, J.D. (2013). *Latin American television industries.* London: Palgrave Macmillan.
Vianna, H. (1999). *The mystery of samba: Popular music and national identity in Brazil.* Chapel Hill: University of North Carolina Press.

References

Albuquerque Júnior, D.M. (2009). *A invenção do nordeste e outras artes.* São Paulo: Editora Cortez.
Beechno, K. (2017). Religion, rights, and violence against women: Negotiating the tensions between faith and feminism in Brazil. PhD dissertation. King's College London.
Bouchard, D. (2017). Communities of ruin: Humanitarian violence and the Amazon's uncontacted tribes. *Culture, Theory and Critique,* 58(1), 62–76.
Buarque de Holanda, S. (2012). *Roots of Brazil.* Translated by G.H. Summ. Notre Dame, IN: University of Notre Dame Press.
Burdick, J. (1993). *Looking for God in Brazil: The progressive Catholic Church in urban Brazil's religious arena.* Berkeley: University of California Press.

Caldeira, T.P.R. (2012). Imprinting and moving around: New visibilities and configurations of public space in São Paulo. *Public Culture*, 24(2 67), 385–419.

Chaui, M. (2000). *Brasil: Mito fundador e sociedade autoritária*. São Paulo: Fundação Perseu Abramo.

Chestnut, R.A. (1997). *Born again in Brazil: The Pentecostal boom and the pathogens of poverty*. New Brunswick: Rutgers University Press.

DaMatta, R. (1986). *O que faz o brasil, Brasil?* 2nd ed. Rio de Janeiro: Rocco.

Downie, A. (2010). Abortions in Brazil, though illegal, are common. *Time*, 2 June. Available at: http://content.time.com/time/world/article/0,8599,1993205,00.html [accessed 28 March 2018].

Ethnologue: Languages of the world, 2017. [online] Available at: www.ethnologue.com [accessed 4 March 2018].

Fausto, B. (1999). *A concise history of Brazil*. Cambridge: Cambridge University Press.

Freston, P. (1994). Brazil: Church growth, parachurch agencies, and politics. In: G. Cook (ed.), *New face of the church in Latin America: Between tradition and change*. New York: Maryknoll, pp. 226–242.

Garmany, J. (2013). Slums, space, and spirituality: Religious diversity in contemporary Brazil. *Area* 45(1), 47–55.

Garmany, J., and Gerhardt, H. (2015). Global networks and the emergent sites of contemporary evangelicalism in Brazil. In: S.D. Brunn (ed.), *The changing world religion map*. Netherlands: Springer, pp. 2011–2024.

Garrand-Burnett, V. (1993). Conclusion: Is this Latin America's reformation? In: V. Garrand-Burnett and D. Stoll (eds), *Rethinking Protestantism in Latin America*. Philadelphia: Temple University Press, pp. 199–210.

Goldstein, D.M. (2003). *Laughter out of place: Race, class, violence, and sexuality in a Rio shantytown*. Berkeley: University of California Press.

Hamburger, E. (2007). Violência e pobreza no cinema brasileiro recente. *Novos Estudos*, 78 (Julho), 113–128.

Hemming, J. (1987). *Amazon frontier: The defeat of the Brazilian Indians*. London: Macmillan.

IBGE (2017). *Instituto Brasileiro de Geografia e Estatística*. Available at: www.ibge.gov.br [accessed 26 November 2017].

La Ferrara, E., Chong, A., and Duryea, S. (2008). Soap operas and fertility: Evidence from Brazil. *Inter-American Development Bank Working Paper Series*, 633, pp. 1–47.

Langfur, H. (2002). Uncertain refuge: Frontier expansion and the origins of the Botocudo War in late colonial Brazil. *Hispanic American Historical Review*, 82(2), 215–256.

Lavalle, A.G., and Castello, G. (2004). As benesses desse mundo: Associativismo religioso e inclusão socioeconômica. *Novos Estudos*, 68(Março), 73–93.

Mann, K., and Bay, E.G. (2001). *Rethinking the African diaspora: The making of a Black Atlantic world in the bight of Benin and Brazil*. New York: Taylor and Francis.

Mariz, C. (1994). *Coping with poverty: Pentecostals and Christian base communities in Brazil*. Philadelphia: Temple University Press.

Martin, D. (1990). *Tongues of fire: The explosion of Protestantism in Latin America*. Oxford: Blackwell.

McCann, B. (1999). The invention of tradition on Brazilian radio. In: R.M Levine and J.J. Crocitti (eds), *The Brazil reader: History, culture, politics*. Durham, NC: Duke University Press, pp. 474–482.

Neri, M.C. (ed.). (2011). *Novo mapa das religiões*. Rio de Janeiro: Fundação Getulio Vargas (Centro de Políticas Sociais).

Page, J. (1995). *The Brazilians*. Reading: Perseus Books.

Pew Research Center (2014). *Religion in Latin America: Widespread change in a historically Catholic region*. Washington: Pew Research Center. Available at: http://assets.pewre search.org/wp-content/uploads/sites/11/2014/11/Religion-in-Latin-America-11–12-PM-full-PDF.pdf [accessed 4 March 2018].

Philippou, S. (2005). Modernism and national identity in Brazil, or how to brew a Brazilian stew. *National Identities*, 7(3), 245–264.

Prandi, R., and Santos, R.W. dos (2017). Quem tem medo da bancada evangélica? Posições sobre moralidade e política no eleitorado brasileiro, no Congresso Nacional e na Frente Parlamentar Evangélica. *Tempo Social*, 29(2), 187–213.

Reis, J.J., and Gomes, F. dos Santos (1996). *Liberdade por fio: história dos quilombos no Brasil*. São Paulo: Companhia das Letras.

Ribeiro, D. (2000). *The Brazilian people: The formation and meaning of Brazil*. Gainesville: University Press of Florida.

Rocha, C. (2017). *John of God: The globalization of Brazilian faith healing*. Oxford: Oxford University Press.

Romo, A.A. (2010). *Brazil's living museum: Race, reform, and tradition in Bahia*. Chapel Hill: University of North Carolina Press.

Schmidt, B.E., and Engler, S. (2016). *Handbook of contemporary religions in Brazil*. Leiden, Netherlands: Koninklijke Brill.

Schwarz, R. (1988). Brazilian culture: Nationalism by elimination. *New Left Review*, I/167, 77–90.

Schwarz, R. (1992). *Misplaced ideas: Essays on Brazilian culture*. London: Verso.

Schwarz, R. (2001). *A master on the periphery of capitalism: Machado de Assis*. Translated by John Gledson. Durham, NC: Duke University Press.

Sinclair, J., and Straubhaar, J.D. (2013). *Latin American television industries*. London: Palgrave Macmillan.

Skidmore, T.E. (2010). *Brazil: Five centuries of change*. 2nd ed. Oxford: Oxford University Press.

Stoll, D. (1990). *Is Latin America turning Protestant? The politics of evangelical growth*. Berkeley: University of California Press.

Vianna, H. (1999). *The mystery of samba: Popular music and national identity in Brazil*. Chapel Hill: University of North Carolina Press.

10 Foreign policy and international diplomacy

Introduction

In the 1990s and the 2000s, Brazil experienced a geopolitical and diplomatic rise. It became more active in its own region, forming new multilateral organizations. These include the Mercosul trade bloc, created in 1991 by Argentina, Brazil, Paraguay, and Uruguay; the Union of South American Nations (Unasur in Spanish, Unasul in Portuguese), with 12 South American nations as members, created in 2008; and the South American Defense Council, linked to Unasur and established in 2010. Brazil also became more active in resolving disputes in the region. For example, it hosted negotiations between Peru and Ecuador after their brief border war in 1995, defused an attempted coup in Paraguay in 1996, helped to ease tensions after Colombian forces attacked a camp of the FARC (*Fuerzas Armadas Revolucionarias de Colombia*) in Ecuador in 2008, and took sides in the constitutional crisis in Honduras in 2009.

Globally, Brazil became more active as well. It joined the expanded G20 group of nations after the financial crisis of 2008–2009. It formed part of the IBSA group of democratic emerging powers (India, Brazil, and South Africa), whose first summit was in 2006. In 2009, Brazil participated in the first BRIC summit of large emerging market nations (Brazil, Russia, India, and China), which, in 2011, added South Africa (Stuenkel, 2017), and, in 2014, it contributed to the establishment of the BRICS-managed New Development Bank.[1] Brazil also expanded its diplomatic presence in Africa in the 2000s, opening several new embassies there. Brazil has also been a prominent voice in international negotiations over, and initiatives involving, global finance, trade, climate change, poverty alleviation, global health, peacekeeping, and internet governance.

At the same time, domestically, Brazil is internationalizing. It is receiving immigrants from Bolivia, Paraguay, Peru, Haiti, Syria, and other countries. More of its people now travel abroad and more of them learn English, especially young people. Direct investment, both into and from Brazil, is robust. If you have recently eaten a Burger King meal, drunk a Budweiser beer, or flown on an Embraer jet, you are consuming or visiting a product of Brazilian investment and Brazil's internationalization.

Figure 10.1 Presidents Obama and Lula pictured here in Washington D.C. in March 2009. Foreign Minister Celso Amorim and Abraham Lincoln look on in the background.

Source: www.whitehouse.gov, Wikimedia commons: https://commons.wikimedia.org/wiki/File:President_ Barack_Obama_meets_with_President_Luiz_Inácio_Lula_da_Silvia.jpg

Brazil's rise in the 1990s and 2000s received wide recognition. When President Obama of the USA saw Brazilian President Lula at the G20 Summit in London in April, 2009, he greeted him by saying, "This is my man right here! I love this guy." He later remarked that Lula was "the most popular politician on earth", attributing this to his "good looks"[2] (see Figure 10.1). The Brazilian press commented widely on Obama's praise of Lula. Such a moment, however, generates several questions. What was behind Brazil's apparent recent rise in prominence and influence in world affairs? Why did that rise apparently stall after 2010? What does Brazil want in global affairs, and how does Brazil's foreign policy establishment see its country and the world? What are the major disagreements on foreign policy in Brazil, and what are the country's major challenges in dealing with the world?

This chapter explores these questions. It first describes Brazil's distinctive diplomatic tradition and doctrine. It then compares and contrasts the different foreign policies of two administrations in which presidents were active in shaping policy: those of Fernando Henrique Cardoso (1995–2002) and Lula (2003–2010), in order to highlight some of the debates about foreign policy in the country and describe the ups and downs of Brazil's global influence. Then, in the conclusion, it summarizes the main challenges of Brazilian foreign policy.

Brazil's diplomatic tradition and experience

As noted in Chapter 2, Brazil is an iconoclastic country with few national heroes. Among the heroes that *do* exist, very few are military figures. This is different from other countries, such as the USA and the UK, where military leaders have long been celebrated as national heroes. One of the few military figures venerated in Brazil is the Duque de Caxias, who won most of his awards putting down secessionist rebellions in Brazil in the nineteenth century.

Brazil's diplomats tend to be more fêted than its military leaders. Like its former colonizer, Portugal, Brazil is a country with a relatively weak armed forces, and thus "must, perforce, rely more on guile than on strength".[3] For former diplomat and government minister Rubens Ricupero, understanding how Portugal survived as an independent country in Western Europe up to the present day is key to understanding Brazilian diplomacy. The Portuguese–Brazilian "diplomacy of weakness" involved compensating for military inferiority by other means, including "the search for alliances and the influence of intangible factors, such as knowledge, intellectual arguments, careful preparation for negotiations, and the ability to negotiate from unfavorable positions" (Ricupero, 2017, p. 37). This is what Ricupero calls smart power, or power based on intellectual and cultural resources rather than military force (see also Burges, 2017, p. 241).[4]

In the pantheon of Brazil's diplomatic heroes, Alexandre de Gusmão has a special place. He is valued for negotiating the Treaty of Madrid in 1750 (see Pimentel, 2013, pp. 53–85; Ricupero 2017, pp. 57–69). This treaty ended armed conflict between Spain and Portugal in the region that is now Southern Brazil, Uruguay, and northeastern Argentina. It allowed Brazil to expand the borders of the country westwards, beyond the limit originally established in the Treaty of Tordesillas in 1534. If the latter treaty had remained in effect, São Paulo and the lands west and south of it would have been in Spanish hands, and two-thirds of the current national territory would have been outside the country's borders. This makes Brazil very unlike the USA, which acquired territory largely through purchase and military conquest. In the words of Rubens Ricupero (2017, p. 27), "Few countries owe as much to diplomacy as does Brazil."

Another key figure in the history commemorated by Brazil's Foreign Ministry is Rui Barbosa de Oliveira. In 1907, he participated in a peace conference in The Hague where he argued for a rules-based international order founded on the principle of the equality of sovereign states, a recurrent theme in Brazilian diplomacy, for which he earned the nickname (at least among Brazilians) "the eagle of The Hague" (Cardim, 2008; Lafer, 2009, pp. 6–7; Pimentel, 2013, pp. 489–527; Stuenkel, 2016, p. 57). Eager to uphold the principle articulated by Rui Barbosa at The Hague, Brazil joined the League of Nations in 1920 and contributed to the creation of the post-First World War international order. It left the organization in 1926, however, because it was not awarded a permanent seat on the Council, the principal governing body of the League of Nations.[5]

The patron saint of the Brazilian diplomatic corps is the Baron of Rio Branco, José Maria da Silva Paranhos Junior (1845–1912 – see Figure 10.2).[6] He was a diplomat, historian, politician, and professor. He was also a royalist who lamented the end of the monarchy in 1888 and used his title throughout his life even though this was supposed to be prohibited by the government.

Figure 10.2 A monument depicting the Baron of Rio Branco that stands in the Praça da Alfândega in central Porto Alegre, RS.

Source: Ricardo André Frantz, Wikimedia commons: https://commons.wikimedia.org/wiki/File:Mon umento_ao_Barão_do_Rio_Branco_1.jpg

Upon returning to Brazil after serving diplomatically in Europe, Rio Branco became involved in the settlement of border disputes between Brazil and its neighbors. He took a scholarly approach to these conflicts and studied geography and history to press Brazil's claims. He negotiated treaties with Argentina over the border between Argentina and the Brazilian states of Santa Catarina and Parana (1895), and with France over the border between the Brazilian territory of Amapá and French Guyana (1900). Rio Branco became Foreign Minister in 1902 and served in that role until 1912. During that time, he continued to negotiate Brazil's borders, with Bolivia over the area that is now the state of Acre in the Brazilian Northwest (1903), and with Ecuador over a disputed region of the Amazon (1904). He is credited with consolidating the Brazilian nation by establishing the present-day borders, and doing it through peaceful negotiations rather than military force (Pimentel, 2013, pp. 263–299, pp. 405–438; Ricupero, 2017, pp. 27).[7]

Rio Branco also realigned Brazilian strategy to make the country closer to the USA. The USA was a rising power in the early twentieth century and it had become the largest foreign buyer of Brazilian coffee, Brazil's most important export at that time. Rio Branco established the first Brazilian Embassy in the USA in Washington, DC in 1910, and sent one of his top diplomats, Joaquim

Nabuco, former Minister in London, to head the Embassy as Ambassador. Brazil's good relations with the USA were an important asset to it in the border disputes with France, Argentina, Bolivia, and Ecuador.

The Baron of Rio Branco and his role in national consolidation forms part of the official narrative promoted by Brazil's Foreign Ministry (known as *Itamaraty*, after the palace in Rio where it was originally housed). In essence, this narrative is that Brazil is *sui generis* and has a distinctive approach to diplomacy. For Rubens Ricupero, Brazil is a country that is satisfied with its territorial status, at peace with its neighbors, confident in international law, accustomed to, and skilled in, the achievement of negotiated solutions, and keen to be recognized as a constructive, moderating force in world affairs, working to make the international system more democratic and egalitarian, but also more peaceful and balanced (Ricupero, 2017, p. 31; see also Patriota, 2010).

Celso Lafer, a former Brazilian Foreign Minister, makes similar points about the essence of Brazilian foreign policy. He emphasizes how Brazilian diplomats search for the Aristotelian mean (between rich and powerful states, on one hand, and poorer and weaker ones, on the other), articulate consensus, and use international law and multilateral institutions to seek solutions to conflicts (Lafer, 2009, p. 115).[8] For Lafer and many other analysts, Brazil's key characteristics are its isolation from the centers of global power and its condition as a developing country. In consonance with these conditions, the thread of continuity in Brazilian foreign policy is the concern for autonomy in order to pursue national economic development (Lafer, 2009, pp. 101–119; Vigevani and Cepaluni, 2009, pp. 1–9).

The thinking of the sociologist Gilberto Freyre (1900–1987) was influential in the creation of Itamaraty's core doctrine (Freyre, 1946). Freyre's book *Casa Grande e Senzala* (in English, *The Masters and the Slaves*), published in 1933, challenged negative assessments of Brazil's racially mixed society. It argued for Brazil to be considered a new and hybrid civilization that combined, in the Americas, the contributions of European, African, and indigenous civilizations (Vieira, 2018, p. 156).[9] In later works, Freyre described this civilization as "lusotropical." For Freyre, the Brazilian people were essentially generous, happy, sensual, peaceful, orderly, tolerant of racial and religious differences, and at peace with the world (Chaui, 2017, p. 37). Freyre also saw in the Baron of Rio Branco a representative of these values (Ricupero, 2017, pp. 709, 711).

For some, Itamaraty's core doctrine, high degree of professionalism, and relative insulation and autonomy from other government agencies and from civil society make it a uniquely effective government ministry. The examination to enter Itamaraty is famously difficult, giving the ministry prestige. (This characteristic gives rise to the criticism that the diplomatic corps is distant from the concerns and culture of ordinary Brazilians.) For Ricupero (2017, p. 30), the Foreign Ministry and its role in foreign policy have been met with almost universal approval inside Brazil (2017, pg. 30). Itamaraty has overcome some of the deficiencies found in other parts of the Brazilian state and, in a boxing metaphor often used by diplomats, consistently "punched above its weight." Similarly, for the political scientist Philippe Schmitter, "No other 'third world peripheral' state has such a consistently well-trained and autonomous diplomatic service. Whatever regime or government in power, Itamaraty had always guaranteed a high degree of continuity in its foreign policy" (Schmitter, 2009, p. x).

Other analysts identify Brazil's ambiguous identity as a key asset in its diplomacy. For example, is Brazil "Western" or "non-Western"? For some, Brazil is a country that is comfortable being, at the same time, both.[10] Much of its population has European ancestry. The indigenous population is small, with fewer than one million people in a population of 207 million. Moreover, there are no records of large-scale indigenous civilizations (similar to the Incas in Peru or the Aztecs in Mexico) in Brazil before European conquest. Brazil's institutions look Western to European or North American eyes. On the other hand, roughly half of the population has some African ancestry, and Brazil has one of the largest black populations in the world outside of Africa. At the level of the general population, there are beliefs, practices, and customs that some would describe as non-Western, especially in the interior of the country and in indigenous reserves. Brazil also has a colonial history, giving it affinities with the more recently decolonized countries of Africa and Asia. This gives Brazilian diplomats a unique ability to dialogue with counterparts across the main dividing lines in global politics, including West and non-West, North and South. According to the political scientist Matias Spektor, many Brazilian diplomats are critical of the role of race in determining who gets access to decision-making in institutions of global governance, and some of them at the United Nations even refer to US and European officials, as well as their allies, as "the whites" (Spektor, 2016, p. 32).

Not all observers share a positive assessment of the Foreign Ministry, its portrayal of Brazil, and its role in articulating and implementing Brazilian foreign policy abroad. For philosopher Marilena Chaui, for example, the Freyrian vision of Brazil's peaceful and harmonious national development is a myth. She argues that some of Brazil's most important political changes, such as the creation and end of both the first republic (1889–1930) and the Estado Novo (1937–1945), were the result of military coups d'états. Furthermore, Brazilian history is littered with the violent repression of popular rebellions (Chaui, 2017, p. 36).[11]

The Itamaraty narrative of Brazil's peaceful history also glosses over the Paraguay War (1865–1870), a bloody conflict that led to the reduction of Paraguayan territory to about half its previous size and the destruction of much of the male population of that country. It also ignores inequalities of power. Brazil did not have to use force in dealing with many of its smaller neighbors because it was so much more powerful than they were. In the dispute over Acre, for example, Brazilians invaded the area and the Bolivians felt they had very little choice but to demand compensation for the loss of their territory, which was already a *fait accompli* (Jacobs, 2012). The Baron of Rio Branco himself recognized that his success in negotiations depended, at least in part, on the threat posed by the Brazilian Navy (Alsina Jr., 2014).

For political scientists Sean Burges and Jean Daudelin, the Brazilian Foreign Ministry has historically been "oligarchic." This is because Itamaraty monopolized decision-making within an "old boys' network" (Burges and Daudelin, 2017, p. 224), and also because the interests represented by the Foreign Ministry were narrow, often benefiting a small circle of "national champion" firms like Odebrecht (construction), Petrobras (oil), Vale (mining), the state-owned Bank of Brazil, and a handful of others.

In the view of international relations scholar Marco Vieira, Brazilians' ambiguous or hybrid identity masks deep-seated anxiety and a desire to measure themselves "according to largely unattainable standards of Western modernity" (Vieira, 2018, p. 162). In the time of the Baron of Rio Branco, according to Vieira, this resulted in a "whites-only" policy of recruitment to the Foreign Ministry (Vieira, 2018, p. 156). For Vieira, even Freyre's "lusotropicalism" is still "centered on the 'desire' to be of the West, even if different or even better than conventional Western civilizational standards" (Vieira, 2018, p. 163). For critics such as Vieira, Itamaraty represents a patriarchal and elitist society, and its portrayal of Brazil largely reflects the interests and experience of the upper, largely white strata of that social order. Ricupero gives ammunition to such critics when he reminisces that his enchantment with the Foreign Ministry reached its pinnacle when, during his examination to enter the diplomatic corps in the Itamaraty Palace in 1958, "servants in gloves and white uniforms with golden buttons served us coffee in elegant cups with gold trim and the coat of arms of the republic". According to the former Ambassador, who had grown up in a working-class neighborhood in São Paulo, he never lost this "love at first sight" of the Foreign Ministry (Ricupero, 2017, p. 24).

Despite the continued relevance of the debate between critics and defenders of Itamaraty, it is true that in South America war has been less important and much smaller in scale than in many other parts of the world. As Andrés Malamud argues, state formation in South America was "softer" than in other regions such as Europe and South Asia. Wars and the destruction of states have been relatively rare and limited, and borders have often been demarcated peacefully (Malamud, 2017, p. 153). Today, the whole of Latin America and the Caribbean is a nuclear-free zone, the result of the Treaty of Tlatelalco in 1968. And Brazil is a relatively rule-abiding and peaceful global actor, even in the region that it dominates. In the words of Rubens Ricupero, it is a dinosaur, but a "vegetarian dinosaur."[12] For example, Petrobras's gas facilities in Bolivia were nationalized by the government of Evo Morales in 2006. Some countries might have saber rattled, sent troops to the border, and issued threats. Brazil simply negotiated compensation for the loss of Petrobras's assets (Burges, 2017, p. 242).

There is another important element to Brazil's foreign policy tradition. This is its role in shaping the post-Second World War order, whose institutions are still important in twenty-first century global politics. The view of Brazil's Foreign Ministry is that Brazil's special role in shaping that order make it deserving of access to the highest tables of global governance. Before and at the beginning of the Second World War, Brazil's President Getúlio Vargas played a "double game", maintaining cordial relations with fascist Italy and Nazi Germany, as well as the USA. When he felt that he had been forced to choose sides, Vargas chose the Allies, and Brazil was the only Latin American country to send troops to fight in the Second World War. Brazil sent 25,000 soldiers to Italy to fight under US command in Tuscany and Emilia-Romagna (Hilton, 1979; McCann, 1995). Brazil also allowed the USA to establish air bases in Recife and Natal in the Northeast during the Second World War. These bases were vital to getting supplies to North Africa. Brazil also signed agreements pledging to sell natural resources to the USA as part of the war effort. As a result of Brazil's declaration of war against the Axis powers on 22 August 1942, it lost shipping to German U-boats. Thirty-three of its ships were sunk and more than 1,000 people lost their lives in these attacks (McCann, 1995).

Brazilian policymakers believed that their loyalty to the Allied war effort – which took time but was eventually wholehearted – would bring them rewards at the end of the Second World War. Brazil did receive military assistance and private investment from the USA after the war, but Latin America was not a priority for the USA and no Marshall Plan-type aid was supplied to Brazil (Hilton, 1981). Brazil strengthened its military and became the most important industrial power in South America after the war, but its aspirations for international recognition were thwarted at the United Nations, created in 1945. Brazil pressed for, but failed to win, a permanent seat in the Security Council. The Soviet Union and Great Britain successfully argued that a seat for Brazil would give the USA a second vote in the body, since the USA and Brazil were closely aligned at the time. Since that time, Brazil has continued to press for a reform of the United Nations and its inclusion as a permanent member of the Security Council. In recent times, it has joined the G4, with India, Japan, and Germany, who also would like permanent membership of the Security Council, to lobby for this reform (Patriota, 2010, p. 22).

In Brazil's post-Second World War diplomacy, its relationship with the USA looms large as a major concern. This relationship is asymmetric: it is far more important to Brazil than it is to the USA. The ties have at times been very close, as under the Presidency of Castelo Branco (1964–1967), the leader of a military regime, when Brazil sent troops to participate in the USA's occupation of the Dominican Republic in 1965. USA–Brazil relations were again close in the early 1970s during the Nixon administration in the USA and the Médici administration in Brazil (Spektor, 2009).[13] But they have also been more distant under governments of various ideological complexions, such as during the independent foreign policies of presidents Jânio Quadros (1961) and João Goulart (1961–1964) (Loureiro, 2017). President Ernesto Geisel (1974–1979), another military president, also had a cool relationship with the USA due to tensions over West German cooperation with Brazil in the development of the latter's nuclear energy industry, and criticisms of Brazil's human rights record by the Carter administration (1977–1980).[14]

More recently, Brazilian foreign policymakers have worked hard to retain autonomy *vis-à-vis* the USA, making sure not to align automatically with it, but also maintaining cordial and meaningful relations. Under President Lula, the Foreign Minister, Celso Amorim, talked about a foreign policy that was "active and assertive" (*ativa e altiva*; see Amorim, 2015, 2017). Scholars debate the extent to which Brazilian foreign policy has been genuinely autonomous of the USA. For example, Maria Regina Soares de Lima argues that Brazil's default position is a foreign policy of prestige (or status-seeking), the claiming of a special position in the international hierarchy due to Brazil's unique character-istics. This default position does not challenge the international status quo and seeks only a special position for Brazil, not a structural change in the rules and institutions of the global order. For Soares de Lima, the only really autono-mous foreign policies in Brazil's republican history were the brief "double game" of President Vargas at the beginning of the Second World War, the independent foreign policies of Presidents Quadros and Goulart in the early 1960s, and the active and assertive foreign policy of President Lula.[15] However, this typology seems too restrictive to other observers, and neglects other moments of autonomy, such as those that occurred during the Geisel presidency and described above.

In summary, Brazil is a country with a strikingly consistent foreign policy doctrine and a remarkably professional Foreign Ministry, one which, historically, has had broad autonomy to devise and implement policy. Numerous debates surround Itamaraty, such as whether its portrayal of Brazil as fundamentally peaceful is accurate, to what extent it represents a broad "national interest" or, instead, the interests of an oligarchy, whether Brazil's ambiguous identity is an asset or a hindrance to it, and whether its aspirations can be matched by its resources. In recent years, Itamaraty's monopolization of foreign policy has been challenged by two developments. These are the increasing activism of civil society, reflecting a population with rising levels of education and interest in foreign affairs, and the involvement of Brazilian chief executives who have on occasion "presidentialized" foreign policy (Cason and Power, 2009). In the next section, the administrations of two presidents who are said to have presidentialized foreign policy will be examined in order to highlight some of the recurrent tensions in Brazil's approach to world affairs.

Foreign policy under Cardoso and Lula

The foreign policies of President Fernando Henrique Cardoso (1995–2002) and Luiz Inácio "Lula" da Silva (2003–2010) reflect two different views of the international order and the best way for Brazil to behave within that order. In the view of international relations specialists Tullo Vigevani and Gabriel Cepaluni (2009, pp. 53–80, 81–100), these contrasting visions can be summarized as autonomy through participation under Cardoso and autonomy through diversification under Lula.

The Cardoso administration's orientation is captured in President Fernando Henrique Cardoso's second inaugural address on 1 January 1995. On that occasion Cardoso said:

Brazil is respected abroad again. Foreign investment has multiplied, generating new horizons for Brazilians. Again on the external level, Brazil is reaping the benefits of democracy, economic stability and a renewed confidence in the potential of our market. The country has become more relevant to the world. At the same time, the world has become more relevant to the well-being of Brazilians … The national interest, today, is not achieved through isolation. We affirm our sovereignty by participating and by integrating, not by distancing [ourselves]. This is what we are doing in MERCOSUL – an irreversible priority of our foreign policy. It is what we are achieving with the creation of an integrated space of peace, democracy and prosperity shared with South America. And it is reflected in our vision of hemispheric integration and more solid relations with the EU, Russia, China and Japan, without taking away from our historic links with Africa.

(Quoted in Bonfim, 2004, pp. 427–428)[16]

The Cardoso administration's foreign policy is associated with the traditionalist wing of the Foreign Ministry, represented by Cardoso's two Foreign Ministers, Luiz Felipe Lampreia and Celso Lafer. It sought the Aristotelian mean and the "constructive moderation" advocated by Lafer (2009, p. 115), generally accepting the rules of global capitalism. It implemented neoliberal reforms domestically, lowering tariff barriers and privatizing state-owned industries. It generally respected the international hierarchy of states and the rules of various international regimes. For example, it controversially signed the nuclear non-proliferation treaty (NPT) in 1998, despite the fact that the Foreign Ministry had denounced the NPT for years. When the Brazilian government signed the NPT, Itamaraty abandoned the position that the treaty reflected Cold War inequalities because it was mainly used to prevent nuclear proliferation rather than to reduce the arsenals of the already existing nuclear powers (Vieira, 2018, p. 158).

The Cardoso administration prioritized relations with traditional partners such as the USA and the European Union, despite occasional complaints about "asymmetrical globalization" (USA unilateralism) by President Cardoso. Its foreign policy generally met with the approval of commentators who are comfortable with the existing distribution of power within the international system. Mares and Trinkunas (2016, p. 66), for example, see Cardoso's foreign policy as prudent and effective (see also Gordon, 2001). Brazil maintained good relations with the USA while resisting the USA's project of a Free Trade Agreement for the Americas (a hemispheric economic union), quietly strengthened ties with China, India, and South Africa, and on occasion defended democracy in South America without provoking too much criticism from neighbors about Brazilian interventionism.

The Lula administration had a different and more critical approach to the global order. This can be captured in Lula's first inaugural address of 1 January 2003:

Our foreign policy will reflect also the hopes for change that are being expressed on our streets. In my government, Brazil's diplomatic action will be oriented towards a humanistic perspective and will, above all, be an instrument for national development. Through external commerce, the capture of advanced technology, the search for productive investments, Brazil's external relations must contribute to an improvement in the life conditions of the Brazilian woman and man, raising levels of income and generating dignified jobs ... The democratization of international relations without hegemonies of any kind is as important to the future of humanity as the consolidation and development of democracy within each state ... The resolutions of the Security Council must be faithfully complied with ... We are beginning today a new chapter in the history of Brazil, not as a submissive nation, abandoning its sovereignty, not as an unjust nation, watching passively the suffering of its poor, but as a proud (*altiva*) nation, noble, courageously affirming itself in the world as a nation of all, without distinction of class, ethnicity, sex, and belief.

(Quoted in Bonfim, 2004, pp. 449–453)

While there is a debate about to what extent Lula's foreign policy represented a departure from that of his predecessor, this speech contains an insistence that the global order should not permit "hegemonies of any kind," and that Brazil is not a "submissive nation." During the Lula era, one tradition of Brazilian foreign policy became more accentuated. That is the criticism of global inequalities of power and resources, in which 85% of the world's income goes to the richest 20% of the world's population (Hurrell, 2007, p. 11). For Spektor,

The core belief [of Brazilian foreign policymakers] is that the USA and its European allies should treat non-Western states with greater respect and some degree of "equality." In the Brazilian view, U.S. behavior is often imperialistic, unilateral, and dismissive of third countries and of the United Nations – in sum, illiberal.

(Spektor, 2016, p. 34)[17]

Acting on the basis of this view, the Lula administration diversified foreign relations in order to increase autonomy from the US and Europe, though it usually avoided openly clashing with these powers. In fact, in sending troops to Haiti and assuming command of MINUSTAH, the United Nations' peacekeeping operation in that country, Brazil supported US strategy in the Caribbean. (Brazilian troops were stationed in Haiti from 2004 to 2017 – see Figure 10.3.) Lula's "South–South" diplomacy was intended to complement, not substitute, Brazil's relations with its traditional partners. Brazil opened new embassies in Africa, strengthened the integration of South America, and sought allies in the developing world. It also carefully cultivated relations with China, which became Brazil's biggest trade partner, supplanting the USA.[18]

There were times, however, when conflicts with the USA flared up. For example, Brazil, acting with India and other developing countries, rejected a US proposal at the Cancun meeting of the World Trade Organization in 2003,

Figure 10.3 A Brazilian soldier undertaking peacekeeping operations in Haiti in 2010.
Source: United States Navy, Wikimedia commons – https://commons.wikimedia.org/wiki/File:
US_Navy_100316-N-9116F-001_A_Brazilian_U.N._peacekeeper_walks_with_Haitian_children_
during_a_patrol_in_Cite_Soleil.jpg

drawing the ire of then US Trade Representative, Robert Zoellick. President
Lula's foreign policy advisor, Marco Aurelio Garcia, a long-standing member of
the Workers' Party (*Partido dos Trabalhadores*, or PT), built alliances with other
center-left governments in Latin America. When Honduran President Manuel
Zelaya, a leftist leader, was removed from office and sent into exile in 2009,
Brazil was one of the strongest critics of the new interim government and even
sheltered Zelaya in the Brazilian Embassy in Tegulcigalpa, the Honduran capital,
for several months in 2009–2010. Brazil took longer to recognize the subsequent
elected government in Honduras than did many other countries in the region,
finally doing so in May 2011. Brazil was also criticized by some observers for not
being sufficiently constructive in finding a solution to the crisis (Casas-Zamora,
2011; Pereira, 2017b; Roett, 2011, p. 146).

During this time, Brazil also dissented from the evolving international
doctrine of Responsibility to Protect, or R2P. First articulated in 2000, R2P
asserted the right of the international community to intervene in the affairs of a
sovereign state in order to prevent genocide, war crimes, ethnic cleansing, and
crimes against humanity (Bierrenbach, 2011, p. 206). Sparked by misgivings
over the UN's failure to act in response to the genocide in Rwanda in 1994 and

the Srebenica massacre in Bosnia in 1995, and influenced by concerns about terrorism in the wake of the 9/11 attacks in the USA, R2P was adopted at the UN General Assembly in 2005.

The Brazilian response to R2P was to call for caution. Brazilian diplomats conceded the principle that sovereignty does not excuse governments for failing to respect the rights of their citizens. But they pointed out that the application of R2P was inevitably political, and that the instruments of its application, usually armed forces, could pose a risk to the people they were supposed to protect.[19] For Brazil's Foreign Ministry, states had a duty to weigh the costs and benefits of intervention and refrain from intervention if the former exceeded the latter. This was not simply an invocation of traditional sovereignty, but a concern with the unintended consequences of intervention conducted in the name of humanitarianism, and a fear that the big powers could use R2P as a cover for aggressive interventionism in their own interests (Beirrenbach, 2011, pp. 14–15, 203–211; Kenkel and Stefan, 2016, p. 43).[20]

The foreign policy activism of the Lula administration reached its apogee on 17 May 2010, when Iran, Turkey, and Brazil signed the Tehran Declaration, an agreement that placed limits on Iran's nuclear power program. Hailed as a breakthrough by Brazilian Foreign Minister Celso Amorim, the deal was condemned by the USA and then ultimately rejected in the United Nations Security Council, when China and Russia joined the UK, France, and the US in tightening economic sanctions against Iran (Reid, 2014, p. 240).[21] The Tehran Declaration sparked heated debates. The disagreements centered on the perceived wisdom and effectiveness of Lula's foreign policy, but also on whether Brazil was essentially a system-supporting or a system-challenging actor in the global system. "Does it only want a seat at the table, or does it want to change the menu?" was a question asked of Brazil by many international observers, using a culinary metaphor to frame the country's global aspirations. The question has generated heated debate, with observers often projecting their own hopes – whether for change or an upholding of the status quo – on to Brazil.

With regard to the Lula administration, critics lined up to condemn the Tehran Declaration as unhelpful showboating in an area outside of Brazil's traditional area of influence. Prominent diplomats from the Cardoso era condemned the "ideologization" of foreign policy, lamenting the influence of advisor Marco Aurelio Garcia, whom they accused of being "anti-American" and criticizing Foreign Minister Celso Amorim's decision to join the PT (Hunter, 2010, p. 159; Ricupero, 2010, p. 41). These critics abhorred the images of Lula celebrating the Tehran agreement with then Iranian President, Mahmoud Ahmadinejad, and Turkish President, Recep Tayyip Erdogan, and decried the authoritarian tendencies of these two leaders (see Figure 10.4). Rubens Ricupero claimed that the Tehran Declaration and other examples of overreach by the Lula government reflected the excessive personal involvement of Lula in policy-making, and the president's lack of ethical and democratic values (Ricupero, 2010, pp. 41–42).

Figure 10.4 President Lula with Iranian president Mahmoud Ahmadinejad, pictured here in 2009, several months before the Tehran Declaration was officially signed.

Source: Agência Brasil, Wikimedia commons: https://commons.wikimedia.org/wiki/File:Mahmoud_Ahmadinejad_and_Luiz_Inácio_Lula_da_Silva_2009.jpg

Defenders of Lula's foreign policy responded that the charges of "ideologization" missed the point, and that all Brazilian governments had ideological and political perspectives from which they viewed the world. They objected to what they saw as the conformism and quietism of the diplomatic old guard, and argued that Brazil was correct to challenge the status quo of global governance. For these observers, Brazil had every right to negotiate the Tehran Declaration. As a country that had developed a nuclear power program for its energy needs but had decided, in tandem with Argentina, not to build a bomb, it had the necessary technical expertise to talk to the Iranians about their nuclear program. In this view, far from being an unhelpful intrusion by Brazil, the Iran–Turkey–Brazil negotiations were a constructive attempt to break a deadlock that was endangering global security, and they did so within guidelines laid down by the US. In the words of Celso Amorim,

> The arrogance of the P5, including China and Russia, which negotiated exemptions in accordance with their own exclusive interests, has prevailed over the conciliatory efforts of two outsiders [Brazil and Turkey]. The global

political system is still incapable of absorbing the changes [that have taken place] in the geometry of power. But inevitably that will happen, even if [the wait] lasts twenty or thirty years. And [when it happens] it will help bring peace to the world.

(Amorim, 2017, p. 66)[22]

Brazilian foreign policy going forward

With regard to Brazil's stance towards the international system today, opinion is divided. For some commentators, Brazil is a mildly reformist power that is largely system supporting. For Spektor, Brazil's primary aim is "accruing power and influence"; it does not have a grand strategy, or "an explicit and comprehensive vision of the reformed global order" it would like to see constructed (Spektor, 2016, p. 35).[23] Burges concurs, arguing that

> elements of the revisionist structural game being advanced by Brazil thus take on system-supporting characteristics that further entrench the norms of market economics, democratic political processes and security provision in a way that could almost be likened to a traditional middle power but for the Brazilian tendency to not privilege the interests of core Northern countries.
>
> (Burges, 2017, p. 243)[24]

Brazilian diplomat and former Foreign Minister Antonio Patriota has a similar analysis. For him, one of the most striking features of the contemporary world order is that China – a non-European, non-Western power – will become the world's biggest economy in future decades. Brazil appears comfortable with this, and the trend towards multipolarity – the diffusion of power away from a single hegemon towards a variety of competing and cooperating states – is already advanced. For Patriota:

> It is wrong to imply that the rising powers aspire to create a radically different world order. Visibly, for the majority of the international community – rising powers included – the real issue is one of compliance by all with existing rules, without unilateralism, and with expanded opportunity for participation in decision-taking … it is possible to affirm that the contemporary world order, rather than being "Western" or "American-led" already reflects a plurality of influences and is not single-handedly led by anyone. Clearly, rising powers are more attached to it than those who feel a nostalgia for unipolar unilateralism.
>
> (Patriota, 2017, p. 18)

Other analysts argue that as Brazil rises, it might clash with more powerful states more frequently, and is at least potentially a system-challenging actor. For Milani, Pinheiro, and Soares de Lima (2017), for example, Brazil faces a "graduation dilemma" that could take it in one of several different possible directions. The graduation dilemma only applies to a handful of non-nuclear rising powers: Brazil, South Africa, Turkey, Mexico, Nigeria, Saudi Arabia, and South Korea. These powers aspire to "graduate" from being rule-takers to rule-makers in the international system, but they are dependent on recognition by other actors. Established powers may contest their positions, and the leaders of neighboring countries could see them as bullies. They often attempt to use regional integration to enhance their own global prominence, a process that generates tensions. The leaders of these states must try to convince both domestic and international audiences that they should graduate, but they may encounter criticism and resistance both at home and abroad.

According to Malamud (2017), Brazil's rise in the 1990s and 2000s was facilitated by two sets of favorable factors. Internationally, the commodity boom enhanced the value of Brazil's exports such as iron ore, soybeans, and meat. The rise of China and the shift of the locus of global economic power spurred the demand for Brazilian commodity exports. Brazil's peaceful region helped also, allowing Brazilian policymakers to prioritize global issues while furthering integration with their neighbors. Domestically, Brazil benefited from good leadership during the Cardoso and Lula administrations and a high degree of consensus about policy priorities. What is striking is that several of those factors no longer existed in the 2010s. The commodity boom ended and Chinese growth slowed down. Brazilian leadership changed under the presidencies of Dilma Rousseff (2011–2016) and Michel Temer (2016–2018), and the prior policy consensus broke down under the weight of economic recession and political crisis in 2015–2016. The Carwash anti-corruption investigation implicated several of the national champions that had been beneficiaries of Brazilian foreign policy, including the Odebrecht construction company. Some observers, including Mello and Spektor (2018), argue that the evidence produced by Carwash requires a thorough re-evaulation of Brazilian foreign policy, including the alleged autonomy of Itamaraty.[25] While it is not within the scope of this chapter to conduct such a re-evaulation, this is an important topic that will no doubt attract researchers in the future.

It is not clear whether Brazil will "rise" again after this period of relative stagnation in the 2010s. Brazil is unusually dependent for its influence on favorable external perception of its political and economic model. As Fernando Henrique Cardoso said in 1995,

> I believe that Brazil has a place reserved amongst the successful countries of the planet in the next century. I am convinced that the only important obstacles that we face to occupy this place comes from our internal disequilibria – the inequalities between regions and social groups.
>
> (Quoted in Bonfim, 2004, p. 411)

This is, in part, because Brazil is not seen as a military power. Unlike fellow BRICS countries China, India, and Russia, it lacks the capacity to project military power beyond its own borders and within its region (with the exception of its peacekeeping deployments). Admittedly, this is partly because Brazil has not needed to project military power in its region, but in a world in which hard power matters, this limitation is important. Brazil's armed forces are used exclusively to defend the national territory and help with public security and social welfare inside the country.[26] Because of this dependence on external perception, and because of the cyclical nature of its economic and political development, Brazil is perhaps destined to be something of a "yo-yo" country, rising and receding in international influence in accordance with its image abroad. While Spektor (2016, p. 35) is right that behind the scenes Brazil's diplomatic infrastructure remains impressive, and "Brazilian leaders and diplomats now have the clout to facilitate or complicate collective action as never before", this pattern of boom and bust could endure for the short and medium term.

Conclusion

Brazil at the start of the 2020s appears to be neither a rising nor a declining power, but one paralyzed – perhaps only temporarily – by its own contradictions and internal conflicts. In its foreign policy it stands for peace, but internally, it is wracked by high levels of violence. It insists in global fora on the need for non-intervention, multilateralism, and a rules-based order, but in its own region it often prefers *ad hoc* maneuvers that preserve its own autonomy, and its dominance sometimes leads to accusations of interference by its neighbors.[27]

Brazil had a period of rising influence in the 1990s and especially the 2000s, but this was followed by an economic and political crisis. Both the governments of Dilma Rousseff (2011–2016) and Michel Temer (2016–2018) were preoccupied with their own survival and the domestic economic and political situation. Neither government evinced much interest in an activist foreign policy, and not even a humanitarian crisis on its own northern border triggered by the meltdown of the Chavista regime in Venezuela was enough to rouse the Brazilian foreign policy establishment to action.

Brazil is a power that does not project military force abroad in an offensive fashion. It prefers to build up its military capability for defensive purposes. Its priorities are to guard the green Amazon, the fresh water and biodiversity of the Amazon basin, and the so-called blue Amazon, the offshore oil deposits of the South Atlantic coast in the southeast. It also uses selected components of its military for international peacekeeping, as in Haiti in 2004–2017. Because of its distinctive profile, Brazil's global influence depends – to a much greater extent than regional military powers such as China, India, and Russia – on the perceived attractiveness of its economic and political model. When that model appears to be successful, as it did under President Lula (2003–2010), reasonable levels of economic growth of three and four percent per year were accompanied by social inclusion, the reduction of poverty, and even a slight dip in levels of income inequality. During this period, Brazil's visibility and influence rose significantly. But when Brazil appears to be politically polarized and in economic crisis, as it did in 2015–2016, its claims to greater global prestige and decision-making power look less plausible, and are less likely to be accepted by other actors.

In the best-case scenario, Brazil would reset its political and economic model after the 2018 presidential election and resume an activist foreign policy, reclaiming its place at the table in the numerous multilateral fora in which collective problems are confronted. If that were to occur, its diplomatic capacity in areas such as global finance, trade, climate change, poverty alleviation, global health, peacekeeping, and internet governance, which has risen steadily despite the vicissitudes of its domestic politics, would be augmented by a coherent strategic vision and a clearer voice in international affairs. Brazil can contribute, and has contributed, to the improvement of global governance. To what extent it will reclaim this role, and whether it will develop a clearer grand strategy to guide its international relations – and whether it will largely be a status quo or reformist power – remain open questions.

Notes

1 The BRIC acronym was coined in a 2001 report by Goldman Sachs economist Jim O'Neill, who was trying to attract investors to these large countries. See O'Neill, 2011, pp. 11–23, 239. The first BRIC Summit was proposed by the Russian government.
2 See Saxenal, 2010.
3 The quote is from a letter written in 1749 by the Marquis of Alorna in Goa, to King João V of Portugal. Cited in Hatton, 2011, p. 44.
4 Burges complements Ricupero's view of Brazilian foreign policy. "Rather than wielding power through imposition or coercion, the attempt is to reorient the policies and actions of other states through engagement and discussion" (Burges, 2017, p. 241). Some analysts follow Joseph Nye (2005) in calling this "soft power", but we prefer the term smart power in this context. Soft power, or the power of attraction rather than economic or military "hard power", is used frequently with reference to Brazilian foreign policy but in a variety of inconsistent and sometimes confusing ways, which is why we avoid using it here.
5 The Brazilian government of the time, led by President Artur Bernardes, issued a note in 1926 declaring its intention to withdraw from the League of Nations, and then refused to return in 1928. See The League of Nations, 1928. See also Leuchars, 2001.
6 A more recent figure in Brazilian diplomacy, someone who worked for the United Nations rather than the Brazilian Foreign Ministry, is Sergio Vieira de Mello (1948–2003). He worked for the United Nations for 34 years and was the Special Representative of the UN Secretary General in Iraq in 2003 when he was killed in a bombing in Baghdad. See Power, 2008.
7 Even though we think of Brazil as a relatively new country, its contemporary borders are actually older than those of the UK and some other European nations.
8 Lafer calls these "Grotian" solutions, meaning oriented towards international law. This is a reference to Hugo Grotius (1583–1645) a Dutch jurist and philosopher of international law and society. See Hurrell, 2007, p. 13, pp. 83–84 and "Hugo Grotius" in the *Stanford Encyclopedia of Philosophy*. Available at: https://plato.stanford.edu/entries/grotius/[accessed 19 February 2018].
9 For more on Gilberto Freyre and views of race in Brazil, see the chapter on race and ethnicity in this volume.

10 For an argument that Brazil is an important player in the construction of a "post-Western" world order, see Stuenkel, 2016. Brazil's identity as a Latin American country can also be seen as ambiguous. See Bethell, 2010.

11 These rebellions include the movement for independence in Minas Gerais in 1789 (the *Inconfidência Mineira*), the liberal and federalist revolt in Pernambuco from 1848–1850 (the *Revolução Praiera*), the community of runaway slaves in what is now Alagoas between 1605 and 1694 (*Palmares*), the settlement led by a messianic leader in Bahia in 1897 (*Canudos*), the revolt of peasants and rural workers in Paraná and Santa Catarina between 1912 and 1916 (the *Contestado*), the revolt of Rio Grande do Sul from 1835 to 1845 (the *Revolta Farroupilha*), the uprising of enlisted seamen against corporal punishment in the Brazilian Navy in 1910 (the *Revolta da Chibata*), the armed column of renegade military officers that traveled the country from 1925 to 1927 (the *Coluna Prestes*), the attempted Communist uprising in 1935 (the *Intentona*), and the guerrilla movements of the 1960s and 1970s. See Chaui, 2017, p. 36.

12 Comment made during a presentation at the Brazil Institute, King's College London, 23 October 2012. The presentation was entitled "Smart Power, Rio Branco and Brazilian Diplomacy in the Early Twentieth Century".

13 For an analysis of US–Brazilian relations from the point of view of a former Brazilian Ambassador to the USA, see Barbosa, 2015.

14 For evaluations of the more recent pattern of US–Brazilian relations, see Hirst and Pereira, 2016, and Whitehead 2010.

15 From a lecture by Professor Maria Regina Soares de Lima of the State University of Rio de Janeiro (UERJ), University of São Paulo, 26 April 2018.

16 In these and other instances, the authors have translated the Portuguese text into English.

17 Burges (2017, p. 242) echoes the point made by Spektor: "... the fundamental critique Brazil brings to its engagement with multilateral structures is that the norms driving the system and the rules used to enforce them are designed to privilege the North and limit the policy autonomy needed throughout the South to advance national developmental priorities."

18 For the impact of the rise of China and the decline of US hegemony on Latin America, see Dominguez, 2016. For a more positive view of the impact of China on the region, see Li and Christensen, 2012.

19 R2P was invoked at the UN Security Council in 2011 in Resolution 1973, authorizing the use of force to prevent the slaughter of civilians in Benghazi by the regime of Muammar Gaddafi. Brazil abstained from the vote on Resolution 1973, along with Germany, and invoked the idea of a Responsibility while Protecting. In the Brazilian view, Resolution 1973 was an intervention by NATO forces that began as a humanitarian effort, but was transformed into an act of regime change, as NATO-backed rebels toppled the Gaddafi regime and eventually killed Gaddafi himself. In the eyes of some Brazilian diplomats, the chaos in the post-Gaddafi environment in Libya justified Brazil's position in 2011. For the international relations theorists Kai Kenkel and Cristina Stefan, Brazil's invocation of RwP, while never fully developed, contributed to the evolution and refinement of the concept of R2P. See Kenkel and Stefan, 2016.

20 Brazilian diplomat Ana Maria Bierrenbach implies that Brazilian concerns about R2P might have been driven partly by a worry that the high bar for intervention – genocide, ethnic cleansing, war crimes, and crimes against humanity – could eventually be lowered, exposing Brazil to the risk of outside interference to mitigate human rights abuses in the country. Bierrenbach, 2011, p. 207.

21 According to Celso Amorim, Hillary Clinton telephoned him on 11 May 2010 and urged him not to go to Tehran (Amorim, 2017, p. 73).

22 The P5 are the five permanent members of the UN Security Council: Russia, China, France, the UK, and the USA.
23 For an attempt by the Temer government (2016–2018) to articulate a grand strategy, see Presidência da Republica, 2017. The attempt is not very convincing, and the Temer government was not generally seen as having a well-defined foreign policy.
24 Middle powers are states that are not great powers but that have more influence than small or weak states, both regionally and globally. They tend to work through multilateral institutions and informal coalitions of states and avoid unilateral actions. The category usually includes Brazil, Mexico, South Africa, South Korea, and Turkey as well as Canada, New Zealand, Norway, and the Netherlands. See Cooper, 2011.
25 It is also unclear to what extent the Carwash anti-corruption investigation and the information it has uncovered about bribes paid by Brazilian firms has damaged Brazil's image abroad. See Gaspar, 2017.
26 It is not correct to see Brazil as an entirely non-military power. The country has invested in its military technology, including in a nuclear submarine program undertaken with the French and the purchase of Swedish fighter planes. Its defence budget is one of the 15 largest in the world. See SIPRI: Brasil e o 12o Orcamento Defesa, 13 Abril 2014. Available at: www.defesanet.com.br/defesa/noticia/14978/SIPRI—Brasil-e-o-12o-orcamento-Defesa/ [accessed 19 January 2018]. However, Brazil's claims to global influence largely rest on its ability to live in peace with its neighbors and encourage peaceful international dialogue.
27 For a polemical analysis of Brazil's problems with its neighbors, see Malamud, 2011.

Suggested English readings

Amorim, C. (2017). *Acting globally: Memoirs of Brazil's assertive foreign policy*. Lanham, MD: Hamilton Books.
Burges, S. (2017). *Brazil in the world: The international relations of a South American giant*. Manchester: University of Manchester Press.
Lafer, C. (2009). Brazil and the world. In: I. Sachs, J. Wilheim, and P. S. Pinheiro (eds), *Brazil: A century of change*. Chapel Hill: University of North Carolina Press, pp. 101–119.
Mares, D., and Trinkunas, H. (2016). *Aspirational power: Brazil on the long road to global influence*. Washington, DC: Brookings Institution Press.
Milani, C., Pinheiro, L., and Soares de Lima, M.R.S. (2017). Brazil's foreign policy and the "Graduation Dilemma". *International Affairs*, 93(3), 585–605.
Patriota, A. (2017). Is the world ready for cooperative multipolarity? *Rising Powers Quarterly*, 2(2), 15–29.
Spektor, M. (2016). Brazil: Shadows of the past and contested ambitions. In: W. Hitchcock, M. Leffler, and J. Legro (eds), *Shaper nations: Strategies for a changing world*. Cambridge: Harvard University Press, pp. 17–35.

References

Alsina Jr., J.P. (2014). Rio Branco, grand strategy and naval power. *Revista Brasileira de Política Internacional*, 5(2),9–28.
Amorim, C. (2015). *Teerã, ramalá e doha: Memórias da política externa ativa e altiva*. São Paulo: Benvirá.
Amorim, C. (2017). *Acting globally: Memoirs of Brazil's assertive foreign policy*. Lanham, MD: Hamilton Books.

Barbosa, R. (2015). *The Washington dissensus: A privileged observer's perspective on US–Brazil relations.* Nashville: Vanderbilt University Press.

Bethell, L. (2010). Brazil and "Latin America". *Journal of Latin American Studies,* 42(3), 457–485.

Bierrenbach, A. M. (2011). *O conceito de responsabilidade de proteger e o direito internacional humanitário.* Brasília: Fundação Alexandre de Gusmão.

Bonfim, J.B.B. (2004). *Palavra de presidente: Discursos de posse de deodoro a Lula.* Brasília: LGE Editora.

Burges, S. (2017). *Brazil in the world: The international relations of a South American giant.* Manchester: University of Manchester Press.

Burges, S., and Daudelin, J. (2017). Democracy postponed: A political economy of Brazil's oligarchic foreign policy. In: P. Kingstone and T. Power (eds), *Democratic Brazil divided.* Pittsburgh: University of Pittsburgh Press, pp. 211–229.

Cardim, C.H. (2008). *A raiz das coisas: Rui Barbosa: O Brasil no mundo.* Rio de Janeiro: Civilização Brasileira.

Casas-Zamora, K. (2011). The Honduran crisis and the Obama administration. In: A. Lowenthal, T. Piccone, and L. Whitehead (eds), *Shifting the balance: Obama and the Americas.* Washington, DC: Brookings Institution Press, pp. 114–131.

Cason, J.W., and Power, T.J. (2009). Presidentialization, pluralization, and the rollback of Itamaraty: Explaining change in Brazilian foreign policy in the Cardoso–Lula era. *International Political Science Review,* 30(2), 117–140.

Chaui, M. (2017). *Sobre a violência.* Belo Horizonte: Autêntica Editora.

Cooper, D.A. (2011). Challenging contemporary notions of middle power influence: Implications of the proliferation security initiative for "Middle Power Theory". *Foreign Policy Analysis,* 7(3), 317–336.

Domínguez, J. (2016). The changes during the international system during the 2000s. In: J. Domínguez and R.F. de Castro (eds), *Contemporary US–Latin American relations.* New York: Routledge, pp. 1–29.

Freyre, G. (1946). *The masters and the slaves.* Translated by Samuel Putnam. New York: Knopf.

Gaspar, M. (2017). Uma história do Peru: A ascensão e queda da Odebrecht na América Latina. *Piauí,* 130(11),18–28.

Gordon, L. (2001). *Brazil's second chance: En route toward the First World.* Washington, DC: Brookings Institution Press.

Hatton, B. (2011). *The Portuguese: A modern history.* Northampton, MA: Interlink Books.

Hilton, S. (1979). Brazilian diplomacy and the Washington–Rio de Janeiro "Axis" during the World War II era. *Hispanic American Historical Review,* 59(2), 201–231.

Hilton, S. (1981). The United States, Brazil and the Cold War, 1945–1960: End of the special relationship. *Journal of American History,* 68(3), 599–624.

Hirst, M., and Pereira, L.B.V. (2016). The unsettled nature of US–Brazilian relations. In: J. Domínguez and R. Fernandez de Castro (eds), *Contemporary US–Latin American relations.* New York: Routledge, pp.106–127.

Hunter, W. (2010). *The transformation of the Workers' Party in Brazil, 1989–2009.* Cambridge: Cambridge University Press.

Hurrell, A. (2007). *On global order.* Oxford: Oxford University Press.

Jacobs, F. (2012). How Bolivia lost its hat. *New York Times,* 3 April. Available at: https://opinionator.blogs.nytimes.com/2012/04/03/how-bolivia-lost-its-hat/ [accessed 22 February 2018].

Kenkel, K., and Stefan, C. (2016). Brazil and the "responsibility while protecting" initiative: norms and the timing of diplomatic support. *Global Governance*, 22(1), 41–78.

Lafer, C. (2009). Brazil and the world. In: I. Sachs, J. Wilheim, and P.S. Pinheiro (eds), *Brazil: A century of change*. Chapel Hill: University of North Carolina Press, pp. 101–119.

Leuchars, C. (2001). Brazil and the league council crisis of 1926. *Diplomacy and Statecraft*, 12(4),123–142.

Li, X., and Christensen, S.F. (2012). The rise of China and the myth of a China-led semi periphery destabilization. In: L. Xing and S.F. Christensen (eds), *The rise of China: The impact on semi-periphery and periphery countries*. Aalborg: Aalborg University Press, pp. 31–58.

Loureiro, F. (2017). The alliance for progress and President João Goulart's Three-Year Plan: The deterioration of US–Brazilian relations in Cold War Brazil. *Cold War History*, 17(1), 61–79.

Malamud, A. (2011). A leader without followers? The growing divergence between the regional and global performance of Brazilian foreign policy. *Latin American Politics and Society*, 53(3), 1–24.

Malamud, A. (2017). Foreign policy retreat: Domestic and systematic causes of Brazil's international rollback. *Rising Powers Quarterly*, 2(2), 149–168.

Mares, D., and Trinkunas, H. (2016). *Aspirational power: Brazil on the long road to global influence*. Washington, DC: Brookings Institution Press.

McCann, F. (1995). Brazil and World War II: The forgotten ally: What did you do in the war, Zé Carioca? *Estudios Interdisciplinarios de América Latina y el Caribe*, 6 (2). Available at: http://eial.tau.ac.il/index.php/eial/article/view/1193/1221 [accessed on 28 March 2018].

Mello, E., and Spektor, M. (2018). Brazil: The costs of multiparty presidentialism. *Journal of Democracy*, 29(2), 113–127.

Milani, C., Pinheiro, L., and Soares de Lima, M.R.S. (2017). Brazil's foreign policy and the "Graduation Dilemma". *International Affairs*, 93(3), 585–605.

Nye, J. (2005). *Soft power: The means to success in world politics*. New York: Public Affairs.

O'Neill, J. (2011). *The growth map: Economic opportunity in the BRICs and beyond*. London: Portfolio Penguin.

Patriota, A. (2010). O Brasil no início do século XXI: Uma potência emergente voltada para a paz. *Política Externa*, 19(1), 19–25.

Patriota, A. (2017). Is the world ready for cooperative multipolarity? *Rising Powers Quarterly*, 2(2),15–29.

Pereira, A.W. (2017a). Brazil: Geopolitical challenges in a multipolar world. *Rising Powers Quarterly*, 2(2),7–13.

Pereira, A.W. (2017b). Nothing succeeds like failure? Honduras and the defense of democracy in Brazilian foreign policy. *Rising Powers Quarterly*, 2(2), 83–103.

Pimentel, J. V. de S. (ed.). (2013). *Pensamento diplomático Brasileiro: Formuladores e agentes da política externa (1750–1964)*, Vols. I–III. Brasília: Fundação Alexandre de Gusmão.

Power, S. (2008). *Chasing the flame: Sergio Vieira de Mello and the fight to save the world*. New York: Penguin Press.

Presidência da República (2017). Brasil: Um país em busca de uma grande estratégia. *Relatório de Conjuntura*, Número 1, Secretaria Especial de Assuntos Estratégicos, Brasília (May).

Reid, M. (2014). *Brazil: The troubled rise of a global power*. New Haven: Yale University Press.

Ricupero, R. (2010). Carisma e prestígio: A diplomacia do período Lula de 2003 a 2010. *Política Externa*, 19(1), 26–42.

Ricupero, R. (2017). *A diplomacia na construção do Brasil: 1750–2016*. Rio de Janeiro: Versal Editores.

Roett, R. (2011). *The new Brazil*. Washington, DC: Brookings Institution Press.

Saxenal, S. (2010). Why Lula is the man. In: *Times of India*, 9 April 2010. Available at: https://timesofindia.indiatimes.com/edit-page/Why-Lula-Is-The-Man/articleshow/5775158.cms [accessed on 22 February 2018].

Schmitter, P. (2009). Foreword. In: T. Vigevani and G. Cepaluni, *Brazilian foreign policy in changing times*. Lanham: Lexington Books, pp. ix–x.

Spektor, M. (2009). *Kissinger e o Brasil*. Rio de Janeiro: Zahar.

Spektor, M. (2016). Brazil: Shadows of the past and contested ambitions. In: W. Hitchcock, M. Leffler, and J. Legro (eds), *Shaper nations: Strategies for a changing world*. Cambridge: Harvard University Press, pp. 17–35.

Stuenkel, O. (2016). *Post-Western world: How emerging powers are remaking global order*. Cambridge: Polity Press, pp. 1–28.

Stuenkel, O. (2017). *BRICS e o futuro da ordem global*. Rio de Janeiro: Paz e Terra.

The League of Nations (1928). Brazil out. *Time*, 21 May. Available at: content.time.com/time/magazine/article/0,9171,731754,00.html [accessed 20 February 2018].

Vieira, M. (2018). (Re-)imagining the "self" of ontological security: The case of Brazil's ambivalent postcolonial subjectivity. *Millenium: Journal of International Studies*, 46(2), 142–164.

Vigevani, T., and Cepaluni, G. (2009). *Brazilian foreign policy in changing times*. Lanham: Lexington Books.

Whitehead, L. (2010). Obama and the Americas: Old hopes, new risks. In: A. Lowenthal (ed.), *Shifting the balance: Obama and the Americas*. Washington, DC: Brookings Institution Press, pp. 165–181.

11 Soccer in Brazil

Introduction

The first goal went in during the 11th minute of the match. The Germans took a corner, swinging the ball into an unmarked Thomas Müller, who side-footed it past Brazil's goalkeeper Júlio César. Twelve minutes later, Miroslav Klose scored another goal for Germany. And then a catastrophe occurred. In six frantic, almost unbelievable minutes, Germany scored three more goals against Brazil while the fans in the stadium and the nation watching on television were stunned into an anguished silence. Brazilians' dream of winning the World Cup at home, 64 years after losing the final in Rio in 1950, was over. It was 8 July 2014, and the semi-final played in the Mineirão stadium in Belo Horizonte ended 7–1 (Barbassa, 2015, pp. 277–279). This was Brazil's worst defeat ever in a World Cup finals, dubbed the *Mineiraço* by the press.

Understanding the devastation of the *Mineiraço* to many Brazilians is impossible without an appreciation of the importance of football (*futebol* in Portuguese), or soccer, to Brazilian national identity. Soccer has deep roots in the country and dominates the sporting landscape, with millions playing the game and following their club and national team. Wearing the yellow shirt of the national team is an instantly recognizable sign of "Brazilianness". Brazil is associated by outsiders with soccer due to the strong reputation of some of its most famous clubs, players, and its national side, the *Seleção*. The Brazilian national team is the only one in the world to qualify for all 20 of the World Cup finals held since the first in 1930, and the first (and at present the only) to win the tournament five times, the last being in 2002 (Batty and Murray, 2014, p. 12).

This chapter analyses how soccer became such an integral part of the Brazilian way of life, tracing the origins of the game in the late nineteenth century, through the state-sponsored attempts to use soccer as an instrument of national prestige in the mid-twentieth century, and into the globalized soccer landscape of the early twenty-first century. It explores a number of questions, including why Brazilians have such passion for soccer, not only for their clubs, but for the national team. Why has the Brazilian national team's record at the World Cup been so successful? How have soccer and politics been intertwined in Brazil? And how has globalization changed the nature of soccer?

Our reasons for focusing solely on soccer in this chapter – and men's soccer at that – are threefold. First, there are, of course, other sports and leisure activities that are important to Brazilians, but soccer is king. Sports such as volleyball, Formula 1 motor racing, basketball, surfing, Brazilian jiu-jitsu, and handball are also popular, but all of them finish a distant second to soccer. There is also capoeira, a martial art that combines music and dance and traces its origins to Brazilian slave culture. Historically practiced in secrecy, capoeira has grown popular in Brazil as well as globally in recent years. As such, rather than try to address all of these activities in one chapter, here we focus our analysis on one sport (i.e., soccer) in order to explain why it is so crucial for making sense of contemporary Brazil.

Our second reason for considering soccer and soccer alone – and by that, specifically, we mean men's soccer and not men's *and* women's soccer – highlights an even more significant issue: problems of gender inequality in Brazil. According to the United Nations Human Development Index, Brazil's Gender Inequality Index (GII) was rated at 0.414 in 2015, meaning that inequality faced by women and girls in Brazil is more than twice what it is in the USA (GII = 0.203), and between four to *ten times* more than in several European countries (e.g., the GII in the UK ranks 0.131, and in the Netherlands, Denmark, Sweden, and Switzerland, below 0.050). That women's soccer today in Brazil receives only a fraction of the attention that men's soccer does reflects broader and more troubling trends regarding the lack of opportunities and resources for women and girls. When it comes to soccer – and, for that matter, a host of other pursuits – women and girls have rarely been encouraged to play and/or provided opportunities to do so. There has been change in recent years, with the emergence of real phenomes such as Marta Vieira da Silva (see Figure 11.1), but the change has been slow. For these reasons, when it is said that soccer is hugely significant to Brazilians, implicit here is the understanding that *futebol* (i.e., soccer) almost always means men's soccer. Any discussion of Brazilian soccer should therefore raise questions of gender inequality, including the ways women's labor is undervalued and unrecognized in Brazil and beyond.[1]

Finally, our third reason for focusing on soccer at the expense of other sports relates to one of our primary goals in this book: to provide insight into key social, political, cultural, and economic issues in contemporary Brazil. Soccer provides an important and unique entry point to these topics, and by analyzing one sport rather than several, we are better able to hone our critical focus. The aim is not only to help explain Brazil's abiding obsession with soccer, but to help explain *why* this obsession is also important for making sense of other issues and debates in Brazil.

The origins of futebol

Everyday speech in Brazil is full of expressions that come from soccer. If you want to concede something to another person, you *dá bola*, or give the ball to them. If you make a mistake, you *pisou na bola* (stepped on the ball). If you come

Figure 11.1 Marta Vieira da Silva, shown here playing in the 2016 Olympic Games, is widely considered the best ever female soccer player.

Source: Agência Brasil, Wikimedia commons:https://commons.wikimedia.org/wiki/File:Marta_-_Brasil_e_Suécia_no_Maracanã_(29033096805).jpg

close to achieving your aim but did not quite make it, you *bateu na trave*, or hit the post. A situation that is polarized is a *Fla-Flu*, the game between two rival soccer clubs in Rio, Flamengo and Fluminense. Doing something great is to *marcar um golaço*, or score a great goal. Language in Brazil reveals the extraordinary importance of soccer in the popular imagination.[2]

The game has British origins (Norridge, 2008, pp. 187–189). Charles Miller (1874–1953), a Scottish–Brazilian, is seen as the founder of the game in Brazil. He was born in São Paulo to John Miller, a Scottish railway engineer and a Brazilian mother of English descent, Carlota Fox. In 1884, at the age of nine, he was sent to Banister Court School (a private boarding school) in Southampton, England, where he learned to play cricket and soccer. When Miller came back to Brazil in 1894, he brought with him two soccer balls and a set of the Hampshire Football Association rules. He helped set up the São Paulo Athletic Club and the Liga Paulista, the first soccer league in Brazil. São Paulo Athletic Club won three championships, in 1902, 1903, and 1904, with Miller as their striker (Duarte, 2014, pp. 8–9; Fontes and Buarque de Hollanda, 2014, p. 115; Guterman, 2009, pp. 14–16).

Soccer in this period was an elite sport, played in private clubs where members played other sports such as rowing and tennis. The boots (cleats) and balls were imported, making them expensive. These elite origins can be seen in the original crests of some of today's biggest clubs. Flamengo, for example (one of the most popular in the country), has in its original crest of 1895 a pair of crossed oars and an anchor. Sport Club Recife, founded in 1905, has a rowing oar and tennis racquet in its crest. Corinthians, the São Paulo club with the biggest organized fan group in the country, was named after the English club the Corinthian Casuals, which toured Brazil in 1909, and has an anchor and oars in its original crest.

However, soccer soon became, as it did in Britain, a working-class game (Norridge, 2008, p. 190). As in Britain, the growth of soccer was tied up with industrialization and urbanization, and eventually became a professional sport for the mass public rather than an amateur sport for elites in exclusive clubs. Balls and soccer boots began to be produced in Brazil, making them cheaper. Starting in 1931, live commentaries of soccer games were transmitted on the radio. Television coverage of games began in the 1950s. Teams were sponsored by factories, whose managers often saw soccer as a cheap way to keep workers fit and happy. Many people played in empty lots (in Brazil called *futebol de várzea*, floodplain football), or in *peladas*, improvised games on the beach, on cement, on asphalt, or whatever surface that was available. (One of the notable things about Brazil today is the number of improvised soccer pitches that can be seen all over the country.) Children often learned to play barefoot, using whatever materials they could find for a ball. As adults, if they were selected for a factory team, the company would provide them with a uniform and boots.

Immigrant groups set up clubs that reflected their origins. Portuguese immigrants established Vasco da Gama in Rio in 1898 (Goldblatt, 2014, p. 18), and Italians created Palmeiras in São Paulo in 1914. (Palmeiras was originally

Palestra Italia, but this name was changed in 1942 when the government banned the use of any symbols associated with the Axis Powers.) Italians also founded Palestra Italia in Belo Horizonte, and that became Cruzeiro in 1942. German immigrants helped to found Grêmio in Porto Alegre in 1903.

Bangu Athletic Club, founded in 1904 in Rio by the British directors of a textile company, was credited with being the first to admit working-class players, some of whom were non-white (Goldblatt, 2014, pp. 18–19). Some clubs discriminated against black players, but many clubs started to accept them. Club de Regatas Vasco da Gama of Rio de Janeiro is today remembered as a pioneer in this respect.[3] Elsewhere, in Porto Alegre, Sport Club Internacional accepted black players in the 1920s, while its rival Grêmio at first did not. Class as well as racial divisions often separated the teams. In many cities, rival clubs still have historical associations with either elites or more popular followings; clubs with elite origins include Fluminense in Rio de Janeiro, Cruzeiro in Belo Horizonte, São Paulo in São Paulo, and Grêmio in Porto Alegre, while more popular clubs include Botafogo and Vasco da Gama in Rio, Atlético in Belo Horizonte, Corinthians in São Paulo, and Sport Club Internacional in Porto Alegre.

In the 1930s and 1940s soccer was played across class and racial lines and the state promoted the sport as an outlet for popular passion and a source of national self-esteem. (The fact that it is called *futebol* in Brazil is testament to the elasticity of Brazilian Portuguese. Brazilians regularly import words from other languages, especially English.) The Vargas regime of 1930–1945 used soccer, as it used samba and Carnival, "as a tool for promoting national identity and integration" (Giulianotti, 2014, p. xiv). Brazil had become, in the words of the journalist and playwright, Nelson Rodrigues, "the country in soccer boots" (*a pátria em chuteiras*) (Rodrigues, 1994).

The *Seleção*

The Brazilian national team, which competed in its first game in 1914 against the visiting Exeter City Football Club (Duarte, 2014, p. 1), competed in the 1930, 1934, and 1938 World Cups. It finished third in the latter tournament, held in France. Brazil was knocked out by Italy in the semi-final and beat Sweden 4–2 for third place. Gilka Machado, a Brazilian poet, wrote in a poem of the 1938 team, "The soul of Brazil/Lays down a kiss/On your heroic feet" (quoted in Bellos, 2002, p. 41).

After the Second World War Brazil gained the right to host the 1950 World Cup, which was the first World Cup tournament since 1938. The government built the enormous Maracanã stadium, finishing it just in time for the tournament. (Maracanã has, as its official name, the Estádio Jornalista Mário Filho, in honor of a famous soccer journalist and author. It is still a shrine for soccer fans the world over; see Foer, 2004, pp. 128–130 as well as Figure 11.2.) Brazil played Uruguay in the final, and, under the rules of the competition at that time, all they had to do was tie to win the cup for the first time, on home soil. 173,850 people entered the

Figure 11.2 The Maracanã national stadium in Rio de Janeiro, pictured here in 2009 as it was originally configured between 1950–2010. A major overhaul was undertaken beginning in 2010 in preparation for the 2014 World Cup.

Source – Arthur Boppré, Wikimedia commons: https://commons.wikimedia.org/wiki/File:Maracanã_Stadium_in_Rio_de_Janeiro.jpg

stadium with a ticket that had been paid for – a world record for a sporting event at that time. Journalists, officials, and guests pushed the total crowd close to 200,000 (Bellos, 2002, p. 49). Many Brazilians were extremely confident about the match. The first edition of the Rio newspaper *O Mundo* printed a picture of the Brazilian team with the caption "These are the world champions" (Bellos, 2002, p. 49). But in the 79th minute, the Uruguayan player Ghiggia scored what turned out to be the winning goal. He said later, "Only three people have, with just one motion, silenced the Maracanã: Frank Sinatra, Pope John Paul II, and me" (quoted in Bellos, 2002, p. 52). The game finished 2–1 to Uruguay and became known in Brazil as the *Maracanaço*.

Losing this game was devastating for many Brazilians because they had invested so much of their hope and self-esteem in being champions (Goldblatt, 2014, p. 94; Reid, 2014, p. 282). The journalist Fernando Duarte calls the aftermath of the *Maracanaço*, "one of the longest post-mortems in the history of sport" (Duarte, 2014, p. 34). The white uniform used by the team in the 1950 final was discarded, never to be used again (Barbassa, 2015, p. 255); Brazil subsequently adopted the now familiar kit of yellow shirt with green trim, blue shorts, and white socks. Nelson Rodrigues wrote, "Everywhere has its irremediable national catastrophe, something like a Hiroshima. Our catastrophe, our Hiroshima, was the defeat by Uruguay in 1950" (quoted in Bellos, 2002, p. 43). (The Uruguayan players, on the other hand, including captain Obdulio Varela, are still heroes in Uruguay. That is the last time they won the World Cup.) Roberto DaMatta, a Brazilian anthropologist, wrote that the 1950 World Cup final

> is perhaps the greatest tragedy in contemporary Brazilian history. Because it happened collectively and brought a united vision of the loss of a historic opportunity. Because it happened at the beginning of a decade in which Brazil was looking to assert itself as a nation with a great future. The result was a tireless search for explications of, and blame for, the shameful defeat.
>
> (Quoted in Bellos, 2002, p. 45)[4]

Many narratives of the 1950 disaster note that blame for the defeat came to rest on three players. These were the goalkeeper, Barbosa, who had let in a relatively weak shot from Ghiggia, the defender, Bigode, who had supposedly not reacted to a slap from the Uruguayan captain Varela, and the midfielder, Juvenal, who was seen as not having done enough to defend against the Uruguayan attackers. All three of these players were black (Duarte, 2014, p. 34). Today, this scapegoating is seen by most commentators as a shameful reminder of racism, at a time when many other factors and individuals could have been singled out as responsible for the historic loss.

Brazil competed in the 1954 World Cup finals in Switzerland but were beaten by the Hungarians in the quarter finals. A few years later, they had another opportunity for redemption. On 21 April 1957, Brazil beat Peru 1–0 in the Maracanã to qualify for the World Cup finals in Sweden. According to Nelson Rodrigues (1993, pp. 51–52; pp. 60–61), Rio-based sports journalists were not impressed with the team. Peru was considered a weak side and Brazil won narrowly on a free kick by Didi (whose real name was Waldyr Pereira). The journalists instead admired the Hungarians, the Russians, the Czechs, and the English; they thought that European soccer was the best soccer in the world. Some Brazilians also thought that "the Brazilian players were always guided by their instincts rather than reason, and their behavior was marked by immaturity and nervous instability as opposed to maturity and self-control" (Lopes, 2014, p. 115).

In Sweden, Brazil played well. They drew 0–0 with England in the group stage and beat Wales 1–0 in the quarter final. They beat France 5–2 in the semi-final and Sweden 5–2 in the final. Didi was the midfielder who drove their team. Their most unusual, unpredictable player was Mané Garrincha (Manuel Francisco dos Santos), a right winger with a prodigious ability to dribble around opponents (Rodrigues, 1993, p. 53).[5] His legs were crooked and he delighted in surprising defenders. The coaches considered him psychologically unfit to play for the team when, in a friendly in Italy before the World Cup, he waited for a defender to run back into the goalmouth before dribbling around him and scoring. Only reluctantly did they put him in the team. Garrincha captured the love and admiration of many fans and he seemed to express the joy of the amateur player, the young man who played for fun in a casual game or for his factory team. The final also saw action from the 17-year-old Pelé (Edson Arantes do Nascimento). He scored two goals, including one in which he received the ball on his chest, kicked it over the head of the advancing defender, and volleyed it with his right foot past the goalkeeper into the net (Foer, 2004, p. 122). (What he did to the defender the Brazilians call a *chapéu*, or hat.) Mario Zagallo, who was later to coach Brazil, also scored in the final (Guterman, 2009, pp. 128–130).

The 1958 World Cup was the coming of age of Brazil as a soccer nation. Their play delighted the world and news of the team's victory, which reached Brazilians by radio, was received with tremendous enthusiasm (Goldblatt, 2014, p. 100). Nelson Rodrigues declared that because of the team's success in 1958, Brazilians could finally overcome what he called their "mongrel" complex (*complexo de vira-lata*; see Rodrigues, 1993, pp. 51–52, 60–61).

What made the Brazilians special in the sport was a topic of debate, often revealing notions of racial essentialism common at the time (and even still today). For example, in the 1930s, the Brazilian anthropologist, Gilberto Freyre, argued it was due to a combination of cultural and racial factors.

> The Brazilians play [soccer] as if it were a dance. This is probably the result of the influence of those Brazilians who have African blood or are predominantly African in their culture, for such Brazilians tend to reduce everything to dance, work and play alike.
>
> (Quoted in Bellos, 2002, p. 27)

Freyre also described Brazilian soccer as a reflection of a folkloric Brazilian character, the mixed-race artful dodger, or *malandro*. He wrote, in 1938,

> Our style of playing soccer contrasts with the Europeans because of a combination of qualities of surprise, malice, astuteness and agility, and at the same time brilliance and individual spontaneity ... Our passes ... our dummies, our flourishes with the ball, the touch of dance and subversiveness that marks the Brazilian style ... seem to show psychologists and sociologists in a very interesting way the roguery and flamboyance of the mulatto that today is in every true affirmation of what is Brazilian,
>
> (Quoted in Bellos, 2002, p. 36)

The journalist and writer, Mario Filho, brother of Nelson Rodrigues and the man whose name graces the Maracanã stadium, popularized Freyre's ideas in a book first published in 1947, *O Negro no Futebol Brasileiro* (*The Black in Brazilian Football*; see Goldblatt, 2014, p. 85).

There is another, more prosaic explanation of Brazil's success in soccer and victory in 1958 that does not depend on essentialist notions of culture and race. This perspective focuses on the state's promotion of soccer and careful investment in, and planning for, the national team's competitions. The 1958 delegation was the most professional group that went from Brazil to a World Cup up to that time. Its key figure was João Havelange, who, in early 1958, had become head of the Brazilian Confederation of Sports (*Confederação Brasileira de Desportos*, or CBD, which, in 1979, became the CBF, the *Confederação Brasileiro de Futebol*, or Brazilian Football Confederation).[6] Havelange would be there for more than 16 years, and was able to use his leadership of the CBD to jump to the presidency of FIFA (the *Fédération Internationale de Football Association*), world soccer's governing body in 1974, and stay there until 1998.

Havelange appointed the São Paulo businessman, Paulo Machado de Carvalho, as head of the Brazilian delegation to the 1958 World Cup. Machado de Carvalho was an owner of radio and TV stations who carefully prepared for the Cup. For the first time, the delegation included a psychologist, a nutritionist, and a dentist. Twenty-five location scouts were sent to Sweden to find a base for the squad (Goldblatt, 2014, p. 99). Havelange also appointed the coach, Vicente Feola, who selected the players in consultation with Machado de Carvalho, the doctor, Hilton Gosling, and the psychologist, João Cavalhares. As the journalist David Goldblatt (2007, p. 359) notes, "the Brazilians devoted scientific, psychological and economic resources to the development of domestic and international football and to winning, especially the World Cup."

The period from 1958 to 1970 was perhaps a golden age for Brazilian soccer. Brazil won three of the four World Cup finals in that span of thirteen years, in 1958, in 1962 in Chile, and in 1970 in Mexico. In keeping with the rules, they retained the Jules Rimet Trophy, the original World Cup trophy, after winning it for the third time in 1970. (The Cup was stolen from the CBF in 1983 and never recovered.) In this period, all the players in the national team played for Brazilian clubs such as Santos, Corinthians, São Paulo, Palmeiras, Botafogo, Flamengo, Fluminense, Grêmio, Cruzeiro, and Atlético Mineiro. They were known and loved by Brazilian fans, and relatively unknown (with the exception of Pelé) and exotic to fans outside of Brazil.

The 1970 team may have been the best ever for Brazil. Brazil won the final 4–1 in the Azteca stadium in Mexico City with some mesmerizing play and memorable goals, especially the last goal by the captain, Carlos Alberto. A long period of Brazilian possession was finished off by Jairzinho running towards the middle of the pitch from the left, passing to Pelé, who stood just outside the penalty area, and who then teed up his captain by laying the ball off to his right. Carlos Alberto, running up the right side of the pitch, met the pass perfectly with his right foot, hitting a low, hard shot past the Italian goalkeeper into the left corner of the goal. This was soccer that, in its artistry, fluency, and mastery, met the dreams of many fans all over the world.

1970 was the first World Cup final that Brazilians were able to watch on television. The way the team played was admired by many observers. The style was called by some football-art, or *o jogo bonito*, the beautiful game, and it reflected the high technical ability of the Brazilian players, who played on all kinds of surfaces, as well as their tendency to rely on technique and finesse rather than mere physical force. At this time, the generally larger and more physically robust northern Europeans played on muddy fields and put the ball in the air more than their South American counterparts. The Brazilian style of play was more distinctive from the European than it is in the twenty-first century, in part because the game was not as globalized then as it is now. For many Brazilian fans at that time, European soccer was boring and predictable, more about tactics and physicality than grace and finesse. (Some Brazilian fans would still say that now.) But their own team expressed their ability to improvise and make the game more of a dance. In the journalist Franklin Foer's words, "where the European style was prose, the Brazilian was poetry" (Foer, 2004, p. 120).

The British sports journalist, Hugh McIlvanney, wrote of the 1970 World Cup final:

> Those last minutes contained a distillation of their football, its beauty and elan and undiluted joy. Other teams thrill us and make us respect them. The Brazilians, at their finest give us pleasure so natural and deep as to be a vivid physical experience ... the qualities that make football the most graceful and electric and moving of team sports were being laid before us. Brazil are proud of their own unique abilities but it was not hard to believe that they were anxious to say something about the game as well as themselves. You cannot be the best in the world at a game without loving it and all of us who sat, flushed with excitement, in the stands of the Azteca sensed that we were seeing some kind of tribute.
>
> (Quoted in Goldblatt, 2007, p. 359)

The British historian, Eric Hobsbawm, wrote, "who, having seen the Brazilian national football team in its heyday, can deny its claim to the status of art?" (quoted in Fontes and Buarque de Hollanda, 2014, p. 2). Reflecting on this period, the anthropologist, Roberto DaMatta wrote about the link between Brazilian national identity and soccer:

> In futebol there is art, dignity, genius, bad luck, Gods and Demons, freedom and fate, flags, hymns, and tears, and above all the discovery that although Brazil is bad at a lot of things, it is good with the ball. It is a football champion which is very important. After all, it is better to be a champion in samba, carnival and football than in war and the sale of rockets.
>
> (Quoted in Goldblatt, 2007, p. 357)

For some, though, Brazil's 1970 World Cup victory was tainted by the attempts of the government, a dictatorship headed by General Emílio Garrastazu Médici, to exploit soccer success for its own benefit. Such practices had a long tradition in Brazil. President Getúlio Vargas told the national team before they traveled to Switzerland for the 1954 World Cup finals "not to forget that abroad you will represent the ability, the force and the resistance of a people (*raça*). If you win, Brazil will be victorious. If you lose, it will be Brazil that will lose" (quoted in Guterman, 2009, p. 106). President Juscelino Kubitschek invited the national team to the presidential palace and drank champagne out of the Jules Rimet trophy in 1958, and President João Goulart associated himself with the victorious 1962 team in a similar way.

The Médici government, however, brought the political control and exploitation of the national team to a new level in 1970. The head of the Brazilian delegation to Mexico was Army Brigadier Major Jerônimo Bastos. Bastos' chief of security was Army Major Roberto Câmara Lima Ipiranga dos Guaranys. Even the physical trainer was an Army Captain, Claudio Coutinho (Guterman, 2009, p. 183). In addition to the militarization of the delegation, the President of the then CBD, João Havelange, conferred with the head of the intelligence agency the SNI (*Serviço Nacional de Inteligência*), General Carlos Alberto da Fontoura, the head of the military cabinet, General João Baptista de Oliveira Figueiredo, and the President's Chief of Staff, João Leitão de Abreu about the preparations and progress of the national team (Guterman, 2009, p. 171).

President Médici and his advisors were directly involved in the preparations for the World Cup, because they regarded it as an issue of the utmost importance. When CBD President João Havelange fired the team's coach, João Saldanha, in March of 1970, replacing him with Mario Zagallo, many people, including the player Jairzinho, believed that this was done at the behest of the government. Saldanha had been a member of the Communist Party, and was said to be uncomfortable with his role of coach of the national team under a dictatorship (Guterman, 2009, p. 169). Once the World Cup games began, President Médici, who had played for Grêmio de Bagé in Rio Grande do Sul in his youth, listened to them avidly on the radio, telegramming or telephoning his congratulations to the team afterwards (Guterman, 2009, pp. 175–176).

The Médici government tried to portray the 1970 World Cup victory as validation of its project for the country. The President told the *Folha de São Paulo* newspaper the day before the final between Italy and Brazil that it would be 4–1 for Brazil, and the newspaper ran the story under the headline, "In the presidential palace, the hypothesis of a defeat is not accepted" (Guterman, 2009, p. 178). When the team returned to Brazil, Médici was photographed raising the Jules Rimet trophy alongside the players, and issued a press release that said:

> I identify in the success of our national team the victory of unity and the convergence of forces, the victory of intelligence and bravery, confidence and humility, persistence and serenity, technical capacity, physical preparation and moral consistency. But it is necessary to say, above all, that our players won because they knew how to be a harmonious team in which, as well as individual talent, they affirmed a collective will. In this moment of victory, I bring to the people my tribute, identifying myself with the happiness and emotion of the streets, to celebrate, in our incomparable national football team, the affirmation of the Brazilian man.
>
> (Quoted in Guterman, 2009, pp. 183–184)[7]

In this way, the Médici government, which was engaging in fierce repression of dissidents and opponents, tried to show that the military dictatorship was popular. The government tried to use the World Cup victory to win votes for its political party ARENA (the *Aliança Renovadora Nacional*, or National Renovatory Alliance) in the Congressional elections of October 1970.

After the 1970 World Cup, the government pressured the CBD to reorganize the national league in the country. Before this time, competitions had been largely state-wide or, at most, regional. In 1971, the CBD created a national league that is now known as the *Campeonato Brasileiro* or Brazilian Championship (Guterman, 2009, p. 180). The basic format of Brazilian club competition has remained the same since this time, even though the specific organizational details have changed. Part of the season is taken up by the state championships, while the other part is the national league (with four divisions, A, B, C, and D) and a national cup competition (*Copa do Brasil*). Clubs from the states of Rio de Janeiro, Minas Gerais, Rio Grande do Sul, Paraná, and especially São Paulo dominate the national competition.[8]

In 1974 and 1978, the national team experienced frustration and eclipse in world soccer, as the Dutch revolutionized tactics, and the Germans and Argentines won World Cup trophies on home soil in 1974 and 1978, respectively. But, in 1982, Brazil presented another world-class team to the world, in a side that included gifted players such as Socrates, Falcão, Eder, Zico, and Júnior. The team lost 3–2 to Italy in a pulsating quarter-final match in the Sarrià stadium in Barcelona. The Brazilian press dubbed the defeat "the Sarrià Tragedy" (Duarte, 2014, p. 131). This team is still remembered fondly in Brazil, perhaps more fondly than later teams that won the competition (Duarte, 2014, p. 130). Its captain, Socrates, became a national figure in the early 1980s when he, alongside some of his teammates in the Corinthians team, publicly campaigned for a return to direct elections for the presidency of the country and for democracy within the club in a movement dubbed Corinthians Democracy (Downie, 2017, pp. 196–206; Duarte, 2014, pp. 110–111 – see also Figure 11.3).

After a 24-year hiatus, the Brazilian national team won the World Cup again in 1994, in the USA. This team had little of the artistry and flair of the 1970 team, and the period has been baptized the "Dunga era" by some observers, in recognition of the importance of the captain of the 1994 team, the defender Carlos Caetano Bledorn Verri, whose nickname is Dunga (Duarte, 2014, p. 130). Coached by a conservative and defense-minded tactician, Carlos Alberto Parreira, the 1994 team specialized in mopping up opposition attacks, stifling opponents in midfield, and snatching a 1–0 victory with a late goal. (This was the score of its winning round of 16 match against the USA and its semi-final against Sweden.) Brazil won the final of the 1994 World Cup against Italy after a scoreless stalemate was decided on penalties. At this point, Brazilian soccer had changed markedly. Only half of the squad of 22 players in the national team played in Brazil, and most of the best players, such as Mauro Silva, Bebeto, Romário, Dunga, and the goalkeeper, Taffarel, were playing in Europe. In 2002 Brazil repeated this feat with its fifth World Cup victory. This

Figure 11.3 Dr Sócrates, one of Brazil's all-time greats and famous for his social activism, participating here in the Diretas Já protests for direct presidential elections in 1984.

Source: Jorge Henrique Singh, Wikimedia commons: https://commons.wikimedia.org/wiki/File: Socrates_(futebolista)_participando_do_movimento_pol%C3%ADtico_Diretas_Já.jpg

squad looked similar to the 1994 group, in that many of its best players, including the captain Cafu, Roberto Carlos, the striker and top goal scorer Ronaldo, Rivaldo, and Ronaldinho Gaucho, were playing in Europe.

Cafu, the captain of the 2002 team, did something during the post-match celebrations that highlighted the inequalities that are part of the modern game in Brazil. He wrote on his shirt, "100% Jardim Irene", in honor of the neighborhood in São Paulo where he grew up. Jardim Irene is a poor and violent neighborhood in the eastern part of the city, and Cafu had said in an interview that many of his childhood friends had been killed in gun violence. Cafu's tribute to his old home revealed the odds against upward mobility for the poor in Brazil, and the gratitude of a particularly gifted player for his escape from poverty. At Cafu's side for much of the celebration was Ricardo Teixeira, the son-in-law of João Havelange and President of the CBF, someone who had married into a wealthy Swiss–Brazilian family and who epitomized the privilege and power of the *cartolas* (literally, top hats) or bosses who run Brazilian soccer.

In contemporary Brazil, there are polemics around the wearing of the yellow shirt of the *Seleção*. Because some people who protested in favor of the impeachment of President Dilma Rousseff (2011–2016) in 2015 and 2016 wore the shirt, it has become something of a political symbol. For some supporters of President Rousseff and the Workers' Party (*Partido dos Trabalhadores*, or PT), the wearing of the shirt is associated with conservatives who try to use patriotism against the PT. For others, the shirt is still a supra-political symbol of national identity (Sebba, 2018).

It is also remarkable that, in a country traditionally seen as soccer mad, the Confederations Cup, the FIFA mini-tournament held a year before the 2014 World Cup finals in Brazil, was the object of nation-wide protests in June–July 2013. In protests that were diffuse, pluralistic, and difficult to interpret, the largely young protestors objected to the government's lavish expenditure on the World Cup despite serious shortcomings in the public health and education systems, as well as public transportation and security.[9] These concerns were well placed, as Brazil spent $11.6 billion on the World Cup, more than Germany and South Africa, the hosts of the 2006 and 2010 finals, respectively, put together (Barbassa, 2015, p. 280). Furthermore, many stadiums, such as those built in Brasília, Manaus, and Recife, were destined to become under-used white elephants, either because of their location or the lack of a team with a large enough following. The protestors demanded "FIFA-standard" hospitals and schools, and decried the corruption associated with the building of the infrastructure for the World Cup.

Once the World Cup began in June 2014, however, many Brazilians still wanted the national team to win, despite the serious questions that had been raised about the wisdom of holding the tournament in the country (Barbassa, 2015, p. 270). This accounts for the trauma of the 7–1 defeat by Germany in the semi-final with which this chapter began. It remains an open question as to how the Brazilian national soccer team will be seen in the future, and whether Brazilians will continue to put aside their differences to support their team in future international competitions.

The modern game

Brazilian soccer has changed with the globalization of the country. Many clubs specialize in nurturing young players and then selling them off for a profit to European clubs. They are exporting raw material, not refining the finished product. For example, it was estimated in the early 2000s that roughly 5,000 Brazilian soccer players had contracts with clubs outside of Brazil (Foer, 2004, p. 131). This is also reflected in the national team. Among the Brazilian squad of 23 for the 2014 World Cup, only four players played for Brazilian clubs. The rest were *estrangeiros*, or foreigners, some of whom had never played in Brazil as adults.[10] Brazil's World Cup squad in 2018 was similar to the 2014 squad: only three of its players played for Brazilian clubs.[11]

The top five European leagues (in England and Wales, Spain, Italy, Germany, and France) rake off most of the profits from global soccer (including television rights, ticket sales, and merchandising), while the Brazilian league remains outside this gilded arena. Brazil's clubs are, with some exceptions, badly managed and often corrupt (Barbassa, 2015, p. 279; Foer, 2004, p. 120). (Though bribery, money laundering, and other illicit practices are also part of soccer outside of Brazil, as the corruption scandal in FIFA shows.) Wrote Juca Kfouri, a Brazilian soccer journalist,

> In Brazil, there is still the ideology of "rouba mas faz" – it's OK to steal if you get things done. In football, this is stretched to the most far-reaching consequences. Everything is forgotten in the light of victory. I have always said that God put the best players here and the worst bosses to compensate.
> (Quoted in Goldblatt, 2007, p. 794)

The former player, Romário, who was elected to the Senate in 2014, established a Congressional committee to investigate corruption in the game. This committee issued two reports in 2015, one by the majority of committee members, and a minority report signed by Senator Romário (PSB – Rio de Janeiro) and Senators Randolfe Rodrigues (REDE – Amapá) and Paulo Bauer (PSDB – Santa Catarina). While the majority report attempted to protect the directors of the clubs from accountability, the minority report alleged that corruption in FIFA had links with corruption in the CBF, and involved millions of dollars in bribes. The report, which contained more than 1,000 pages, was sent to Brazil's Prosecutor General, Federal Police, Ministry of Justice, and FIFA. It alleged that the CBF housed a mafia that used Brazil's principal sporting patrimony for its own benefit (Romário, 2017, pp. 238–239). The report recommended the indictment of CBF officials Marco Polo Del Nero, José Maria Marin, Ricardo Teixeira, and six other officials, as well as structural changes to the management of soccer in Brazil (Romário, 2017, pp. 231, 216–230). José Maria Marin, a former CBF President, was convicted of corruption and imprisoned in New York in 2018 and his successor, Marco Polo Del Nero, has been unwilling to travel abroad since 2015 because of the risk of his being arrested (Sebba, 2018, p. 15).[12]

Brazilian clubs generally seem content to compete in a league with few international followers, and specialize as suppliers of some of the best players in the world to other clubs. The two most expensive transfers ever (as of early 2018) have involved Brazilian players. Neymar, a player who began his career in Brazil with Santos, was transferred from Barcelona to Paris St. Germain in 2017 for $273 million dollars. And his countryman, Philippe Coutinho, a former youth player at Vasco da Gama in Rio de Janeiro, was transferred in 2018 from Liverpool to Barcelona for $202 million dollars (cf. Udeme, 2018). However, when Deloitte's published its list of the 30 richest soccer clubs in the world (the Money League), not a single Brazilian club made the list.[13]

The World Cup in 2014, staged in Brazil and held in twelve different capital cities around the country, showed how much the modern game had changed in Brazil. Ticket prices were high (Barbassa, 2015, p. 257) and the crowds were largely affluent and white, reflecting changes in club soccer as well. According to the geographer, Christopher Gaffney, ticket prices for games in Brazil are some of "the most expensive in the world relative to the minimum wage"

(Gaffney, 2014, p. 200). From 2007 to 2012, average attendance at Brazilian Serie A (first division) games decreased by 15.8%, while during the same period ticket prices rose by an average of 88% (Gaffney, 2014, p. 200). Fans in Brazil have become accustomed to watching games on the *Rede Globo* television network and seeing half-empty stadiums behind the players on the pitch (see also Foer, 2004, p. 130).

If *futebol* was created and sustained by *o povo*, the Brazilian people, it has, to some extent, been neoliberalized, repackaged, and reformed to fit the lifestyles and preferences of the middle and upper classes. In the words of sociologist Richard Giulianotti, the "commercialization and sanitization of football stadiums ... has clearly had a negative effect on the social and cultural foundations of the game" (Giulianotti, 2014, p. xvii). How to respond to this development is contested. For some, the game should be returned to its working-class roots, made cheaper and more accessible, and therefore – at least potentially – more popular. For others, such a solution is both undesirable and impossible. Soccer around the world has moved in a neoliberal direction, with more luxurious stadiums that include executive boxes, more expensive tickets, bigger deals with television networks, and an expanding worldwide audience. In such a competitive environment, it is incumbent upon the CBF and the clubs to continue to modernize the game in order to capture a greater share of the global industry's profits. The only thing that people from these two perspectives agree on is that corruption is not good for the game. An example of the corruption that has been uncovered came after the 2014 World Cup when Sergio Cabral, the former Governor of Rio de Janeiro state, was convicted of taking bribes from the construction company responsible for the renovation of the Maracanã stadium (Affonso, Brandt, Macedo, and Vassallo, 2017). Even the jewel in the crown of Brazilian soccer was not free from the taint of corruption.

Conclusion

The news anchor, William Bonner, tells a story that reflects the abiding passion for soccer in Brazil. After the presidential election of 2002, Bonner was scheduled to interview Luíz Inácio "Lula" da Silva in the studios of *Jornal Nacional*, the news program of Rede Globo, Brazil's largest television network. He planned to ask Lula, a fan of the São Paulo team Corinthians, which was the biggest thrill for him, his election to the presidency or the goal by Basílio, a goal in 1977 that won Corinthians their first Sao Paulo state championship in 23 years. His editors talked Bonner out of starting the interview in this way, feeling that it was inappropriate. But after the interview, in the elevator with Bonner, Lula, unprompted, said about the election, "Look, aside from the goal by Basílio, I think I've never had an emotion like that in my life!" (Bonner, 2009, pp. 209–211).

In some ways, soccer represents both the best and the worst of Brazil. It reflects the *joie de vivre*, the creativity, the improvisation and athleticism of the people. It is a tremendous force for sociability, solidarity, and togetherness, and for mutual celebration. But soccer also represents the ills of Brazilian society, including corruption in the management of clubs and the National Football Confederation and the predatory selling of players to clubs abroad. It is not surprising that soccer, the world's most globalized game, reflects problems with Brazil's experience with globalization. And, once one understands the deep roots soccer has in Brazilian society and social life, it is easy to understand the trauma of the 7–1 defeat by Germany in the World Cup, a defeat that, according to the journalist Juliana Barbassa (2015, p. 280) "didn't just lift the proverbial rug; it ripped it right off and exposed the gap between Brazil's aspirations and its ability to achieve them, on the field and beyond."

The story of soccer in Brazil is closely connected to elites and their political projects. Politicians saw the mass appeal of soccer and could not resist trying to exploit it for their own ends, whether that was a vision of national integration, national development, or an upcoming election. At the same time, soccer also mirrors the development of Brazilian democracy. It started as an elite sport in private clubs, and it became a sport for everyone, including the poor and the non-white. Through force of will, marginalized people made the game their own. For a lucky few players, soccer became a means of social mobility, while for millions of fans, it was an outlet for their joys and fears, and a means of identifying with fellow citizens and the nation. Despite disagreement and debates about which direction the national game should take in the future, almost everyone agrees that the management of soccer – like the management of the country – should become more transparent and accountable. Whether it will or not is an open question.

Notes

1 Not to be overlooked here is the distressing state of gender inequality in the USA. While better off than Brazil, the USA has one of the highest rates of gender inequality among highly developed countries, according to the United Nations.

2 English has its own sports metaphors, of course; see Norridge, 2008, p. 195. But they tend to come from a multiplicity of sports rather than, as in Brazilian Portuguese, one sport.

3 The authors thank Fabio Luiz for bringing this to our attention.

4 These overwrought statements are reminiscent of the words attributed to Bill Shankley (1913–1981), the legendary manager of the Liverpool Football Club, who is supposed to have said something along the lines of, "Some people think football is a matter of life and death. I assure you, it's more serious than that."

5 The nickname "Garrincha", or wren, was said to have been given to him by his sister, Rosa (Bellos, 2002, p. 97).

6 The CBD split into several different units in 1979. This was partly a response to FIFA's decision to require that its affiliated national bodies should only be for soccer, and not for other sports. At that point, the CBF was created and became responsible for managing the game in Brazil (Downie, 2017, p. xiii).

7 These and other translations from the Portuguese are by the authors.

8 In the 15-year period 2003 to 2017, São Paulo teams won the Série A (First Division) of the Brazilian Championship nine times, with the other champions coming from Minas Gerais and Rio de Janeiro. The São Paulo winners were Corinthians, Palmeiras, São Paulo, and Santos. Cruzeiro, a team from Belo Horizonte, Minas Gerais, won three championships; the Rio team Fluminense won twice; and the Rio team Flamengo won once. Note the complete absence of teams from the south, centerwest,

north and northeast in this list. In the Brazilian Cup, in the eight-year period between 2010 and 2017, the winners have come from Rio Grande do Sul (Grêmio in 2016), São Paulo (Palmeiras twice, and Santos), Rio (Flamengo and Vasco da Gama), and Minas Gerais (the Belo Horizonte teams Atlético Mineiro and Cruzeiro). Again, no teams from the centerwest, north or northeast won the competition in this period, and there was only one winner from the south.

9 For insights into the protests, see Avritzer, 2016, pp. 65–82 and Alston, Melo, Mueller, and Pereira, 2016, pp. 209–213.
10 Brazil Squad for the 2014 World Cup. *Guardian*, 5 June 2014. Available at: https://www.theguardian.com/football/2014/jun/05/brazil-squad-2014-world-cup [accessed 3 February 2018].
11 Roger Gonzalez, Brazil at the 2918 World Cup, CBS Sports, 3 July 2018, available at https://www.cbssports.com/soccer/world-cup/news/brazil-at-the-2018-world-cup-schedule-scores-how-to-watch-neymar-tv-and-live-stream-players-to-watch/ [accessed 4 July 2018].
12 For more information on José Maria Marin's conviction, see Do Luxo ao Cárcere, 2017. For more on Marco Polo Del Nero, Marin's successor as President of the CBF, see Fernandez, 2017. Both Marin and Del Nero were investigated as part of the FIFAgate investigation led by the USA's Department of Justice and the Federal Bureau of Investigation.
13 See Deloitte's Football Money League. Available at: https://www2.deloitte.com/uk/en/pages/sports-business-group/articles/deloitte-football-money-league.html [accessed 31 January 2018]. In 2018, 14 of the 30 richest clubs were English, with Spanish clubs Real Madrid, Barcelona, and Atletico Madrid, the French club Paris Saint Germain, German clubs Bayern Munich, Borussia Dortumund, and FC Schalke 04, and Italian clubs Juventus, Internazionale, and Napoli also listed.

Suggested English readings

Bellos, A. (2002). *Futebol: The Brazilian way*. London: Bloomsbury.
Downie, A. (2017). *Doctor Socrates: Footballer, philosopher, legend*. London: Simon and Schuster.
Duarte, F. (2014). *Shocking Brazil: Six games that shook the World Cup*. Edinburgh: Arena Sport.
Fontes, P., and Buarque de Hollanda, B. (eds). (2014). *The country of football: Politics, popular culture and the beautiful game in Brazil*. London: Hurst.
Goldblatt, D. (2014). *Futebol nation: A footballing history of Brazil*. London: Penguin.

References

Affonso, J., Brandt, R., Macedo, F., and Vassallo, L. (2017). Sérgio Cabral condenado a 14 anos e 2 meses por corrupção e lavagem. *O Estado de São Paulo*, 13 June. Available at: http://politica.estadao.com.br/blogs/fausto-macedo/sergio-cabral-condenado-a-14-anos-e-2-meses-por-corrupcao-e-lavagem/ [accessed 4 February 2018].
Alston, L., Melo, M., Mueller, B., and Pereira, C. (2016). *Brazil in transition: Beliefs, leadership, and institutional change*. Princeton: Princeton University Press.
Avritzer, L. (2016). *Impasses da democracia no Brasil*. Rio de Janeiro: Civilização Brasileira.
Barbassa, J. (2015). *Dancing with the devil in the city of God: Rio de Janeiro and the olympic dream*. New York: Touchstone.

Batty, C., and Murray, J. (2014). *The big book of the World Cup: The complete guide to the 2014 finals in Brazil*. Kingston upon Thames, UK: Vision Sports.

Bellos, A. (2002). *Futebol: The Brazilian way*. London: Bloomsbury.

Bonner, W. (2009). *Jornal Nacional: Modo de fazer*. Rio de Janeiro: Editora Globo.

Do Luxo ao Cárcere (2017). *Rádio Peão Brasil*. 27 December. Available at: http://radio peaobrasil.com.br/do-luxo-ao-lixo-ex-presidente-da-cbf-marin-esta-preso-em-peniten ciaria-dos-eua [accessed 3 February 2018].

Downie, A. (2017). *Doctor Socrates: Footballer, philosopher, legend*. London: Simon and Schuster.

Duarte, F. (2014). *Shocking Brazil: Six games that shook the World Cup*. Edinburgh: Arena Sport.

Fernandez, M. (2017). Após revelações nos EUA, investigação sobre Del Nero na FIFA avança. *O Globo*, 14 December. Available at: https://globoesporte.globo.com/blogs/ bastidores-fc/noticia/apos-revelacoes-nos-eua-investigacao-sobre-del-nero-na-fifa-avanca.ghtml [accessed 3 February 2018].

Foer, F. (2004). *How soccer explains the world: An unlikely theory of globalization*. New York: HarperCollins.

Fontes, P., and Buarque de Hollanda, B. (eds). (2014). *The country of football: Politics, popular culture and the beautiful game in Brazil*. London: Hurst.

Gaffney, C. (2014). A World Cup for whom? The impact of the 2014 World Cup on Brazilian football stadiums and cultures. In: P. Fontes and B. Buarque de Hollanda (eds), *The country of football: Politics, popular culture and the beautiful game in Brazil*. London: Hurst, pp. 187–206.

Giulianotti, R. (2014). Preface. In: P. Fontes and B. Buarque de Hollanda (eds), *The country of football: Politics, popular culture and the beautiful game in Brazil*. London: Hurst, pp. xiii–xvii.

Goldblatt, D. (2007). *The ball is round: A global history of football*. London: Penguin.

Goldblatt, D. (2014). *Futebol nation: A footballing history of Brazil*. London: Penguin.

Guerman, M. (2009). *O futebol explica o Brasil: Uma história da maior expressão popular do país*. São Paulo: Contexto.

Lopes, J.S.L. (2014). The "people's joy" vanishes: Meditations on the death of Garrincha. In: P. Fontes and B. Buarque de Hollanda (eds),4 *The country of football: Politics, popular culture and the beautiful game in Brazil*. London: Hurst, pp. 103–127.

Norridge, J. (2008). *Can we have our balls back, please? How the British invented sport (And then almost forgot how to play it)*. London: Penguin Books.

Reid, M. (2014). *Brazil: The troubled rise of a global power*. New Haven: Yale University Press.

Rodrigues, N. (1993). *À sombra das chuteiras imortais: Crônicas de futebol*. São Paulo: Companhia das Letras.

Rodrigues, N. (1994). *A pátria em chuteiras: Novas crônicas de futebol*. São Paulo: Companhia das Letras.

Romário (2017). *Um olho na bola, outro na cartola: O crime organizado no futebol Brasileiro*. São Paulo: Planeta.

Sebba, J. (2018). Amor à camisa. *TAB*, 22 January 2018. Available at: https://tab.uol.com. br/camisa-selecao [accessed 31 January 2018].

Udeme, C. (2018). Coutinho makes 10 most expensive transfers of all-time list. *FCNaija*, 7 January. Available at: http://fcnaija.com/coutinho-makes-10-most-expensive-transfers-of-alltime-list [accessed 4 February 2018].

Afterword – Brazil's 2018 presidential election

Many of the key moments leading up to Brazil's 2018 presidential election are detailed elsewhere in this book, and, thus, not addressed in this brief Afterword. Instead, here we focus on the immediate runup to the election, the outcome and what it means for Brazil, and what tensions revealed in this election indicate for Brazilian democracy. If lessons from the past four years offer any insight to the next four, it is that more turbulence is likely ahead for Brazilian domestic politics.

With only weeks to go before the first round of general elections, it was still unclear who would be the top candidates. In April 2018, former president Lula began serving a prison sentence for corruption that was every bit as contentious as Dilma Rousseff's impeachment two years earlier. Later, in August 2018, the United Nations Human Rights Committee recommended to the Brazilian government that Lula's candidacy should not be prevented while his appeal process was ongoing, but Brazil's Superior Electoral Court denied the appeal, putting an end to Lula's presidential ambitions. When he withdrew from the race in early September, he was the most popular candidate according to all major national polls.

Lula then tried to shift his electoral support to his preferred successor and vice-presidential running mate, Fernando Haddad, the former Workers' Party (PT) mayor of São Paulo. Haddad's official campaign slogan, "Haddad is Lula," unambiguously emphasized their connection. The tactic worked, and within days the race narrowed to Haddad and far-right candidate, Jair Bolsonaro, of the Social Liberal Party (PSL). As the election neared, observers worried the result might rip Brazil apart: the winner would likely be Haddad, from the PT, a party now toxic to many Brazilians on account of the Carwash (*Lava Jato*) political corruption scandal; or Bolsonaro, a candidate *himself* toxic to many Brazilians on account of his political views.

So what about Bolsonaro, the former army captain who fancies himself a political outsider despite nearly 30 years in Brazil's federal congress? His comments reflect misogynistic, homophobic, racist, and authoritarian views so extreme that in September 2018, he was denounced on the front cover of *The Economist* as "Latin America's latest menace" (2018). In the final days leading up to the election, millions of people (overwhelmingly women) took to streets nationwide under the banner "*Ele Não*" (Not Him) to protest his candidacy. So extreme was Bolsonaro, many thought, he would lose to whichever candidate faced him in the second round.

Then, on 7 October 2018, Bolsonaro won 46 percent of the total valid vote – nearly enough to win the election outright in the first round – sending him through as the clear frontrunner to the second round. Haddad finished a distant second with 29.3 percent of the total valid vote, setting up a runoff election against Bolsonaro only three weeks later. This was the matchup Bolsonaro hoped for, as so polarized had Brazil become, the only PT candidate that seriously threatened him was Lula. Granted, many of Bolsonaro's core supporters are drawn to his right-wing rhetoric, and he is supported by some elites who despise the lower classes and would have voted for almost anyone who could prevent the PT from returning to the presidency (c.f., Chomsky, 2018). Important, too, was the influence of social media, the spread of misinformation (i.e., fake news), and voter manipulation using online resources (Cowie, 2018). Bolsonaro also received widespread support from Brazil's growing evangelical population, who tend to support his ultra-conservative social agenda (Schipani and Leahy, 2018). Added to this is the issue of public security, and Bolsonaro's promise to reduce restrictions on gun ownership, and assurances to police officers they will not be investigated if they kill while on duty. This hard-line rhetoric explains why surprising numbers of the urban poor support Bolsonaro: he addresses head-on something they confront on a daily basis (Richmond, 2018).

What is harder to discern, however, is how many Brazilians voted for Bolsonaro not necessarily because they support *him*, but more so they could vote *against* the PT. In addition to the Carwash scandal, the PT shoulders the blame for mismanaging Brazil's economy between 2003-2016, making little effort to address structural problems such as Brazil's regressive tax policies, pension reform crisis, and privileges for business elites. As Borges and Vidigal argue, anti-PT sentiment comes not only from the right; this is a group that is highly diverse and ideologically heterogeneous (2018). Lula would likely have won the election were he not in prison – his appeal to voters remains strong despite the downfall of his party – but in hindsight, no other PT candidate realistically stood a chance. On 28 October 2018, Bolsonaro won 55.1 percent of the total valid vote in the runoff election to become Brazil's next president.

So what does this mean for Brazil, and Brazilian democracy more generally? The immediate economic outlook is grim, and Bolsonaro will struggle to reduce the federal government's fiscal deficit. He has promised to privatize or abolish fifty state-owned enterprises, though if he reduces long-held protections for Brazilian businesses, he will likely butt heads with economic elites. He also wants to reduce environmental protections, particularly in the Amazon, but this will undermine Brazil's international diplomacy, and more importantly, further endanger indigenous groups in the region. Other campaign promises include ending affirmative action in Brazil's federal universities, ensuring abortion remains illegal, and the possibility he might challenge Brazil's same-sex marriage law. How he intends to do this, however, without resorting to Brazilian "politics as usual" (viz., favors and patronage) – something he consistently rallied against during his campaign – remains an open question.

More broadly, Brazil's current state of political polarization is worrying for more fundamental reasons. For example, in their book *How Democracies Die*, Levitsky and Ziblatt argue that "informal rules" and "institutional forbearance" are necessary for sustaining democracy (2018). "They amount to the same thing," notes David Runciman (2018): "resisting the temptation to take every cheap shot going." Levitsky and Ziblatt focus mostly on the United States, but as Anthony Pereira observes (2018), the same also goes for Brazil. One need only look to the last election in 2014 to see a clear downward trend. It was from this context, in which tactics and rhetoric that would have been unthinkable only a few years beforehand became alarmingly commonplace, that Bolsonaro emerged.

What this suggests is that individuals like Bolsonaro are, perhaps, not so much the cause of Brazil's political polarization, but rather symptoms of deeper, structural democratic problems. This is concerning, and Brazil, of course, is today not the only country facing extreme political polarization. With hindsight, this could be what 2018 is most remembered for in Brazil: not Bolsonaro the president, but rather the context that enabled his candidacy, and how his election signalled a decisive and polarizing split. This has been, and continues to be, an excruciating election for Brazil, and what happens next will likely have long-term and profound implications.

References

Borges, A. and Vidigal, R. (2018). Do lulismo ao antipetismo? Polarização, partidarismo e voto nas eleições presidenciais brasileiras. *Revista Opinião Pública*, 24(1), 53-89.

Chomsky, N. (2018). I just visited Lula, the world's most prominent political prisoner. A "soft coup" in Brazil's election will have global consequences. *The Intercept*, 2 October. Available at: https://theintercept.com/2018/10/02/lula-brazil-election-noam-chomsky/ [accessed 22 October 2018].

Cowie, S. (2018). Brazil: Fake news scandal hits country's presidential election. *Aljazeera*, 20 October. Available at: https://www.aljazeera.com/news/2018/10/bolsonaro-continues-lead-polls-fake-news-scandal-181019220347524.html [accessed 22 October 2018].

Levitsky, S. and Ziblatt, D. (2018). *How democracies die: What history reveals about our future*. New York: Viking.

Pereira, A.W. (2018). Brazil's democracy is on the ropes – and now a dreaded election begins. *The Conversation*, 30 August. Available at: https://theconversation.com/brazils-democracy-is-on-the-ropes-and-now-a-dreaded-election-begins-102283 [accessed 22 October 2018].

Richmond, M. (2018). Bolsonaro's conservative revolution. *Jacobin*, 17 October. Available at: https://jacobinmag.com/2018/10/brazil-election-bolsonaro-evangelicals-security [accessed 22 October 2018].

Runciman, D. (2018). *How democracies die* review – Trump and the shredding of norms. *The Guardian*, 24 January. Available at: https://www.theguardian.com/books/2018/jan/24/how-democracies-die-review [accessed 22 October 2018].

Schipani, A. and Leahy, J. (2018). Jair Bolsonaro courts Brazil's evangelical Christians. *Financial Times*, 19 October. Available at: https://www.ft.com/content/d9939a48-d33d-11e8-a9f2-7574db66bcd5 [accessed 22 October 2018].

The Economist (2018). Jair Bolsonaro, Latin America's latest menace. 20 September, available at: https://www.economist.com/leaders/2018/09/20/jair-bolsonaro-latin-ameri cas-latest-menace [accessed 31 October 2018].

Index

Brazilian Confederation of Football (CBF) 216, 220, 222–3
Brazilian Confederation of Sports (CBD) 216, 218–19
Brazilian Empire 42
Brazilian Institute of Environmental and Renewable Nature Resources (IBAMA) 156
Brazilianness 13, 208
BRICS *see* Brazil, Russia, India, China, South Africa
Brocos, M. 89
Buarque de Holanda, S. 3, 88
Bumba meu boi 169
Burdick, J. 176
Burges, S. 191, 199

Cabral, S. 49, 223
Cadastro Único (CadUnico) 73
Cafu (Marcos Evangelista de Morais) 220
caipirinhas 22
Caixa Econômica Federal (Federal Savings Bank) 73, 112, 115
Caldeira, T. 110
Campaign of Nationalization 24
Campeonato Brasileiro 219
Candomblé 175–6, 181
Canudos War 19, 126, 149
capitalism 4–5, 9, 14, 59, 62–3, 65–6, 68–9, 73, 78, 103, 105–7, 144, 149–50, 154, 160, 176, 181, 194
Capoeira 172, 209
captaincies 15–16, 41
Cardoso, F.H. 39, 47, 60, 64–5, 71–2, 93, 186, 193–4, 197, 200
Carnival 9, 22–3, 163, 212, 217
cartolas (football bosses) 220
Carvalho, P.M. de 216
Castelo Branco, H. de A. 192
Catholic Church 125, 130, 137, 175–7, 179, 181
Catholicism 177, 179
Cavalhares, J. 216
Central Bank 67, 72
César, J. 208
Chang, H. 60, 62, 64
Chaui, M. 3, 13–14, 91, 190
citizens' constitution 66
citizenship 7, 33, 44, 50
Civil Police 110
civil rights 28, 92–3, 132, 134, 139
class 5, 8–9, 21, 45, 47–8, 50, 74, 92, 94, 96, 105, 107–8, 110, 112–14,

122–3, 127–9, 131–6, 170, 191, 195, 211–12, 223, 228
Clean Hands investigation (Italy) 53
climate change 9, 68, 70, 109, 116, 157–8, 160, 185, 202
coalitional presidentialism 34, 38
coffee 17, 20, 42–4, 58, 62, 65–6, 69, 88, 103, 145, 188, 191
Coimbra University 42
Cold War 25, 46, 129, 139, 194
collective bargaining 24
collective mobilization 8, 121, 123–4, 126–7, 129–31, 135–9
Collor de Mello, F. 47, 64, 71
colonization 1, 4, 13–15, 29, 33, 41, 86, 90, 103, 124, 144–5, 149, 152, 164, 174, 180–1, 187
colorism 97
Communism 23, 129
Communist Party 47, 129, 218
comparative advantage 62, 65, 67, 146
Complexo de Vira-Lata (Mongrel Complex) 13, 215
Comte, A. 43
Comunidades Eclesiais de Base (CEBs) (Ecclesiastical Base Communities) 130, 137, 176
Conditional Cash Transfer (CCT) 73–6
Confederação Operária Brasileira (Brazilian Workers Confederation) 127
Congress, National 34–7, 45
Conselheiro, A. 19
Consolidated Labor Laws (1943) 66
Constitutions 7, 26–7, 33, 36, 38–40, 43, 47, 50, 52–3, 66, 69–70, 107, 125, 128, 130–1, 133, 156, 185; Amendments 34, 49, 77, 95
Copa do Brasil 219
Corinthians 211–12, 216, 219, 223
Coronéis (Colonels) 15
corporatism 23
corruption 3, 7, 26, 33, 38–9, 41, 47–9, 51–3, 64, 66, 71, 88, 111–12, 121, 136, 179, 200, 221–4, 227
cortiços 107
coups 10, 25, 38, 44, 46, 53, 185; military coups 21–4, 69, 128–9, 190
Coutinho, P. 222
crentes 179
crime 8, 38, 40, 49, 52, 102, 109–11, 117, 196
Crivella, M. 50
Cruzeiro 212, 216